AF759523

For those readers who have not yet had the pleasure of reading Illan rua Wall's highly original brand of critical legal theory: you are in for a real treat. Paradoxically, this jostling theoretical maelstrom of a book makes you sit still in wonder. By turns funny, erudite, playful and intensely creative on every single page, this is a masterful account of atmosphere, of the politics of the crowd, and of sovereignty.

— Ben Golder, University of New South Wales, Australia

Law and Disorder is many books. It is a theory of protest, an exploration of the shifting affects of crowds, a methodological weapon and a moving manual for resistance. It explores the subversion of sovereignty as well as the ways that it makes itself present. It is best read with an openness to the political quality of Wall's writing and its destabilising reimagining of possibilities.

— Carolina Olarte, University of the Andes,
Bogotá, Colombia

This is a rare feat of a book, managing to be both politically rousing and affectively engaging, both revolutionary and quietly eavesdropping on the world's goings-on. Illan rua Wall has produced a text of deep sensitivity, enabling us to rethink the atmospheric affects of public order as an integral part of the sovereign mechanism; placing crowds and protest at the core of the affective life of the populace.

– Andreas Philippopoulos-Mihalopoulos,
University of Westminster, UK

LAW AND DISORDER

Focusing on the moment when social unrest takes hold of a populace, *Law and Disorder* offers a new account of sovereignty through an affective theory of public order and protest.

In a state of unrest, the affective architecture of the sovereign order begins to crumble. The everyday peace and calm of public space is shattered as sovereign peace is challenged. In response, the state unleashes the full force of its exceptionality, and the violence of public order policing is deployed to restore the affects and atmospheres of habitual social relations. This book is a work of contemporary critical legal theory. It develops an affective theory of sovereign orders by focusing on the government of affective life and popular encounters with sovereignty. The chapters explore public order as a key articulation between sovereignty and government. In particular, policing of public order is exposed as a contemporary mode of exceptionality cast in the fires of colonial subjection. The state of unrest helps us see the ordinary affects of the sovereign order, but it also points to *crowds* as the essential component in the production of unrest. The atmospheres produced by crowds seep out from the squares and parks of occupation, settling on cities and states. In these new atmospheres, new possibilities of political and social organisation begin to appear. In short, crowds create the affective condition in which the settlement at the heart of the sovereign order can be revisited. This text thus develops a theory of sovereignty which places protest at its heart, and a theory of protest which starts from the affective valence of crowds.

This book's examination of the relationship between sovereignty and protest is of considerable interest to readers in law, politics and cultural studies, as well as to more general readers interested in contemporary forms of political resistance.

Illan rua Wall is Reader at the University of Warwick Law School, UK.

LAW AND DISORDER

Sovereignty, Protest, Atmosphere

Illan rua Wall

Routledge
Taylor & Francis Group
LONDON AND NEW YORK

First published 2021
by Routledge
2 Park Square, Milton Park, Abingdon, Oxon OX14 4RN

and by Routledge
52 Vanderbilt Avenue, New York, NY 10017

Routledge is an imprint of the Taylor & Francis Group, an informa business

© 2021 Illan rua Wall

The right of Illan rua Wall to be identified as author of this work has been asserted by him in accordance with sections 77 and 78 of the Copyright, Designs and Patents Act 1988.

All rights reserved. No part of this book may be reprinted or reproduced or utilised in any form or by any electronic, mechanical, or other means, now known or hereafter invented, including photocopying and recording, or in any information storage or retrieval system, without permission in writing from the publishers.

Trademark notice: Product or corporate names may be trademarks or registered trademarks, and are used only for identification and explanation without intent to infringe.

British Library Cataloguing-in-Publication Data
A catalogue record for this book is available from the British Library

Library of Congress Cataloging-in-Publication Data
A catalog record has been requested for this book

ISBN: 978-0-367-67521-9 (hbk)
ISBN: 978-0-367-33370-6 (pbk)
ISBN: 978-0-429-33042-1 (ebk)

Typeset in Bembo
by Deanta Global Publishing Services, Chennai, India

For Ruán & Odhran

CONTENTS

ACKNOWLEDGEMENTS

This book is dedicated to Ruán and Odhran: a proportion of it was written in the early mornings with Odhran wriggling on my lap, singing his lovely strange tuneless melodies. As the book has developed, his gurgles have turned to words, sentences and paragraphs. Ruán has provided beautiful moments of joyful disorder. Almost every day around them seems to be riotous and tumultuous, as waves of ecstasis, de-individuation and temper sweep across the scene. To my parents, Elizabeth Kirwan and William Wall, for the powerful atmospheres of thoughtfulness, joy, love and calm that they have always exuded. With my brother Oisín, they were my first crowd. To Oisín Wall and Miranda Faye Thomas, for their love, support and kindness.

The Independent Social Research Foundation has provided an inestimable support with their Early Career Fellowship. Inestimable in the sense that they gave me time! – something that cannot be given, taken or held in any way. In particular, my thanks go to them for investing the term 'fellowship' with its literal meaning. I have discovered friends amongst their number.

As with every book there are particular people who were central to the development of the concerns, ideas and feelings enclosed within. James Martel, Carolina Olarte, Dan Matthews, Alison Young, Costas Douzinas, Ben Golder and Andreas Phillipopoulus-Mihalopolous have helped me think and rethink the senses of politics, law, space, affect and atmosphere. They have provided encouragement and support. Their comments on various texts in the becoming of this book have been invaluable. Tara Mulqueen, Claire Blencowe, Goldie Osuri and Christine Schwobel-Patel have been the most wonderful co-conspirators in various Research Centres and Groups. Stephen Connelly's always-open door across the corridor opened onto incredible diagrams of the deep networks of continental philosophy. Jayan Nayar, Laura Lammasniemi, Raza Saeed, Vanessa Munro, Dallal Stevens, Tor Krever, Johanna Cortes-Nieto, Angel Makote-Njagi and

Simon Thorpe have been incredible colleagues and friends – constantly knocking me off balance and subtly insisting upon directions that I could not have conceived of in advance. These have included everything from joyful ontologies, catastrophes, post-election violence and poverty to decolonial subsidence and anarchist constitutionalism. Unbeknownst to them, Nina Gryf and Jakob Sobik helped me to crack the first part of the book on a beautiful April morning in Oxford a long time ago.

There are obviously too many people involved in a project that has lasted nearly a decade: Yvette Russell, Stacy Douglas, Luis Eslava, Swastee Ranjan, Rose Parfitt, Jess Whyte, Chris Butler, Karen Crawley, Nina Power, Elena Loizidou, Máiréad Enright, Bernard Keenan, Aoife O'Donoghue and Daniel McLoughlin. But as ever, this is only the surface, there are so many others. My thanks to my students in Legal Theory and Law and Disorder: their advice to slow down has always proved to be just out of reach. The insights of all of your discussions, presentations, essays and podcasts are everywhere in this book. I'm sure if you ever read it, you will know yourselves in its pages. My particular thanks go to Paula de Wailly, Giuliano Natali, Renee Liew, Shamilka Hewagama and Anoshamisa Gonye, whose research assistance and enthusiasm was contagious. The book was mostly written in Missing Bean, The Bear and Bean, Peloton and Society cafes, as well as the various Bodleian libraries in Oxford. So for me its pages are pervaded by the soft smell of old books and sharp espressos. Early on in the project I visited the University of New South Wales in Sydney with the help of Amelia Thorpe and Ben Golder, and later Universidad del Rosario in Bogotá hosted me with the support of Johanna Cortes-Nieto.

Finally, to Bríd who is always willing to sit me down and talk through whatever crisis has befallen the writing of the book, and to knock some sense into my incoherent ramblings. Everything is shared with you.

INTRODUCTION

The state of unrest

In late 1935, Georges Bataille could feel it. He addressed the *Contre-Attaque* group as Paris was consumed by protest and counter-protest: 'What drives the crowds into the street is the emotion directly aroused by striking events in the atmosphere of a storm, it is the contagious emotion that, from house to house, from suburb to suburb, suddenly turns a hesitating man into a frenzied being'.[1] The city had become the bearer of new affects. The atmosphere of the storm gathered over it. The clouds were dark with threat, anxiety and excitement. As the protests, riots, marches and strikes continued, this crisis of feeling spread. It thickened. It began to stick to bodies, condensing in every little interaction. The affects of the disorder spread through the city, through the country. France was gripped by a state of unrest. This book is about those feelings of the state of unrest. It is about the way in which atmospheres of crowded protest can seep out from protests or occupations. How the streets around a crowded event can fill with different feelings, and how those feelings can very quickly spread out around a city, a country, a region and at times even around the world. It is about how these affects can be *felt* among the populace as the opening of new (exciting and/or terrifying) political, social and legal possibilities. In the state of unrest what is possible or realistic can become radically different.

The state of unrest is a limit situation for the sovereign apparatus, a moment when the habitual relations of peace and calm on which sovereignty relies begin to break down. This makes unrest a particularly useful lens through which to understand sovereignty, because it sensitises us to those relations that have been interrupted.[2] It draws our attention to the ordinary affects of the sovereign order, to habitual obedience and an affective sense of 'public order'. With affect, Brian Massumi explains, 'the political becomes directly felt'.[3] Sovereign affects are those aspects of the state order that the populace *feel*, the sentiments of stability, consent, allegiance, security, obedience, loyalty, docility and peace. These are important because 'power is exercised through and reproduced in our feelings'.[4] These feelings are produced on a collective level through the government of affects. Affects are public sentiments which circulate through and between bodies. Katherine Ibbett helps explain this:

> If an emotion is understood to belong to an individual, to be located in an interior core from which emotions billow up to the surface, then affect has a different configuration, providing a way to think through 'feeling' (including the bodily) without clinging to a particular notion of the subject. It lies somewhere between emotion and experience. It doesn't tally with a neatly bounded self but perhaps holds between such selves, for affect's in-betweenness, its non-distinctions, are variously narrated; and affect might be more bodily than an emotion, but it is not a sensation.[5]

The public sentiments of the sovereign order wax and wane, shifting imperceptibly through different eras. '[A]ffective states generate attachments to leaders, to reigning ideologies, to the existing social structures and hierarchies, and to normative ways of being'.[6] In the state of unrest, these public sentiments are transformed into the site of a crisis. The state of unrest is a series of shifts in the affective life which sovereignty relies upon. It is a glitch in the affective reproduction of sovereign orders.[7]

One of the key drivers of the shifts in affective life of the populace is crowded protest. Crowds produce intense atmospheres, which gradually spill out around the city. These atmospheres are particularly intense affective fields, which sit on the threshold of our consciousness. They operate on our bodies, shifting our capacity to act. We are familiar with them in other circumstances: we might dance in the hot, dark fug of a nightclub; chant in unison with a crowd in the stadium; quietly move around the walls of the art gallery; or perhaps pray in the heavy silence of a cathedral. We come to these spaces with expectations and habits, understandings of the function of the building and the event that will take place there. But once there, the atmosphere impinges on the body. We might think about it as though it were a magnetic or gravitational field. In either, the space around an object that generates the charged field is laden with a force. This might be attraction or repulsion, but objects which enter the field (and in the case of magnetism, react to it) are affected by it. As we will see, affective atmospheres shift the capacity to act. They do not prevent any particular action but shift what each person is likely to do in the space. Atmosphere 'colors nonlinguistic sensory experience by giving it a quantity of intensity, and thus force, that prepares the organism to respond to that which is impinging on it, *but in no predetermined direction*'.[8] This book will focus in particular on atmospheres, but we will also see various formations of public sentiments, national moods, structures of feeling, zeitgeists, ambiences and the popular temper. In short, we will focus on the formations that are produced by crowds as they conserve, intensify and overthrow sovereign orders.

Crowds

Unlike the nation, the people, the multitude, the proletariat or other figurations of collective power, crowds have remained unburdened by the weight of idealisation. In fact, they tend to be dismissed as violent and irrational.[9] However, massive assemblies of people are often the only technology of power available to those who lack access to the corridors of power. Rather than recreate the idealisation of yet another figure of collective power, this book will not assign to the crowd a fundamentally malign or benign essence. Instead, it will suggest that they should be seen as a *political technology*. Crowds gather because of some cause. But they tend to produce feelings that exceed the stated aims of their protest. These excess beliefs and desires shift and turn, sometimes pulling people to confrontation, sometimes drawing people together in new bonds. The excess is a crowd's 'vibrance', its tendency to excite new capacities to action (or inaction). The production of vibrance renders the crowd unpredictable and unstable. But it also gives it a remarkable power.

Quite obviously, crowds are not the sole property of protestors and revolutionaries. They are used to stage all sorts of everyday social, political and economic events, as well as being a by-product of some modes of contemporary social organisation. We might think of funerals, nightclubs, product launches or public transport. In each of these moments crowds are a technology which can effectuate different social, religious or economic ends. The 'Black Friday' sales, for instance, are staged to communicate the beginning of the Christmas shopping season and to associate particular shops with it. To ensure the greatest (and most salacious) coverage of this feeling, shops will attempt to draw large numbers of edgy and competitive consumers. The tense and often violent affects of these crowds are intensified by ensuring they are sleep deprived through early morning opening and over-night queuing, and by celebrating the scarcity of the most desirable or discounted items. When violence does break out, the coverage goes viral, generating the feeling that this particular shop is worth fighting over this holiday season. In this way 'Black Friday crowds' have become an effective economic technology. I do not want to draw any *essential* distinction between these economic crowds and those who gather for more political purposes. It is not helpful to try to fit crowds into distinct categories that are each internally coherent. The classification of crowds, even when undertaken with great insight and care[10] sacrifices close attention to the way they unfold in a reductive quest for a set of category markers. Ultimately, attempts at classification must impose a set of conventions in advance and then measure particular crowds according to these preset ideas.[11]

Crowds may be deployed for any variety of purpose, but this book will mostly focus on crowds as a *political technology*. In this sense, the key question is not the end that a crowd might be aimed at (anything from gender justice, economic redistribution or human rights to racist policies or fascist politicians). By framing crowds as a political technology, the idea is to shift our focus away from the ends that the specific crowds aim at and instead focus on the way the technology might shape the way those ends are reached. We can contrast it with other political and legal technologies such as judicial review, online petitions, letter-writing campaigns or lobbying. Crowded protest quite clearly has a very different set of affective dynamics. It generates atmospheres, stages forms of immediate horizontal bodily communication, collective movement, mood, demeanour and rhythm. Focusing on crowds as a political technology sensitises us to the dynamics of specific crowds. It helps us to see the error of reducing all crowds to a unitary actor. Traditional crowd theory produces an image of 'the crowd' that would be the same across all space and time. Gustave Le Bon is perhaps the greatest culprit in projecting an essentialised, unitary sense of the crowd as irascible, irrational and violent.[12] In this Le Bon goes beyond the identification of common dynamics of the crowd to insist upon 'the crowd' as a unitary subject of history. It is the same in any context, he suggests. But crowds *are* different from one another; they unfold in different ways depending upon their setting, their era, their shape and size, the cause that gathers them, the affective dynamics of the events and a million other factors. There is a crucial methodological difference between identifying a common actor ('the crowd') with a single destiny ('savage violence') and examining the ways that a political technology (crowds) operates (affective atmospheres, valorisation, contagion, etc.).

This distinction is important too when it comes to thinking about the political significance of crowded political action, especially if there is a suggestion that violence is involved. The political systems which have been most closely associated with crowds are the inter-war European fascist states. During the inter-war period these states staged closely managed crowded scenes to release the abject forces that would enervate the dictatorial states and their murderous projects. They also deployed abject crowd violence in the name of racial, social and political purification, both during and after their ascent to power. The logics of nation, race and homeland operated discursively and affectively to connect these particular crowd formations with ideas of the 'masses'. They generated a terrible affective vibrance in the national socialist project. However, while crowds may have been an essential element of European fascism, the reverse is not true. Fascism *is not* essential to every crowd formation. If it were, then every event that operationalised crowds would have to contain the seeds of fascism: every festival, funereal, shopping centre, demonstration or state occasion. Fascism is not necessarily an element of every crowd formation, but fascist violence is certainly a potential of crowded politics. Paraphrasing Foucault, I might say that my point is not that crowds are bad but that they are dangerous.[13] They are not fundamentally fascist, but there is always a certain risk. The affective forces and energies that spill out in crowded scenes are always capable of turning into something destructive. Fascism honed this violent, racist potential of crowds. It habituated the populace to this violence. But the simple association between crowds and fascism is a sort of idealisation. It blinds the analyst to the ways in which liberals, conservatives and radicals of all stripes call upon crowd dynamics.

Sovereignty, government

Achille Mbembe explains that the 'ultimate expression of sovereignty largely resides in the power and the capacity to dictate who is able to live and who must die'.[14] This power to kill or to let live (necropolitics) or to make live and let die (biopolitics) 'constitutes sovereignty's limits', he explains. 'To be sovereign is to exert one's control over mortality and define life as the deployment and manifestation of power'.[15] These liminal moments of life and death are a crucial site in which sovereignty is given form. Since Giorgio Agamben's *Homo Sacer* the limit figures of the *homines sacri* have been given priority in a portion of contemporary critical legal thinking.[16] Theories such as Agamben and Mbembe's that deploy liminal analyses often make two claims: firstly, that the limit helps us understand a concept by tracing its external contours, even if it is groundless (as in deconstruction) or rendered indistinct (as in Agamben). Secondly, these liminal theories tend to claim that the limit does not remain in the limit-moment but is brought within the concept as a form of latency or potentiality. So, for instance, bordering practices do not remain at a checkpoint on the frontier; they are increasingly brought into everyday state practices. Or in the case of sovereignty, the limit case of the *homo sacer* remains the latent potential of every interaction with the state. In this way, the limit sensitises us to a certain quality which patterns everyday relations. This book also relies upon a limit scene. As we saw in the first pages, the state of unrest is a moment when the affective order of sovereignty is disrupted. However, while unrest can help us understand the exceptionality that is often deployed against those who dispute the sovereign order, the limit is also there in 'normal' orderly relations.

As we will see in the first part of the book, crowds often generate the affects, atmospheres and ambiences in which the feelings of sovereignty flow. This is important because sovereignty does not have an obvious referent, a material thing that one could point to in order to explain what it was. It is a bundle of ideas, developed over centuries. It has different shapes, forms and sentiments in different places. To give these meaning they have to be staged – an emergency presidential address, a coronation, a space of national identification, a commemoration or moment of national mourning. Staging sovereignty makes it affectively meaningful. Staging sovereignty with a crowd intensifies and amplifies these affects, but it also makes the scene unstable. Crowds are always capable of producing glitches. The flows of belief and desire that emerge in crowded situations are not necessarily the affects, atmospheres and ambiences in which the sovereign is going to be glorified. To grasp this we must take our cues from political theatre: the costumes, the background, the scenes and the broad movements are important. It is not enough to see merely the narrative; we must begin to understand sovereign *style.* Style is a thick term here, conveying more than fashion or appearance. Rather, it tries to gather the very manner in which a sovereign might deploy their metaphysical inheritance in different ways, and to different effect. The aim here is to insist upon the potential of sovereign concepts to produce radically different affects, even as the same concepts are themselves staged. This means that Edmund Burke's rather singular account of love-and-awe/dignity-and-majesty that we will see in the prologue needs to be pluralised. Love and awe are certainly two key affects of sovereign relations, but it is also far more complex than this. To begin to think these sovereign affects, we must take our eyes off the sovereign with his political theology and examine the relations that are being amplified between the sovereign and its crowds. The argument is ultimately that we can begin to grasp a sense of sovereignty in the molecular flows of belief and desire that gather around moments where it is staged.

Importantly, this also returns us to the *homines sacri*: sovereignty can be staged in crowded moments. The glitches that crowds produce can knock events increasingly out of kilter. In these moments, like the more conventional political disorder of riots and unlawful assemblies, the police arrive in great numbers. They deploy a form of force which comes directly from the sovereign. It is the force of sovereign's peace, a 'sister' to the war power.[17] The sovereign's peace must be enforced against the disorderly crowds. But this is precisely a form of *liminal* force which the state will escalate to ensure the ultimate return of habitual obedience of the populace. The indistinction of rule and exception that constitutes the figure of the *homo sacer* returns here but in different forms. The crowds subjected to the kettle, to gas, to rubber bullets or to live ammunition draw us less towards the paradigm of the camp, than to the colony. In the colony the governmental question was always how to return a restive populace to a state of passivity, and how to generate conditions of docility. In short, we see a play of norm and exception which is similar in some ways to Agamben's analysis but which moves beyond it as well.

The dislocated debate between Michael Foucault and Giorgio Agamben over the relation between sovereign and governmental power is important throughout the book, but also it is achingly familiar in contemporary critical (legal) theory. In *Society Must Be Defended* and again in *Security, Territory, Population* Foucault suggested that governmentality overtakes sovereign power during the eighteenth century, through the framework of political economy of the population.[18] '[G]overning is by no means coextensive with the state, sovereignty or law .... [It is found in] a dispersed range of sites: one governs the sick, one governs one's family, one governs children, one governs the soul, and one governs one's self'.[19] Agamben agrees to a point but argues it is essential to see a much longer genealogy of government. In *The Kingdom and the Glory*, he associates government with *oikonomia*, tracing it through the ancient Greek and early Christian church. He tells us that Xenophon formulates *oikonomia* as 'a functional organisation, an activity of management which is not bound to rules other than that of the orderly functioning of the house (or of the undertaking in question)'.[20]

In the early Christian church, Agamben finds a thinking of the '*oikonomia* of salvation' – the order necessary to lead a good life. He argues the world is 'governed through the coordination of two principles, the *auctoritas* (a power without actual execution) and the *potestas* (a power that can be exercised); the Kingdom and the Government'.[21] On one side, the sovereign reigns but cannot rule, and on the other the government has power but is an-archic. In this way, Agamben argues, instead of competitive modes of power, we can see the essential interrelation of government and sovereignty. Ultimately, the government (the multiple minor agents of sovereignty) sign for the sovereign; they make its structure present in ways that are impossible for the pure sense of *auctoritas*. Here we might pose Patricia Owen's theorisation of economies (*oikonomia*) of force in colonial subjection as a counterpoint to Foucault's government as conduct of population, or Agamben's political and economic theology. Owen traces the power (*oikonomia*) deployed to pacify and control colonised peoples. The colonial forces of para-military policing and the military pacification (a sort of para-policing) both deploy and develop 'household' forms of power. The colony is the point where the power over the household is developed most intensely. This book will deploy all three senses of government (as governmentality, as a way of signing for sovereignty, and as a colonial dynamic). But rather than resolving the theoretical tensions between them here in an abstract sense, I will trace them as they each play out (independently and together) in the field of public order.

People, population, populace

Throughout the book we will see three figurations of collective political power: 'the people', the 'population' and most importantly the 'populace'. The people is the term most closely associated with western sovereignty. As either revolutionary signifier demanded by the masses as they overthrow the sovereign order or as the term used by that order to convey its authority over the mob, the people is a heavily freighted term. Population, on the other hand, is a radical reconfiguration of the problem of the people.[22]

> One of the great innovations in the techniques of power in the eighteenth century was the emergence of 'population' as an economic and political problem: population as wealth, population as manpower or labor capacity, population balanced between its own growth and the resources it commanded. Governments perceived that they were not dealing simply with subjects, or even with a 'people', but with a 'population', with its specific phenomena and its peculiar variables: birth and death rates, life expectancy, fertility, state of health, frequency of illness, patterns of diet and habitation.[23]

Unlike the people, which suggests a unitary political subject, the population is spread out into different phenomena so that it can become the 'technical-political object of management and government'.[24] Foucault suggests that the people presents a unitary question for the sovereign structure; it is either obedient or it revolts. But the life of the population can be disaggregated. It becomes both the object of this technical knowledge and the subject of micro-level changes to optimise whatever aspect is under consideration.[25]

The third term that I will use is 'the populace'. This has an interesting valence that is less frequently explored. Etymologically it stems from the middle French *populace* and Italian *popolaccio* or *popolazzo* (*-accio* or *-azzo* being pejorative suffixes). Both mean the least privileged parts of society, the common people, rabble or mob. In English there are three closely related meanings: the ordinary people; the inhabitants of a particular place (a synonym of population), or a multitude, crowd or throng.[26] Populace and population are synonyms in the sense that both suggest the need for management/government.[27] But into this mix, the populace also adds the pejorative sense of the rabble or the masses. This introduces a key difference. Where 'the population' might be known by statistical collection and managed by carefully crafted social interventions, the populace must be known and managed through a broad sense of 'public order'. The populace is then a version of the population. But where the population also suggests the problems of grain, circulation, disease as Foucault shows,[28] the populace is very particularly a security problem. In particular it is a public order security problem because of its close relation to the problem of crowds and disorder. It is a site of risk. It threatens disorder but in an undifferentiated sort of way. The populace is the great body of people from which the crowds emerge. It cannot be reduced to the crowd, but nor can it simply be disassociated. Because of this association, the populace also carries a strong sense of affect: it is full of the whims, moods, impulses, passions and fads.[29] It requires specific apparatuses developed to manage these affective instabilities. While the populace is close to the population in the sense of its governability, it's relation to crowds also connects it to the people. As we will see in the final part, the violence done by and to crowds sometimes crystallises a new social force. The affective reverberations of the crowd and population open the possibility of an appearance of the people. So unlike population which Foucault shows entails the explicit and fundamental exclusion of the people,[30] crowds connect the populace to the people.

Chapters, parts and the argument

The book has an unusual structure. There are twenty two chapters if you include the excurses, prologue, introduction and conclusion. These are a mixture of substantive chapters developing the key arguments of the book and shorter explanations nestled in between. The chapters are shorter and there are more of them than the genre conventions of this type of academic monograph (usually anything from three to ten chapters). They are meant to crowd together, performing a force of numbers where the collection and articulation of a mass of resonant ideas becomes more powerful by way of its number. Much as I dreamed of producing a book whose structure was entirely organised as a swarm, with non-linear resonating chapters, I realised as I began to write up the research that it would prove unreadable. Unwilling to move back to a standard structure, I have instead organised the book by introducing four distinct parts. While these build upon one another, they are also distinct movements which establish the key elements of the book. The first sketches sovereign affects, the second explores the apparatus of public order, the third thinks about the way that crowded action might affectively 'pattern' the people and the fourth examines the state of unrest through the framework of violence and enmity. The four parts begin with a short introduction and end with an excursus where I double back over a key element of that part of the book. Each substantive chapter also has a very brief digest at the outset.

The book focuses on the affective relations of law and disorder which are experienced in the state of unrest. It produces a theory of sovereign affects, focusing on the crowded scenes which enervate the sovereign order. It insists that rather than an obscure and underwhelming legal sub-discipline, 'public order' is actually an essential attribute of the sovereign order. Ignoring it, as critical (legal) theory has often done, is an important error.[31] Public order is an everyday experience of sovereignty, where the sovereign order claims the peace and calm atmosphere of public space as an iteration of its glory and good government. Exploring public order as an affective state and as a governmental apparatus, we begin to nuance some of the recent theories of sovereignty, exceptionality, and coloniality. What's more, this framework helps us to understand the importance of protest in a way that paradigms like human rights miss. Protest is *not* important because (when expressed in a limited way) it vindicates the citizen's rights to assembly and speech.[32] Nor is it important because it helps to stage the 'marketplace of ideas' which the constituted order might then mediate. It is important because it operates at the articulation of the affective life of the populace and the sovereign order. Protest is important because, sometimes, it radically reconfigures the affective valence of a situation. Protest is important because it can change everything.

Notes

1 Georges Bataille, *Visions of Excess: Selected Writings 1927-1939* (Minneapolis: University of Minnesota Press, 1985), 162.
2 Alison Young, 'Japanese Atmospheres of Criminal Justice', 59.4 *The British Journal of Criminology* (2019), 767.
3 Brian Massumi, 'Histories of Violence: Affect, Power, Violence – The Political is not Personal', *Law Review of Books* (13/11/2017) https://lareviewofbooks.org/article/histories-of-violence-affect-power-violence-the-political-is-not-personal (viewed on 02/04/2020).
4 Deborah Gould *Moving Politics: Emotion and ACT UP's Fight against AIDS* (University of Chicago Press, Chicago, 2009), 3.
5 Katherine Ibbett, 'When I do, I call it affect', 40.2 *Paragraph* (2017) 244–245.
6 Gould, *Moving Politics*, 26.

7 Lauren Berlant explains: 'All times are transitional. But at some crisis times like this one, politics is defined by a collectively held sense that a glitch has appeared in the reproduction of life. A glitch is an interruption within a transition, a troubled transmission. A glitch is also the revelation of an infrastructural failure.' Lauren Berlant, 'The Commons: Infrastructures for Troubling Times', 34.3 *Environment and Planning D: Society and Space*, 393.
8 Ibid. 20 (emphasis in the original). Gould makes this observation about affect in general, but it is particularly acute in the context of affective atmosphere.
9 As noted by Costas Douzinas, *Philosophy and Resistance in the Crisis* (London: Polity Press, 2013), 130; and William Mazzarella 'The Myth of the Multitude, or, Who's Afraid of the Crowd?' 36 *Critical Inquiry* (2010), 697.
10 Elias Canetti, *Crowds and Power* (New York: Viking Books, 1963).
11 For instance, Momboisse is typical of a certain genre of police literature which categorises crowds in order to instruct police how to intervene. Raymond Momboisse, *Riots, Revolts and Insurrections* (Charles Thomas Publisher: Springfield Illinois, 1967).
12 Gustave Le Bon, *The Crowd: A Study of the Popular Mind* (T Fisher Unwin: London, 1903).
13 Michel Foucault, 'On the Genealogy of Ethics: An Over View of Work in Progress' in Hubert Dreyfus and Paul Rabinow, *Michel Foucault: Beyond Structuralism and Hermeneutics* (Chicago, University of Chicago Press, 1983), 256.
14 Achille Mbembe, *Necropolitics* (Duke University Press, 2019), 66.
15 Ibid.
16 Giorgio Agamben, *Homo Sacer: Sovereign Power and Bare Life* (Stanford: Stanford University Press, 1998).
17 *R v Secretary of State for the Home Department* (ex parte Northumbria Police Authority), [1989] 1 QB 26, as per Nourse, LJ.
18 Michel Foucault, *Society Must Be Defended: Lectures at the College de France 1975-76* (New York: Picador, 2003); Michel Foucault, *Security, Territory, Population: Lectures at the College de France 1977-78* (New York: Palgrave MacMillan, 2009).
19 Ben Golder, *Foucault and the Politics of Rights* (Stanford: Stanford University Press, 2015), 53.
20 Giorgio Agamben, *The Kingdom and the Glory* (Stanford University Press, 2011), 18.
21 Ibid., 103.
22 Foucault, *Security, Territory, Population*, 43.
23 Michel Foucault, *The History of Sexuality: Volume 1: An Introduction* (London: Penguin, 1979), 25.
24 Foucault, *Security, Territory, Population*, 70.
25 Marcelo Hoffman, *Foucault and Power: The Influence of Political Engagement on Theories of Power* (Bloomsbury, 2013), 101–107.
26 'populace, n.' OED Online. March 2020. Oxford University Press. www.oed.com/view/Entry/147906 (viewed on 28/03/2020).
27 This is true in the dictionary sense, but we also find it in the work of careful Foucauldians like Thomas Lemke who deploys population and populace interchangeably when discussing post-Foucauldian biopolitics and the government of life. Thomas Lemke, 'Beyond Foucault: From Biopolitics to the Government of Life' in Ulrich Brockling, Susanne Krasmann and Thomas Lemke, *Governmentality: Current Issues and Future Challenges* (Abingdon: Routledge, 2011), 165.
28 Foucault, *Security, Territory, Population*.
29 The Apple dictionary (drawn from the Oxford University Press database) gives the following usage for 'populace': 'the party misjudged the mood of the populace'. We could substantiate this connection with a quick survey of Edmund Burke's usage of the term. In the *Reflections* the populace is animated to plunder, it is filled with 'a black and savage atrocity of mind' (Edmund Burke *Reflections on the Revolution in France, and on the proceedings in certain societies in London relative to that event.* [1790] in Edmund Burke *Revolutionary Writings* (Cambridge: Cambridge University Press,

2014)). In the 'Thoughts on the Cause of the Present Discontents', the populace has a fury that is fierce and licentious; it is licentious and embodying a 'boldness' and shakes the peace of a kingdom. Edmund Burke, *The Writings and Speeches of Edmund Burke, Volume II: Party, Parliament and the American Crisis 1766-1774* (Clarendon Press, 1981). The populace is the moody, affective body of the population.

30 Foucault, *Security, Territory, Population*, 43–44.

31 There are a small number of exceptions to this, in particular the work of Mark Neocleous has repeatedly returned to public order (Mark Neocleous, *The Fabrication of Social Order: A Critical Theory of Police Power* (London: Pluto Press, 2000); Mark Neocleous, *War Power, Police Power* (Edinburgh: Edinburgh University Press, 2014).

32 David Mead, *The* New *Law of Peaceful Protest: Rights and Regulation in the Human Rights Act Era* (Oxford: Hart Publishing, 2010).

PROLOGUE

Sovereign aesthetics

In which we introduce an aesthetic staging of sovereignty – a sense of sovereign majesty and dignity – Burke connects majesty to the sublime/awe and dignity to the beautiful/love.

There is an aesthetic theory of sovereignty which Craig Carson puts most simply: 'Sovereignty, to be efficacious, must be staged'.[1] Sovereignty has to be *made* present, and such a making has its styles and feelings. Acts of state have a certain theatricality; they are put on, performed *for* their audiences. More than this, sovereignty is performed in ways that excite the populace, that engenders their affects. The audience are not passive recipients of these broadcasts. The sovereign seeks out desires, attachments and drives that are embodied in the performance itself. It invites its populace to join in. There are 'moments of state' that stage the theatre of sovereignty for particular audiences: inaugurations, coronations, the state of the union, a papal visit, a royal wedding or jubilee. Rich concepts like 'majesty', 'splendour', 'glory' and 'dignity' that make up the traditional Western metaphysics of sovereignty do not give us singular meanings but instead open differently in particular performances. It is not simply that a unitary sense of sovereignty might be staged in different ways but that different ways of staging sovereignty perform *different* sovereign relations. To take just two key terms, majesty and dignity hold the potential to produce many different affective flows. But these affective constellations give majesty and dignity different meanings. Unlike a theologico-political understanding of sovereignty which takes a deep dive into the genealogy of concepts, '"the aesthetic" can be defined as the sensible presentation of concepts'.[2] An aesthetic approach insists that sovereignty is understood through the relations it engenders. The question becomes: 'What is being staged in this sovereign relation?'

A prologue stands out, before the beginning of the narrative– a sort of prefiguration of the text to come, without being introductory as such. This prologue aims to establish the stakes of the book, examining sovereignty, public order and unrest to understand their affective dynamics. Edmund Burke has been chosen here because of the manner in which he stages sovereign sentiment, often framing sovereign relations against the tumult of unrest. *Reflection on the Revolutions in France* is a central text, because it produces two different stagings of majesty and dignity, and their attendant feelings of the awesome sublime and love of the beautiful. But we can also look before the *Reflections* to develop the key affective terminology of government. In the 'Thoughts on the Cause of the Present Discontent' Burke had introduced the problem of maladministration and the affective unrest that it generates. Between these texts we find a complex and compelling analysis of the affective life of the sovereign apparatus.

On 5 October 1789, between 3,000 and 4,000 Parisian women arrived at the palace at Versailles. They were outraged by the faltering grain supply. Late that night a much larger crowd began to congregate: there were at least 20,000 of the Parisian National Guard, along with a number of companies of infantry and a 'motley band' of up to 800 men armed with muskets, sticks and pikes. The exact purpose of this much larger group remains unclear, but on the morning of 6 October they began to clash with the king's *gardes du corps*.: 'Some demonstrators had managed to enter the *château* and penetrated as far as the antechamber to the queen's apartment'.[3] Following a shot into the crowd which killed a seventeen-year-old volunteer, two of the *gardes du corps* were lynched. Order was restored by the National Guard, but as Rudé puts it: 'To the national guard … there could only be one solution: the king must be made come back to Paris, whether their commander-in-chief was willing or not'.[4]

In the *Reflections on the Revolution in France* (1790) Edmund Burke is transfixed by this moment. He gives it pride of place. The description of those October days helps Burke re-orient the *Reflections*, from the order of inheritable sovereignty and property to the monstrosity of revolution. But as David Collings observes, Burke falsifies the vignette, underlining the most scurrilous accounts of the events and inventing details that were nowhere reported and that did not (as far as we can tell) take place. Burke was evidently horrified by the events; he seems to have found something unspeakable in their transgression of the sovereign's person. He writes that the palace was 'left swimming in blood, polluted by massacre and strewed with scattered limbs and mutilated carcasses'.[5] He titillates the readers with the image of the beautiful Queen jumping almost naked from her bed and fleeing before the crowd. They enter her chamber and pierce her bed 'with a hundred strokes of bayonets and poniards'[6] – a barely concealed trope of rape. Tom Furniss notes that at least some of these embellishments or falsifications were pointed out to Burke as the book went into successive editions, but he never altered his account.[7] The reasons for this are quite clear: the description provides the affective centrepiece of the argument. It crystallises everything that is horrific about the revolution: Their Majesties are violated and the indignity of a terrible new sublime force is unleashed.

Collings suggests that the crowd's actions are much more than a 'political affront' to Burke. In fact, in the most base and quotidian of manners, they break a taboo.[8]

> Through these fictions he depicts what is for him the truth of the crowd's actions. Evidently, one cannot conceive of the revolution apart from mass slaughter, an exemplary image of the dismemberment of the body politic, nor apart from rape, an image that suggests that the crowd physically invaded a space forbidden to it, overwhelmed a few vulnerable people with the force of its amassed bodies, and profaned something for which it should have the greatest respect. To violate the constitution, one must also violate the *body* of the state in an act which, by oversetting the highest things, brings about the universal devastation previously witnessed only in the darkest tragedies.[9]

To convey the metaphysical significance of the events, Burke creates a fantasy of mutilation, dismemberment and rape. He invents the gore in order to represent the significance of the events, precisely because what has been lost is something metaphysical that escapes simple explanation. There is something in that simple proximity of the king and his people that rankles with Burke. Their sublime and beautiful majesties are juxtaposed with the profane bodies of the rabble that reek of blood and sweat. The abject and the majestic stand alongside each other. Worse still, the abject seems to subject the majestic![10]

This scene stages the double sublime of Burke's French revolution: at once the delightful sublime of their sovereign majesties and the terrible sublime of the people. Derrida explains in the first volume of *The Beast and the Sovereign* that

> Majesty is … another name for the sovereignty of the sovereign … . *Majestas* indeed names, as the superlative of magnitude or grandeur, the majority of the great, of the *magnus,* the *major*, the male erection of a grandeur grander than grandeur. The king, the monarch, the emperor is upped [*majoré*], erected … to a height that is majestic, upped, augmented, exaggerated, higher than the height of the great, incomparably higher than height itself, even sublimely higher than height, and this is already the height of the Most High: The Sovereign in its Majesty is most high, greater than great … . This standing, erect, augmented grandeur, infinitely upped, this height superior to every other superiority is not merely a trope, a figure of rhetoric, a sensory way of representing the sovereign.[11]

This height of the sovereign, its majesty, is accessible to the senses, but as Derrida continues, 'the majestic Most High rises above all comparable and sensory height (whereby it is also sublime, or in any case lays claim to being meta-metaphorical and meta-physical, more than natural and more than sensory)'.[12] For Burke, as the sovereignty of the sovereign, majesty is embodied in the king. The proper audience of the sovereign scene would be struck by their awe-some majesty. In the embodied majesty there is something more than sensory, it is a sign of an excess of embodiment. By embodying this sublime and locating the site of excess, it is captured. It is possible to be in its presence, but more importantly it is possible to *leave* its presence. With the royal body, distance is possible. And at a distance, Burke says, the sublime generates delight rather than terror. The king's body bounds this sublime majesty, localises it, places it within an order which is comprehensible. However, it does this without rendering it prosaic and terrene. The king's body is elevated rather than the sovereign majesty being rendered mundane. His majesty is extended through his law, keeping his peace, determining subject positions within the estates. In the English context Burke underlined the manner in which the social constrains the majestic sublime through the ordering that renders it comprehensible.

Burke's fantasy of the crowd in the Queen's bed chamber and the slaughter of the guard conveys a different sense of the sublime. The sublime is delightful only so long as it is *not* everywhere and anywhere. As he had explained in *The Sublime and the Beautiful:* 'When danger and pain press too nearly, they are incapable of giving any delight, and are simply terrible'.[13] The king's body provides a location for the sublime. Only by giving a specific location is it possible to take distance. When the king is decapitated this specific location is removed. Instead, the people is sovereign. Burke writes in the *Letters on a Regicide Peace:* 'Out of the tomb of murdered monarchy in France has arisen a vast tremendous unformed spectre, in a far more terrific guise than any which ever yet has overpowered the imagination and subdued the fortitude of man'.[14] By stripping sovereignty of its dignified robes, 'all the decent drapery of life is to be rudely torn off'.[15] The new sovereign sublime is to be found anywhere the crowd manifests itself. Rather than being localised in the body of the king, the sovereign sublime becomes generalised. It can be localised anywhere that number gathers in the name of the people, and will be used to break apart the social order that Burke claims has restrained the sovereign power. This is a new mode of sovereignty, a sublime that is unrestrained by social convention.

In Burke's early work, the sovereign is sublime in a relatively simple sense. For instance, in *The Sublime and the Beautiful* he insists, 'I know nothing sublime that is not some modification of power'. And that: 'The power which arises from institution in kings and commanders, has the same connection with terror. Sovereigns are frequently addressed with the title of dread majesty'.[16] That slim volume was committed to distinguishing the affects of the sublime from the beautiful. But by the time of the *Reflections* in 1790, Burke insists that sovereignty is not so simple. The state must evince the majesty of the sublime and but also the love borne of the beautiful. The Burkean sublime is a 'kind of terror … [that] crushes us into admiring submission: it thus resembles a coercive rather than a consensual power, engaging our respect but not, as with beauty, our love'.[17] In the *Reflections* alongside the need for a dread majesty, the sovereign also requires beauty. The beauty of the state would 'create in us love, veneration, admiration, or attachment'.[18] Or as Eagleton puts it, law 'must blend terror and kindliness, coercion and consent, in well-calculated proportion'.[19] In the *Reflections* this beauty is personified in the calm beauty of the Queen. But it is also found in the form of tradition, that 'soft collar of social esteem'[20] which limits the sovereign and his people, without compulsion.

In this combination of the sublime sovereign and the beautiful social order (or majesty and dignity as we will see) Eagleton underlines the paradox:

> only love will truly win us to the law, but this love will erode the law to nothing. A law attractive enough to engage our intimate affections, and so hegemonically effective, will tend to inspire in us a benign contempt. On the other hand, a power which rouses our filial fear, and hence our submissive obedience, is likely to alienate our affections and so spur us to oedipal resentment.[21]

Burke rejects the eviscerating moment of a radical break and the attendant Rights of Man, precisely because it sweeps away the social fabric. He saw society as a gradual accretion of tradition over centuries. It is precisely this fabric that is torn to shreds when the Queen is imagined fleeing almost naked from her bed. The new sublime lacks social restraint, and the populace and sovereign are to be governed by terror alone.[22]

Burke had insisted that good, calm, peaceful and effective sovereign orders were marked by a balance between the sublime majesty and the beautiful dignity.[23] Burke had associated the sublime with the masculine and the beautiful with the feminine.[24] In the *Reflections* this gendered aesthetics was applied to sovereignty in such a way as to insist upon the clothing of the sublime in the beautiful. 'The law must coerce like a man but cajole like a woman, chastise like a father but indulge us like a mother'.[25] Thus, Eagleton suggests that Burke's legal theory is epicene: 'It must be a cross-dresser, concealing its true gender. Yet there is always an ugly bulge in its alluring garments'.[26] The sovereign in Burke is *not* simply a sublime power, it must also be beautiful. In this, the sovereign seeks to excite both love and awe. But Eagleton is not queer enough in this reading of Burke. It seems as though he wants to 'demystify' Burke's ugly bulge, to underline the sovereign's terrible violence beneath all of the cajoling and indulgence. But this sort of 'demystification' risks prioritising the awe of the sublime over the love of the beautiful. The robes and symbols of the sovereign are not just a way of staging a quality of the sovereign that is already there; they are the *essential* trappings of the office and without them the office is denuded.[27]

Alongside this intense sovereign aesthetics, in the 'Thoughts on the Cause of the Present Discontents' (1770) Burke introduces the question of affective government. Importantly, this is related to sovereignty, but it is *not the same question.*

Burke's 'present discontents' (of the title) were that the sovereign order had been denuded. The affective bonds of a sovereign order had begun to break down, and the government, which is responsible for *managing* these affects, was to blame. At the outset he lists these 'universally admitted and lamented' facts:

> That Government is at once dreaded and contempted; that the laws are despoiled of all their respected and salutary terrors; that their inaction is a subject of ridicule, and their exertion of abhorrence; that rank, and office, and title … have lost their reverence and effect … that our dependencies are slackened in their affection, and loosened from their obedience.[28]

When the sovereign is perceived as 'odious and feeble', he writes, the consequences will be inevitable 'to our public peace'. He employs a symptomatic reading of public disorder, insisting that when popular discontent is prevalent 'there has generally been something found amiss in the constitution, or in the conduct of government. The people have no interest in disorder'.[29] As government is corrupted, dissent becomes increasingly intense. When the management of that epicene power of sovereignty breaks down and the people are no longer excited to love and awe, an atmosphere of 'sullen gloom and furious disorder prevail by fits: the nation loses its relish for peace and prosperity'.[30]

In this reflection Burke introduces a crucial distinction between the government of affect and sovereign affects. In short, the sovereign order must be staged, but without the government to mediate the sovereign order adequately, it will lose its affective force. Burke introduces an idea that will be essential throughout this book. He writes:

> Nations are not primarily ruled by laws: less by violence. Whatever original energy may be supposed either in force or regulation; the operation of both is, in truth, merely instrumental. Nations are governed by the same methods, and on the same principles, by which an individual without authority is often able to govern those who are his equals or superiors; by a knowledge of their temper, and by a judicious management of it. … The temper of the people amongst whom he presides ought therefore to be the first study of a Statesman.[31]

The 'temper of the people' is an intriguing idea. It points to an affective quality to the life of the populace. Government is an emollient: it can calm and assuage the temper of the people. But bad governance, for Burke at least, is an astringent, irritating their temper, giving rise to unrest. There is little or no 'original energy' in law; it is in the government of popular sentiments that the populace is managed.

The people's temper is what Ben Anderson calls 'affective life';[32] the circulation of affects, atmospheres and moods as they move around and through moments of sovereignty. 'Government' is the techniques by which the temper of the people is managed. Good government may add to the glory of the sovereign, and bad government may lessen it. In the 'Thoughts on the Cause of our Present Discontents' Burke productively deploys the polysemy of 'temper'. Temper conveys anger and unrest. The temper of the people is its ability to become restive when the state malfunctions. But it also suggests a neutralising or countervailing force – the power to temper their anger. The 'temper of the people' is precisely its *capacity* for unrest. Government *with* the temper of the people will prove more effective than attempting to govern against it. For Burke, the temper of the people very obviously comes from below, from the circulation of public sentiments, attachments and identifications. It is something natural, closely related to the 'soft collar' of the customary order that he lauds in the *Reflections* (the customary order that is swept away by the social revolution). A good-tempered people has been well governed.

Burke is clear that the state of discontent in which the popular temper is irritated gives rise to a new breed of agent – an accelerant:

> A species of men to whom a state of order would become a sentence of obscurity, are nourished into a dangerous magnitude by the heat of intestine disturbances; and it is no wonder that, by a sort of sinister piety, they cherish, in their turn, the disorders which are the parents of all their consequence. Superficial observers consider such persons as the cause of the public uneasiness, when, in truth, they are nothing more than the effect of it. [33]

New leaders emerge who crystallise the new symbolic economy of the disturbance. Burke is very clear that such men are not the original cause of disorder, but a symptom and an intensifier of the disorder. In the same way that the government does not create society, the revolutionary is merely an expression of the underlying anger. Once they emerge, however, a new spiral of events unfolds:

> Fierce licentiousness begets violent restraints. The military arm is the sole reliance; and then, call your constitution what you please, it is the sword that governs. The civil power, like every other that calls in the aid of an ally stronger than itself, perishes by the assistance it receives … . Everything partakes of the original disorder. Anarchy predominates without freedom, and servitude without submission or subordination.[34]

Burke describes a spiral from stability through unrest and disorder to the threshold of suppression or revolution. We can read this idea of the temper of the people through the later *Reflections*, where the dignified fabric of sovereignty is torn when the sovereign order fails in its duty to sustain the peace and calm of the people. And sovereignty stripped of its dignity will increasingly fall back on the sublime (terrible) majesty – on its exceptional violence.

In these brief notes, I have begun to sketch the key themes of this book. Burke's aesthetics is never simply a matter of empty representation. The staging of sovereignty is always tied to the affects that might emerge in the populace: the right mixture of love and awe, the pure terror, the tempers rising or the calming governance. Governments intervene in the affective life of the populace. They seek to know it and to manage it. At the same time, Burke is very clear that the risk of failing to know and manage the affective life of the populace leads to the complete breakdown of the sovereign order. He makes clear that both sovereign order and revolutionary movement operate upon the same level. In short, his aesthetic theory of sovereignty sensitises us to the possibilities of an affective analysis.

Notes

1 Craig Carson, 'The King's Virtual Body: Image, Text and Sovereignty in Edmund Burke's "Reflections on the Revolution in France"', 2.2 *Republic of Letters: A Journal for the Study of Knowledge, Politics and the Arts* (2011), 120.
2 Dick Howard, 'Foreword', in Zvi Ben-Don Benite, Stefanos Geroulanos and Nicole Jerr (eds), *The Scaffolding of Sovereignty: Global and Aesthetic Perspectives on the History of a Concept* (Columbia University Press, 2017), xvi (emphasis in original).
3 George Rude, *The Crowd in Popular History: A Study of Popular Disturbances in France and England, 1730-1848* (Oxford University Press: Oxford, 1959), 76.
4 Ibid., 77.
5 Burke *Reflections*, 72.
6 Ibid., 72.
7 Tom Furniss, 'Stripping the Queen: Edmund Burke's Magic Lantern Show', in Steven Blakemore (ed) *Burke and the French Revolution, Bicentennial Essays* (University of Georgia Press, 1992), 69.
8 David Collings, *Monstrous Society: Reciprocity, Discipline and the Political Uncanny at the end of Early Modern England* (Lewisburg: Bucknell University Press, 2009).
9 Ibid., 64.
10 Ibid., 64.
11 Jacques Derrida, *The Beast and the Sovereign Volume 1* (University of Chicago Press, 2009), 215.
12 Ibid., 215.
13 Edmund Burke, *Philosophical Inquiry into the Origin of our Ideas of the Sublime and the Beautiful* (London: Thomas McLean, 1823), 46.
14 Edmund Burke, *Letters on a Regicide Peace, Volume 3* (Liberty Fund, 1999), 65. For an insightful examination of the corporeal and vital forces see Catherine Packham, *Eighteenth Century Vitalism: Bodies, Culture, Politics* (Palgrave 2012).
15 Burke, *Reflections*, 79.
16 Burke, *The Sublime and the Beautiful*, 90.
17 Terry Eagleton, 'Aesthetics and Politics in Edmund Burke', 28.1 *History Workshop Journal* (1989), 57.
18 Burke, *Reflections*, 80.
19 Terry Eagleton, *Holy Terror* (Oxford University Press, 2005), 48.
20 Burke, *Reflections*, 79.
21 Eagleton 'Aesthetics and Politics in Edmund Burke', 58.
22 Eagleton writes: 'The law must not be seen naked, or it will shed its authority along with its garments. This in Burke's view is the real crime of the French Jacobins – that they have ripped the comely veils of hegemony from the law and exposed its phallic barbarism for all to see' (Eagleton, *Holy Terror*, 50).
23 Ibid., 49.

24 William J T Mitchell, *Iconology: Image, Text, Ideology* (University of Chicago Press, 1987).
25 Eagleton, *Holy Terror*, 49.
26 Ibid., 50.
27 It is Thomas Carlyle's infamous *Sartor Restatus: The Life and Opinions of Herr Teufelsdrockh* (1831) (Oxford: Oxford University Press, 2008) that sees this relation between dress and authority most clearly.
28 Edmund Burke, *The Writings and Speeches of Edmund Burke, Volume II: Party, Parliament and the American Crisis 1766-1774* (Clarendon Press, 1981), 253.
29 Ibid.
30 Ibid.
31 Ibid., 252.
32 Anderson, *Encountering Affect.*
33 Burke, *Writings and Speeches Vol II*, 286.
34 Ibid., 286–287.

PART I

Affective sovereignty

Sovereignty appears. That is where we start. Something or someone appears as sovereign. They stand in for an entire apparatus, embodying that authority, that metaphysics. Around them a web of relations is gathered. In the Western tradition, these relations are understood through various metaphysical terms: majesty and dignity adhere to the sovereign body and radiate outwards; glory and splendour are produced for the sovereign by political and economic relations. Once staged, these concepts become more than the sum of their theological associations. They are freighted with aspects of the performance. They can no longer be considered in isolation but require an understanding of the ways they resonate. These moments of appearance give tone and texture to the sovereign order. The aim of this first part is to focus on ways in which sovereignty is staged in order to generate particular affective relations. In the coming chapters, we look to four moments where citizens encounter sovereignty. Each sovereign encounter shows that the styles of sovereign appearance (its aesthetics) are crucial to the transmission of its sovereign affects. Sovereign aesthetics are supposed to generate affective encounters, making sovereignty meaningful for the public.

This part will introduce the idea of sovereign affects and the government of temper. We will see the atmospheres of national mediation, a zombie royal wedding, the image designed to stop a revolt and a governmental apparatus for the management of morale. Each chapter also introduces a different methodological approach to the question of affect. In the first chapter we see the materiality of affective atmosphere. This helps us to explore the idea of affective communication. In the second chapter we see the manner in which the genre analysis of events can help us think about affective expectations, and indeed how the affective scripts might be disrupted. In the third chapter we will see the manner in which affect escapes, in particular engaging with the 'autonomy of affect' thesis. In the fourth chapter we examine an affective apparatus designed to manage popular affect. This fourth chapter also introduces a difference. Instead of taking a contemporary example where sovereignty is staged for the populace, it investigates an important moment of the *government* of affects. The distinction between government and sovereignty is important for this book as we have seen already in Burke. Sovereignty reigns but cannot govern, where government is a form of power without transcendent authority. They operate together, all the while remaining different modalities of power. Sovereignty deploys majesty, dignity and splendour. It seeks to evince affects of loyalty, love and awe. But the government conducts populations; it manages and orders. It intervenes in the life of the population where sovereignty stands above. This is an important distinction which we will continue to return to throughout the book.

1

ATMOSPHERES OF SOVEREIGNTY

In which we introduce an affective account of sovereignty – the state attempts to protect its spaces of national mediation – atmospheres are analysed as the affective tone of space – we meet Teresa Brennan's account of the materiality of atmospheres – and think about the manner in which atmospheres can be created or managed.

On a windy evening in the spring of 2008, a group of eighteen largely white, 'nerdy libertarians' arrived at the Jefferson Memorial in Washington, D.C. Each one of them inserted earphones and began a silent disco. We get a good sense of their dancing from the first of two videos posted by 'freethejefferson1' on YouTube. The camera quickly picks up a gathering of graceless gestures by the rear wall: a balding man in a tee-shirt bounces around; a tall ungainly man wearing a sports coat gesticulates wildly, while others bob more carefully, hands moving this way and that. Soon the park rangers arrive and begin to disperse the dancers. The second video is largely made up of the conversation between a park ranger, the man shooting the video and Ms Mary Brooke Oberwetter – who would later take the case to the District Court. The ranger insists: 'You saw the sign: Quiet!' Oberwetter responds that they were being quiet because it was a silent disco. So the ranger shifts tack: 'You were Dancing in here. That is disorderly'. The conversation continues until the ranger loses patience. After a number of warnings, he arrests Oberwetter and escorts her away. She was detained for five hours and later cited for an unauthorised demonstration and interfering with an agency function.

While no further action was taken by the park rangers, Oberwetter took the case to the District Court for the District of Columbia. Among other things, she sought a declaration that the actions of the park rangers violated the First Amendment of the US Constitution – protection of free speech. The court in *Oberwetter v Hilliard and Salazar* dismissed her claims, finding that the Park Service was entitled to place restrictions on speech because it was a non-public space for the purposes of the First Amendment.[1] Oberwetter's case has little precedential significance. It is an uncontroversial reaffirmation of classic US free speech doctrine. But, it does contain a beautiful moment of insight into the staging of sites of sovereignty. The case concerns the conditions of *encountering sovereignty*. From it, we can begin to draw out the affective conditions of staging sovereignty. It highlights the atmospheric spaces where sovereignty is mediated and made present to a public. This chapter introduces atmospheres, which will become one of the crucial sites for both sovereignty and, later in the book, for the social and political potential of the state of unrest. The aim here is to introduce a material account of affect, underlining the manner in which sovereignty can operate affectively from the background.

The space of the Jefferson Memorial was not 'public' for the purposes of the First Amendment. It was a special enclave, distinct from the public space of the parklands and sidewalks around it. As such, the jurisprudence explains that the Park Services were entitled to place certain restrictions on speech, so long as they were reasonable given the purpose that the regulations sought to effect. The key function of the Park Service's intervention was to protect 'an atmosphere of calm, tranquillity and reverence'. The court explained that the state is entitled to protect the atmosphere in which the dignity and majesty of the state are made present. This makes sense for as long as we do not think too hard about what the court means by 'atmosphere'. But if we do pause on it, the trouble begins, because atmospheres flummox us. They seem so obvious in one's lived

FIGURE 1.1 Alex Grichenko, 'Thomas Jefferson Memorial', public domain.

experience: the electrifying gig, the tension-filled room, the cosy winter's evening before a crackling fire, the football stadium during a local derby – or the atmosphere of majesty and dignity at a national monument. When they are at their most intense, atmospheres are palpable. But once we place them into our traditional epistemologies, they seem to evaporate. A good place to begin is with the leakiness of bodies, things and environments.[2] Objects are not self-contained entities; they interact. Imagine yourself, for a moment, in a forest or a rubbish dump: the smells of timber, damp and vegetation or the sour tang of human detritus, sharp and foetid. These smells come from objects rotting, decomposing and decaying, a process of chemical interaction whereby molecules are released into the air. We become conscious of this sometimes as smell, but most of the time we do not consciously perceive this fug. That does not stop it from affecting us, changing our bodies in ways that we may or may not be attuned to. From the polluted smog of the industrial city to the 'atmospheric purity' imagined by air-conditioning manufacturers,[3] we are constantly interacting with organic and inorganic molecules that make up 'air'. Teresa Brennan asks us to go further here. She argues: 'If I walk … into the atmospheric room … and it is rank with the smell of anxiety, I breathe this in'.[4] The smell that we sense here is a material event.[5] We identify particular molecules exuded by those (organic and inorganic) bodies around us. And we make sense of it as anxiety. That is to say that it changes our body, and we decode this change of bodily state as the feeling of 'anxiety'. What is important here for Brennan is that this is not simply a symbolic identification, a thought about being anxious. It is a bodily communication. The affects exuded by others communicate with our body as we enter the room. Our pulse quickens, we become more alert, we feel slightly queasy as our body begins to produce adrenaline or other hormones. In other words, the molecules exuded unwittingly by those anxious bodies around us facilitate a non-linguistic communication with our bodies. Thus when we sense the anxiety in the atmosphere in the room that Brennan describes, we are making sense of the 'smell' but also of our own bodily reaction. In this account, atmosphere is a sort of communication of matter, a shifting emanation from and to bodies and things. It is a material occurrence and not simply a subjective event.

Alongside this idea of a molecular fug, we can also think about the way that space conducts atmospheres. The cathedral and the stadium, for instance, seek to conduct bodies in very different ways. In the cathedral, the building seeks to silence by way of its grandeur. It conveys enormity, transcendence and the transience of human existence by dwarfing the body. The stadium on the other hand reverses this affect. It encourages collective noise and chants; it pits one crowd against another, stirring up feelings of enmity. One crowd must out-sing the other. There is enormity and grandeur here as well, but it is very definitely *for* the crowd. The stadium is a place where people go to worship themselves and their avatars on the pitch. In both, the orientation of the space itself is important. The stadium faces one crowd against another, as they circle the pitch. A cathedral orients the worshippers below the altar and the pulpit on high. Beneath, they are promised transcendence, a transcendence captured as the height of the roof above seems to capture the heavens. But we must also think about the state of these spaces. The cathedral is darkened, musty, with shafts of light illuminating the enormity. The stadium on the other hand is filled with brilliant white light (natural or artificial). Even away from the amphitheatre bowl, the corridors and passages will have a bright and clean light. Both spaces conduct the bodies that fill them to produce the molecular fug. In turn, the production of this molecular fug intensifies the spatial dynamics.

These are old spaces of atmosphere. They show us that people have been planning and building *for* atmosphere before it was named as such. But one of the first contemporary architects to make atmospheres the centre point of his practice was Peter Zumthor. At the heart of Zumthor's practice is the rejection of 'representational architecture' where buildings tell stories or are functionally determined. Instead he seeks to create spaces of intense affect, conjuring up ambiences and moods. The problem with representational spaces, he implies, is that they lack or cover over the affective nature of the space: they tend not to 'move him'.[6] Instead, he mainly designs achingly calm spaces that will be frequented by the global super-rich, as well as a number of public art galleries and museums. These are spaces that do not need to be efficient or compact but instead can give extensive place to the atmosphere. In response to Zumthor, we might comment that even the most 'representational spaces' that he critiques still have affective atmospheres. Anderson and Ash's beautiful reflection on the ambiences and atmospheres of an Accident and Emergency (A&E) waiting room in the UK is a useful counterpoint. They point to the shifting tone of the space, as people move through it, and as time passes late into the night.[7] The least atmospheric space that you can think of still has an atmosphere. Zumthor is an atmotechnician, and as such he wants to forget the less intense spaces of the budget warehouse supermarket, the disciplining order of the factory floor, or the frenetic movement of the overcrowded shopping precinct on a Saturday afternoon. But an atmosphereless space remains impossible. Atmospheres cannot be switched on or off; they are a condition of our spatio-temporal existence.

There are, however, spaces where the atmosphere is more intense and in which we experience it more readily. We are much more familiar with these concerns in spaces of consumption, where desires are shaped by the environment, than the ambience of an A&E waiting room. In a supermarket or department store: the lighting, piped music and scents; the design of paths and aisles; the layout of rails, shelves and counters; the height of the ceiling and ability to see over or through shelving; and the distribution of products, visual communications of promotions and deals – all contribute to the atmosphere of the space. Environmental psychology and marketing theory begin with the 'affective quality of place' and its manipulability by marketers.[8] The generation of spaces and things becomes a type of technology for selling. This atmosphere may convey feelings of better value (for instance, stripped-out warehouses, in a grid shape, with bright lights and warm colours, etc.) or quality (more open spaces with luxurious colours combined with narrower aisles, soft lights, classical music, etc.).[9] Chris Hudson's work on the ION Orchard shopping mall in Singapore is exemplary of the levels of atmospheric engineering that can be layered into a space of consumption. She details the use of light, sound and smell ('aromatopias') to convey an 'extraordinary shopping experience' at the ION Orchard. There are eight levels of the ION. The lowest basement floor 'is reminiscent of the sort of *pasar* (market) that is common to Southeast Asia. It is noisy, warm, and the general feel is of hustle and bustle, even mild chaos, as people move around deciding which dish they will buy and then look for a place to eat it'.[10] It is filled with Chinese medicine stalls, stocks of preserved meat, people eating. Its workers sweat as they frantically boil, fry and toss woks. However, as you ascend through the higher basement floors the atmospheres begin to change: 'Embodied sensations ... are experienced as less frenetic and without ubiquitous noise of the clattering of cooking utensils'.[11] These floors are populated by Starbucks, H&M, AIX Armani Exchange and other global brands. The first street-level floor is different again. It houses elite goods (Rolex, Saint Lauren Paris, Tag Heuer), and its 'visual, olfactory and aural aspects ... signal a different space and demand different forms of engagement and embodiment'.[12] Hudson talks about the idle sauntering of the urban citizen, who is compelled by the atmosphere. As she moves up onto the first and second floors above ground level, the prices increase. The third floor houses the Sloane Clinic, offering surgical and non-surgical cosmetic procedures: 'All such techniques for enhancement of self and identity management are delivered in an atmosphere of quiet discretion'.[13] Finally then, the fourth floor 'is characterized by grandiloquent spaces in which to stroll and saunter and enjoy the art works scattered around'.[14] As we progress from the subterranean basement to the fourth floor above ground level, the atmospheres gradually shift, signifying a move from the particularity of Singapore to the global elite cosmopolitanism.

> You can eat at any level at ION, but you can only become more beautiful, locate a suitable 'lifestyle', discover custom designed workout programs, buy expensive clothes, join a global brand community, and stage your own lifestyle at the higher levels. Staging lifestyles demands different embodied experiences and responses at the various levels: eating and shopping for necessities and moving on quickly at the lower levels; browsing, window shopping, and strolling in a leisurely manner at the upper levels.[15]

Hudson is describing what I call 'atmotechnics' – an engineering of space to generate atmosphere.[16] We are not supposed to *consciously* read this environmental management, but rather it is intended to affect our comportment, to change the way we act and relate. Thus on B4, one might push through a crowd, queue for food or enter a heated argument. By the time you have entered the hushed calm of L3, such comportment is unthinkable and aberrant. As Hudson suggests: 'Place atmospheres are created, evoked and manipulated to facilitate the social practices expected of consumers and to modify behaviour'.[17]

With this in mind, we can return to our Jefferson Memorial silent disco. In the District Court judgment, Judge Bates quotes the rule that the state 'need not wait until havoc is wreaked' to restrict a type of speech.[18] This is not mere hyperbole, at least as I read the case. The judge is not suggesting that this silent disco is going to cause widespread civil unrest, riot or even revolt. Instead, the Memorial is a significant site of national attachment and imagination. It is invested with the dignity of the foundation. The site is supposed to resonate with citizens as they come face to face with the origins of their state. As Lauren Berlant remarks, this is the function of Washington: 'When Americans make the pilgrimage to Washington they are trying to grasp the nation in its totality'.[19] Washington is a place of 'national mediation'. The Jefferson Memorial is a crucial site in this mediation between the state and the nation. It houses the atmosphere of sovereign dignity and majesty. But until the atmosphere was disrupted by the silent disco, it remained in the background. From the background, it could move bodies, shift behaviours and intensify feelings. The atmosphere of the Memorial exercises its affective forces without ever needing to come to the foreground. In theatre, the background is that part of the scene that fades from view. It is the basis from which something can come to the foreground. But it is *not* where 'the action' happens (foreground), nor is it a space of reason or synthesis (middle ground). The background 'sets the scene', but it is only by fading from attention that it can do its work.[20] In other words, the background works precisely because we are inattentive to it.

Affective atmospheres are everyday material events. However, they tend to hide or dissimulate themselves.[21] We acclimatise or attune to our atmosphere; our body finds a place in the affective space. And so, to us, the atmosphere seems to disappear – it shifts to the background. We enter a throbbing night club or gig, where the excitement is palpable. This atmosphere is vibrant, readily perceptible, but as we settle into the space, perhaps beginning to share the excitement, the atmosphere itself becomes less perceptible. We say things like we are immersed; we let ourselves go in the moment. It is not that the atmosphere has disappeared but that we begin to sit within the affective flow, noticing only when it changes again, perhaps when the house lights are turned on and the music fades at the end of the night. As Andreas Philippopoulos-Mihalopoulos explains: 'At the point of becoming-other … an atmosphere becomes visible, ontologically vibrant. *This vibrance becomes epistemologically accessible as … [a] different atmosphere*'.[22] When atmospheres change, we suddenly notice their vibrance or at least their difference. This might occur as we move into a different atmospheric intensity, or as the atmosphere around us changes, but either way the point is that it becomes perceptible as atmosphere when we are dis-attuned. Attunement then is the process of syncing with an atmosphere, where an atmosphere which has become-other modifies the way we are in the world. Sarah Ahmed remarks that atmospheres stick differently to us depending upon our mood.[23] She insists that we attune differently. But this also works the other way. It is not simply that someone in a sparkly mood enters a sad, blue room, and they simply become at one with the sadness in the room sharing the same affective state – because the person in a sparkly mood might also disrupt the blue atmosphere of the space. Exactly how the atmospheric change will settle depends upon the behaviour, the affective forces and the emotive power of all present, of the space, the time, the symbolic setting, etc.

The Jefferson Memorial works affectively as a site of national mediation because the atmosphere remains in the background. Like the Lincoln Memorial, the Jefferson Memorial is a monumental space, designed to convey the historical significance of the figure. Jefferson towers sternly within the space, holding the Declaration of Independence in his left hand. His dark bronzed figure contrasting against the white marble of the floor and walls, and the brilliant limestone of the cupola. The visitor must approach the building from the tidal basin, climbing the steps to a single portico entrance. As they enter, the space opens up above them, underlining the feeling of enormity. The enclosed height presses down on those who enter, like a cathedral, encouraging hushed tones, careful speech and contemplation of enormity. You enter the cool, quiet space. The Memorial directs you to look at Jefferson, and then to share his stare at the White House and the surrounding tidal basin. But all the while it affects you with the atmosphere of sovereign dignity and majesty. Because by the time you have walked quietly around, you have attuned. This is the context for understanding Judge Bates' worry about 'havoc'. It is not physical disorder but the disruption of the staging of the dignity of foundation that concerns him. A trivial silent disco lessens and potentially destroys the atmosphere of dignity and awe. And so, for the court, the dancers are a legitimate concern. Their actions, which would normally be totally acceptable, are made *disorderly* because they challenge the atmosphere of sovereignty.

The space of the Jefferson Memorial conducts the atmosphere, shaping behaviour. However, it relies upon those within the space to maintain this performance. We can return to the cathedral that we imagined earlier. When worshippers arrive in an orderly fashion, the space conducts their affects. It shapes their ways of being in the space, confirming the modes of behaviour they have come to expect from this space. However, what if the people who arrive into this cathedral are actually the band members of Pussy Riot, on their way to their infamous 2012 gig in the Cathedral of Christ the Saviour in Moscow? Then we might understand the manner in which the atmosphere relies upon those present to reproduce the atmosphere. As they don their signature bright balaclavas we can see that the Cathedral's atmosphere is about to be disrupted. Most atmospheres appear natural and given, but they are in fact extremely fragile. If one is willing to act against the affective grain, the atmosphere can be shifted.

The atmosphere of sovereignty at the Jefferson Memorial operates from the background to shape the feelings that should surround the state's foundation. This is our first set of sovereign affects: the atmospherics of a space of national mediation. This is a specific atmosphere, conducted within a specific place. Its specificity or exceptional status is the point of the litigation. It is a distinct enclave in which the dignity of the foundation is protected. But what is conducted in this particular space is supposed to touch every interaction with and concept of the sovereign order. This may seem like an odd place to begin – given the book's claims to think protest, revolt and unrest. I attach no particular significance to this silent disco, beyond the fact that it precipitates a moment where the state specifically considers the affective conditions of its own staging. Indeed, I have intentionally chosen this as the book's starting point because it is *not* a world historical protest or revolt. It is a decidedly minor event. Its everyday, clunky, libertarian politics have not resonated more broadly. '#FreetheJefferson1' never went viral. But precisely because it is *not* some sort of intensely resonant protest, we can see more clearly the web of minor affects at play. It demonstrates the manner in which sovereignty can be played out from the background. The insult of the silent disco was to perform the space differently, an act that cheapened the atmosphere of majesty and dignity. The silent disco made attunement to the enormity of this state-foundation impossible, by drawing attention to the atmosphere. In this way, it underlines the importance of a focus on those elements of sovereignty that are supposed to remain in the background. The next chapter takes this same set of dynamics but plays it out in a slightly more dramatic setting.

Notes

1 *Oberweter v Hilliard and Salazar* Civil Action No. 09-0588, available at http://voices.washingtonpost.com/crime-scene/jeffersondecision.pdf (viewed on 04/04/2020).
2 Nick Shapiro, 'Unknowing exposure: Toxic emergency housing, strategic inconclusivity and governance in the US Gulf South' in Emelie Cloatre and M Pickersgill (eds) *Knowledge, Technology and Law* (Routledge, 2014), 189.
3 Peter Sloterdijk, *Bubbles: Sphere Volume I: Microspherology* (Semiotext(e), 2011).
4 Teresa Brennan, *The Transmission of Affect* (Cornell University Press, 2004), 68.
5 Margaret Wetherell pours some cold water on this idea of pheromonal communication, suggesting that the literature is not as strong as Brennan argues. Margaret Wetherell, *Affect and Emotion: A New Social Science Understanding* (Sage: London, 2012), 143.
6 Peter Zumthor, *Atmospheres: Architectural Environments – Surrounding Objects* (Birkhauser GmbH, 2006).
7 Ben Anderson and James Ash, 'Atmospheric Methods' in Phillip Vanni (ed.) *Non-representational Methodologies* (Abingdon: Routledge, 2015), 34–51.
8 Mary Jo Bitner, 'Servicescapes: The impact of physical surroundings on customers and employees', *Journal of Marketing*, 56(2): 57–71 (2015).
9 Ibid. See also Alastair Tombs and Janet McColl-Kennedy, 'Social-servicescape conceptual model', 3.4 *Marketing Theory* (2003) 447.
10 Chris Hudson, 'ION Orchard: Atmosphere and consumption in Singapore', 14.3 *Visual Communication* (2015), 301.
11 Ibid. 302.
12 Ibid.
13 Ibid.
14 Ibid.
15 Ibid. 304.
16 Illan rua Wall, 'Policing atmospheres: Crowds, protest and 'atmotechnics', 36.4 *Theory Culture Society* (2019), 143.
17 Hudson, ION Orchard, 304.

18 Oberweter v Hilliard and Salazar, 18
19 Lauren Berlant, *The Queen of America Goes to Washington* (Durham: Duke University Press, 1997), 25.
20 Illan rua Wall, 'The ordinary affects of law', *Law, Culture and the Humanities* (available online, 2019).
21 Andreas Philippopoulos-Mihalopoulos, *Spatial Justice: Body, Lawscape, Atmosphere* (Abingdon: Routledge, 2015).
22 Ibid. 165.
23 Sara Ahmed, 'Happy Objects' in Melissa Gregg and Gregory Seigworth, *The Affect Theory Reader* (Duke University Press, 2010). See also Sarah Ahmed, *The Cultural Politics of Emotion* (Edinburgh University Press, 2014).

2

SWITCHING SOVEREIGN GENRES

In which we see an event where sovereignty is staged – we explore the genres of such a performance, meeting Elizabeth Anker and Bonnie Honig – the sentimental romanticism of a royal wedding – we engage with genre switching – the anxiety of the gothic – and we see the police securing the genres of sovereign performance.

On the 29th of April 2011, the day of the royal wedding between Prince William and Kate Middleton, the zombies began gathering in Soho Square. Or at least, that had been the Royal Zombie Flash Mob plan – a protest and picnic.[1] However, the police closed three of the four entrances to the square and the few zombies that got through initially thought they would be kettled. Giving up on the zombie apocalypse, they left the square. In their own words: 'we were fairly inoffensive members of the undead, who ate some homemade "brainssss" cake earlier in the day, and travelled on to Starbucks'.[2] It was something of a surprise to the innocuous undead to be escorted from Starbucks by the police and detained pursuant to the prevention of a breach of the peace. The zombies – all of good character as the Supreme Court later confirmed – were brought to various police stations and detained until after the wedding had taken place. Along with a number of Republican protesters who had also been detained, the zombies challenged their detention in the High Court. The case gradually travelled through the Court of Appeal, the Supreme Court and finally to the European Court of Human Rights.[3] Each case reaffirmed the common law power to detain pursuant to a breach of the Queen's peace and the preventative detention that such a power facilitated. We will come back to the Queen's peace in Chapter 6, but for now we can observe the Metropolitan police's explanation that the zombie flash mob took on an especial significance because it was supposed to take place in the vicinity of a royal ceremonial event. There was a danger, they claimed, that

FIGURE 2.1 John Robertson, 'A "zombie" with police in Oxford St., London', 29 April 2011, Alamy.

it might diminish the dignity of the event. This would present an affront to the Queen's peace, and on occasions like these, as Waddington noted, 'the full paramilitary potential of modern policing was deployed'.[4] So in a sense, the story of our zombies seems like a familiar one where the police over-react to a creative but unthreatening protest. But the royal wedding and the zombie wedding flash mob also opens a different sense of the affects and atmospheres of sovereignty to those that we saw in the last chapter. Although the Queer Resistance protesters insist that it was never their intention, the zombie royal wedding helps us to see the sovereign affects at play in the royal wedding and opens the possibility of imbuing them with different affects. To show this, let me carefully read one scene of the royal wedding.

The projected romance of the royal wedding is crystallised perfectly in the five-minute balcony scene, where the Prince and the Princess are presented to the crowds at Buckingham Palace. Indeed it is this scene, with its 'public kiss', that metonymically stood for the wedding as it was splashed around the world on front pages and news bulletins. In the UK, both BBC and ITV covered the events live. ITV's coverage, with presenters Julie Etchingham and Philip Schofield, had the greatest insight into the sovereign encounter being staged. We can begin with the rapturous opening of the scene:

Scene: Balcony on the first floor of Buckingham Palace, overlooking the Mall, which is full of thousands of people.

Stage Directions: Ornate doors of the balcony swing open.
Etchingham: Here we go.
Crowd: Cheers … volume rises as they see the couple emerge.
Kate [catching a glimpse of the crowd, murmurs inaudibly]: Oh, wow.
Etchingham: Oh wow, she says. … Oh wow. [laughing joyously]
Stage Directions: Couple wave … . Crowd cheer …

The opening part of the scene establishes the connection between the crowd and the couple. They stand alone on the balcony. Kate's beautiful dress is ornate with complex lace work across her shoulders, the silk clinging to her figure. Her veil and hair are swept back, she wears simple but resplendent earrings and a tiara. The dress is comparatively simple in comparison to Prince William's faintly ridiculous ornate red uniform, blue sash and medal, gold epaulettes, cuffs and collar. The balcony is also dressed with red fabric trimmed with gold.

The camera switches between the couple on the balcony and panning shots of the sea of people below the balcony. The images invisibilise the large empty space at the front of the Palace, knitting the couple and crowd together. The joyous cacophony of the crowd remains throughout the scene, rising and falling as the scene reaches its crescendos.

Stage Directions: After a minute the doors reopen and the Royal family emerge.
Etchingham: And a lovely moment as the Queen has allowed the couple some time on their own for the crowd to take that first glimpse.

The Queen enters the scene, but from the outset she is off centre and largely off screen – the bonds of attachment for the current monarch do not need to be established. The scene introduces the *future* king and queen. The cameras and commentary repeatedly seek to draw out the joyousness of the scene:

Etchingham: And a beautiful shot of the royal couple as they take in the view that they can scarcely have imagined really. Such an extraordinary atmosphere of good will.

Etchingham gestures towards the atmosphere of the space: that massive crowd gathered in glorification of the future monarch. She mediates the feeling of the space that is perhaps missing in the simple images.

The event presents the audience with layers of sovereign affect, each overlapping to create the rich texture of atmosphere. A particularly important moment in the balcony scene is the flyover.

Stage Directions: There is a flyover of three planes from the Second World War (a Lancaster bomber and two fighter planes, a Hurricane and a Spitfire) and then four modern jets (two Typhoons and two Tornados).

FIGURE 2.2 Paul Grover, 'The Royal Kiss with HRH Kate Duchess of Cambridge and HRH Prince William', 29 April 2011, Alamy.

Etchingham: And it is not just the sight, you can feel it, can't you? [*pause*] That thunderous noise, you can feel the ripple of sound as the Lancaster came through.

The planes play two roles here: firstly, they help us to connect the feelings of joy and celebration with the sovereignty being performed. The planes index the sovereign's war power; they underscore the sovereignty at play in the scene. But importantly, you are not simply supposed to see the planes, the royal couple and the crowds. As Julie Etchingham makes explicit: you *feel* them. 'You can feel it, can't you?' Her interrogative is simultaneously aimed at her co-presenters who might actually have felt the noise. But more importantly it is directed at the viewers, who certainly cannot feel the ripples of sound but who are instructed to imagine it. They must also feel it. The vibrations of the engines and the joyousness of the scene are marked as a material feeling that is supposed to be shared between those present and those watching. We are to feel the vibrations of the machines as they crystallise the sovereign scene. The love of the beautiful couple, which we are bound into, is connected with their terrible power of destruction and glory, to their war power.

The planes' second role is underscored by arch-conservative BBC political commentator Andrew Neil (on ITV for the day), who connects the balcony wedding scene to the national glory of the Second World War.

Neil: It's fitting to have these planes too, because they played such a role in the Second World War, and of course at the end of the Second World War, it was on that balcony that the country celebrated, with a Mall full of people, the final end of the war in Europe.

The scene is drawn precisely to echo previous moments of sovereign glory. The two moments fit into one another: the glory of one is connected to the other. The planes are echoes; we are to feel them, feel their vibrations and feel the sense of time and belonging with which they resonate. Remember, the events are carefully choreographed to stage particular affectively intense moments. The media have been thoroughly briefed on the script; their task is to underline it and make sure that its significance is not lost on anyone. In this sense, their representation of the event is a direct window into the intentions of those who sought to stage this as a national affective encounter.

Let us break away from the events of the day to note an insight from Elisabeth Anker's *Orgies of Feeling*. There she explains that political events, ideas, characters, strategies and discourses are told through genres. They are

> mediated by the different modalities in which they are depicted and made legible. Genres of political discourses work as a set of interpretative conventions and affective expectations for public political life. These genres provide norms and anticipations for the trajectory of political events, articulate models for civic morality and citizenship, offer possibilities for the exercise of power, employ temporal schemas for the content of political life, and solicit particular felt experiences in their participants. … [D]ifferent genres resonate at different historical moments and encourage certain actions, subjectivities and legitimations while discouraging others.[5]

Like Anker, Bonnie Honig also asks the genre question, but for Honig, the genre of political analysis and theorising draws 'attention to the reading practices of political theorists'. We read events with 'a set of genre expectations'.[6] The genre conventions of a political discourse structure plotlines and characters, but they also structure the affective dynamics of the political scene.[7]

In the royal wedding balcony scene, our commentators, Etchingham and Schofield, work hard to embed and amplify the genre scripts of modern romance in the scene.

Schofield: But also what a thing for Kate Middleton, for Katherine, her royal Highness now [chuckles], to end up on the balcony of Buckingham Palace. Who would have thought, I mean that really is the most extraordinary fairy tale. She will have driven past it in her car or a cab or on a bus, hundreds of times, and then, there you are, one of the few to have stepped foot on that balcony, and see what so few people see: that sea of people from that point of view, stretching right back towards … [trails off].

Neil: Who would have thought it as she headed off to *St Andrews* [University] for her first term.

Etchingham: [laughing] Exactly, St Andrews must feel a long way away.

Neil: Hoping for a degree, as most of us would simply hope for a degree, and she comes away with a prince.

Laughter

This is supposed to be a happy tale; we are supposed to imagine the royal courtship. It is not the classical fairy tale of the royal wedding of Diana and Charles, which played out through motifs of virginal purity and innocence. Instead, this is a slightly more worldly modern romance with the tensions and intensities of a university romcom. Despite this contemporary genre setting, the fairy-tale subtext is never far from the surface. The balcony scene is the 'happy ever after moment' at the end of a story, something that the narration underlines throughout the day. The ordinariness of this college romance intensifies the drama of the balcony scene. It is put into stark relief by the fact that this is an *actual* prince, and she is becoming an *actual* princess.

If the royal wedding is a modern romance, a fairy tale where a 'mere commoner' is elevated through love, then the zombies appear to switch the genres. In *Antigone Interrupted* Honig explains that genre switching is 'that switch in expectation, reception, and readerly cues that occurs ... when we re-emplot a text in a new genre, when we approach it with different cues in mind than before'.[8] The police were worried that the global televisual audience might read the scene differently. They complained that the presence of the royal wedding zombies ran the risk of lessening the 'dignity' of the royal wedding. The danger is a switch from modern romance to gothic romantic. The gothic presents a strange realism, one where the everyday relations have been infected with a germ of the ineffable. The familiar is cracked open and something terrible leaks out. This is the terrain of anxiety, dread and, potentially, even terror.[9] The zombie costumes mimic Kate's wedding dress, but instead of the flush romance of a princess, their skin is whitened and fake blood drips from the zombies' mouths. The zombies mirror the royal couple. The police's (unfounded) fear was that the zombies would operationalise their genre switch, intruding on the sovereign event by throwing worms and maggots at the wedding party outside Westminster Abbey.[10]

We can trace three key dynamics of this genre switch. Firstly, the marriage is both literal and symbolic. The wedding obviously signifies the bond between the royal couple. But it also stands for the bond between the (future) sovereign couple and their people.[11] This is the opportunity for the people to meet their future sovereigns and to share in their bond of love. The state encouraged everyone to take part, by travelling to London or by closing their roads and holding street parties. The media hyped these street parties in advance and covered them extensively on the day. The joyous celebration in London is thus supposed to mirror events around the country. The crowds are an essential part of this scene. They stand for the great body of people, enthusiastically meeting their royal suitor. The political marriage between the people and this soon-to-be sovereign has been ordained since his birth. By playing the actual royal wedding as a modern romance, the symbolic bond between the sovereign and the people promises happiness and joy. But if we replay the royal wedding as gothic romantic, suddenly that second bond between the sovereign and people is rendered uncertain. 'Tania Modleski explains that the (anti) hero in pure Gothics is always undecidable, "a handsome magnetic suitor or husband who may or may not be a lunatic and/or murderer"'.[12] In the gothic, the sovereign is suddenly potentially malign.

Secondly then, this gothic uncertainty is particularly important when we think of the way that the balcony scene indexed the sovereign war power. In the romantic, the sovereign war power manifests a comforting feeling of protection. The Second World War planes index the justness of the struggle against fascism. But switching genres, in the gothic the uncertainty of the suitor/sovereign reveals the sublime war power in a different light. The state's sovereign power is not benign but potentially a murderous violence. The planes strike an anxious note. It is Iraq rather than Berlin, it is Libya or Syria rather than the beaches of Normandy or the Battle of Britain that are indexed. If a genre switch had been successful, the glorious and sublime feeling of the war power in the scene would be cast again in the fear and anxiety of the war on terror, rather than a sense of glorious and just protection. By introducing the gothic into the scene, the zombies add a note of anxiety and uncertainty into the dignity of the sovereign couple meeting their people, and this infects the reading of the sovereign's war powers.

Thirdly, on a different level, the zombies clarify the affective dynamics of the event. One of the key conventions of zombie fiction is their bite. Zombies are contagious. By trying to stage their own royal wedding, the zombies draw attention to the other contagion of the day. As Etchingham says, we 'feel' the affective dynamics of the day. The nation and the world are supposed to be touched by the love between Wills and Kate, endearing them to their audience. The kiss on the balcony is the key site of this contagion. It is the image that was beamed around the world. It is the moment that would globally index the emotional register of the event. But the zombies also want to kiss. Their kiss infects their victim and binds them to the zombie for life. In short, the mirroring is not simply a matter of costume. The wedding stages a joyous contagion, and the zombies make this visible through the trope of infection. But the zombies insist that the infection is never simply benign.

The royal wedding and its gothic zombie double demonstrate the manner in which we might begin to think about the affective dynamics that are being staged in this moment of sovereignty. The sovereign apparatus seeks out desires, attachments and drives. It weaves these into the performance of sovereignty, attaching itself in different ways to people's projections and attachments. This means that in an everyday sense, terms like 'majesty', 'splendour', 'glory' and 'dignity' do not give us singular meanings.[13] Instead, they point to a variety of popular feelings, shared atmospheres and affects. It is not simply that a unitary sense of sovereignty might be staged in different ways but that different ways of staging sovereignty perform *different* sovereign relations. Crucially, this also means that what appears as an arch-sovereign scene may be switched. Its significance, atmosphere and affective valence may turn against the plans of those who stage the event. With a genre switch, very different affective scripts, beliefs and desires suddenly emerge in the scene.

The royal wedding is useful precisely because we can clearly see the manner in which sovereignty is being produced as an affective constellation within it. The atmospheres of glorification carry over, giving an aura of joy and love to the royal couple. The 'great day out' feeling, where the populace share in the couple's joy binds them all together. At the same time, large numbers of people generate intensities which can be unstable and potentially turbulent. Because of this instability, the police are tasked with careful management of the event's aesthetics:

> acts of protest that would diminish the *dignity of the occasion* are rigorously prevented. A person carrying a tin-whistle that might have been blown during the two minute silence at the Cenotaph on Remembrance Sunday was ejected from the crowd. People thought to be preparing pacifist protests during Trooping the Colour were stopped and searched, and then escorted from the area.[14]

These disruptions do not threaten the sovereign order, in the sense that maggots being thrown at the royal couple is unlikely to suddenly convince the populace that the monarchy was an institution that had already died. But they do threaten the 'magic' of the day. They threaten to break the spell of the event, that suspension of ordinary cares and concerns that comes as the populace share this atmosphere of joy. Now it is time to put the sovereign order in a little more jeopardy.

Notes

1 There were at least two groups planning a zombie wedding in Soho Square on the day. The arrested zombies came to protest the effect of austerity on services for lesbian, gay, bisexual and transgender communities. Queer Resistance pointed out that the state claimed not to be able to find money to spend on those most in need, but it could lavish millions on the royal wedding. Roz Kaveney is credited with the tweet which began the idea (Ruth Pearce, 'Queer Zombies Plan Royal Wedding "Celebration"', http://www.lesbilicious.co.uk/campaigns-politics/queer-zombies-plan-royal-wedding-celebration/ viewed on 28/02/2020).

2 Chris Farnell, 'The Royal Wedding Zombie Flash Mob: Breach of the Peace (of the Dead)' http://chriswritesapocalypses.blogspot.co.uk/2011/05/17-royal-wedding-zombie-flash-mob.html (viewed on 28/02/2020).

3 *R (Hicks and Ors) v Commissioner of Police of the Metropolis* in the [2012] EWHC 1947 (admin), [2014] EWCA Civ 3 and [2017] UKSC 9. At the European Court of Human Rights it is reported at: *Eiseman-Renyard and Ors v United Kingdom* (2019) ECHR, 110.

4 PAJ Waddington, *Liberty and Order: Public order Policing in a Capital City* (UCL Press, 1994), 45.

5 Elisabeth Anker, *Orgies of Feeling: Melodrama and the Politics of Feeling* (Duke University Press, 2014), 20.
6 Bonnie Honig, *Democracy and the Foreigner* (Princeton University Press, 2003), 109.
7 Berlant's work on genre is also instructive: 'For Berlant, a "genre" is an emotionally invested, patterned set of expectations about how to act and how to interpret, which organises a relationship between the acting and interpreting subject, their feelings and impressions, their struggles and their historical present. Genres also organise conventions about what might be hoped for, explicitly or secretly, and the bargains that can be made with life. Genres serve as mooring, or placeholders, for intensities within streaming experience'. Robbie Duschinsky and Emma Wilson, 'Flat Affect, Joyful Politics and Enthralled Attachments: Engaging with the Work of Lauren Berlant', 28 *International Journal of Political Culture and Society* (2015), 179.
8 Bonnie Honig, *Antigone, Interrupted* (Cambridge University Press, 2013), 81.
9 Thus, perhaps unsurprisingly, zombies have proliferated in popular culture since the attack on the twin towers. Kyle Bishop, *American Zombie Gothic* (MacFarland & Co, 2010), 11.
10 See *R (Hicks) v Commissioner of the Police of the Metropolis*, para 13. There was no actual evidence of maggots and worms. There was another unrelated group who had made a throwaway comment at the end of one of their fliers, but none of this group had made it to Soho Square. The 'intelligence' on this other group was presented as creating reasonable suspicion for detention. As 'Hannah Chutzpah', one of the arrested zombies, makes clear on Twitter: 'A brief comment on the "maggot confetti" line that keeps coming up: I get that it's attention grabbing but it's also complete retrospective nonsense that the cops made up. I first heard about it in the police's paperwork for the judicial review'. 'It's gross, it would be a mean thing to do to a couple on their wedding day, and it makes royalists clutch at their pearls. Well done, Met Police spin machine. You came up with a headline-grabbing bit of nonsense'. 'Before we were arrested the police did a stop and search on us (obviously) and they found: cooperative people in fancy dress with bags full of books, water bottles, cameras … nothing that would seem amiss on anyone in London on that silly day'. 'But the 'maggot confetti' line was important to the police because imaginary maggots demonstrated what kind of people they were (apparently) dealing with.' (@Hannah_Chutzpah 28/03/2019, full thread available here: https://twitter.com/Hannah_Chutzpah/status/1111271207868026881).
11 As Honig makes clear, the marriage in female gothic fiction readily stands for the social contract (Honig, *Democracy and the Foreigner*, 110).
12 Ibid.
13 While the royal wedding does not present the traditional sovereign metaphysics in its conventional symbols – the crown, orb, sceptre, ring, etc., – they are, nonetheless, on full show. Just to take two key dynamics, we could think of the dignity of the royal couple and the glory of the scene. Dignity is supposed to adhere to the royals, attaching to their status and the manner in which they bear it. It is a part of them. Thus the symbols and scripts of the day sought highlight this restrained solicitude, bearing and comportment. If dignity was a question of Wills and Kate's carriage in this national moment, the glory of the scene had to be produced *for* the royals. As Agamben makes clear in *The Kingdom and the Glory*, glory does not belong to the sovereign; it must be produced for them. Here he draws on Christian theology to underline that even within the trinity, glory has an economy with the holy spirit and son producing it for the father, for instance. In the context of Western sovereignty, glory tended to be associated with military might and victory in warfare. In the royal wedding, we see that the prior military glory of the Second World War provides an affective afterglow. The current fighter jets provide another site of glorification. But most importantly of all, it is the popular adoration of the loving couple by the crowds, the acclamation of their splendour, that intensifies the sense of sovereign glory at play in the scene.
14 Waddington *Liberty and Order*, 45 (my emphasis).

3

PLAYING FOR HEARTS AND MINDS

In which we shift from stable sites of sovereignty to a revolutionary context – we examine the deployment of an image to shift the affective dynamics of a revolution – we meet Brian Massumi, who introduces us to the way in which sovereign affects might be extra-linguistic, found in the tics and jerks that signal a different field.

The Tunisian Revolution was already in its second week when President Ben Ali visited Mohamed Bouazizi's bedside. The visit was an attempt to calm the popular temper that had gradually risen after Bouazizi's self-immolation in late December 2010. The image of his visit (which I will call 'Bouazizi's Bedside') was carefully curated. It was staged to resonate with those on the streets. It was initially placed in *La Presse Tunisie* before circulating widely in the official and unofficial media. In this chapter I want to look more closely at this image, thinking about it as an intervention in a contest of sovereign affects. The image was a direct intervention in the visual economy of the unrest. Affect oozes from the cracks in its visual rhetoric. I want to suggest that Ben Ali's regime hoped to restage the affective tensions of his sovereign order on that day in January 2011. They hoped to de-escalate the situation by evoking feelings of security and familiarity, desire for predictability, regularity and development.

In the image, Ben Ali stands with his entourage. His hands are clasped at his waist. He wears glasses and seems to stare at the almost mummified Bouazizi. Beside him, a doctor in a white coat is evidently talking. To the right of the picture are three other doctors, all in scrubs – a woman to their front. They stand beside an apparently sophisticated hospital monitor. Behind Ben Ali is his entourage. Ben Ali's head is tilted slightly to one side. The eye is drawn immediately to him. He is distinguished in terms of the colour palette; he wears his trademark dark suit when everyone else is in lighter tones. He lies at the focal point of the

FIGURE 3.1 Tunisian Presidency/AFP, 'Bouazizi's Bedside', 2011.

picture. This is a visual rhetoric of sovereignty, a political iconography[1] to which Ben Ali's regime was always sensitive.[2] But at the same time, nothing is quite right about this photograph. There is a slightly odd, uncanny feeling to it that is present from the first glimpse.[3] Initially, we might put this down to the very obvious tension that is being staged: the contrasting body language of the doctors (arms folded, intense stares) and the sovereign with his entourage (hands clasped in unison, thoughtful expressions). But there is something else as well. Perhaps it is the microphone that juts in, just visible between Ben Ali and the speaking doctor. Whatever it is, the more you examine the image, the more its theatricality seems to emerge. We can imagine the photographer actively posing the photograph: the scene is set, Ben Ali and Bouazizi play themselves, the regime is there in the guise of the advisers and the doctors stand for the public. Dramatically restaging the scene from the streets requires that the same themes and characters are played out, but at the same time something new is introduced.

On the surface, this is all about Bouazizi's survival: the hospital setting, the medical machines, the doctors gathered to treat his charred unconscious body. But in a beautiful reversal, the question being posed is not Bouazizi's survival but that of Ben Ali and his regime. In the image, as in the protests that were occurring just miles away, Bouazizi had already played his last card. All that was left for him was to die. His frustration with the bureaucratic-police apparatus had already resonated across Tunisia. And with this resonance, he drops from the story. Ben Ali is actually the sick man in this photo. The image is addressed to those who will decide his fate on the streets and squares. When we look at the photograph in this sense we can begin to see the visual rhetoric. Ben Ali stands listening. He is quiet and calm, proud rather than supplicant. His governmental 'achievements' are underlined: the position of women (the doctor), the medical technology, the education system.[4] Ben Ali's regime was secured by intense inclusion and exclusion (advancement for those within the system and social death for those beyond, care for the population who can be governed and grinding down the people who might undermine it).[5] In the image he exudes the manifold aspects of his 'care', his pastoral power. At the same time there is a quiet authority. The doctors stand and face him; he is at the centre of things. He is there among the people, but his sovereign majesty also distinguishes him: his trademark suit, the manicured face and hair, all gesture towards the portraits that hung everywhere in pre-revolutionary Tunisia. His body asks the first question: do you risk all of 'our' achievements?[6]

At the same time, Ben Ali's gaze directs the viewer to look at Bouazizi. All that we can see of his body is a blackened upper lip, drawn back to reveal a row of teeth. It is a flash of horror, designed to char the imagination. It overtakes that other image of Bouazizi that was circulating at the time. In this, Bouazizi is handsome and happy, wearing a white shirt beneath a zipped jacket. He half smiles, with his hands drawn back in the air, about to clap. This is the image that would adorn posters of the revolution, and later would be redrawn for official stamps and other merchandise. There is no image of the immolation. But the blackened lip conveys the abjection upon which the revolution was building itself. We must not forget the intensity of the national scene on the day the image was released. The visit occurred ten days into the protests. The unrest had spread from a minor town to the major cities. The protesters had been met with both intense repression and with promises of jobs, food, economic development and future prosperity. The image was another type of intervention.

Certain images are sticky, returning to consciousness over and again. In the context of social media we can think of 'virality' as a way of naming that stickiness. 'Bouazizi's Bedside' aims at precisely this stickiness. In a country gripped by a state of unrest, the president cannot appear on the streets to face down the crowd. But he can restage the dynamics of the streets. And such a restaging needs to stick, or else it looks like weakness. Brian Massumi calls this stickiness 'intensity': 'the strength and duration of the image's effect' on a viewer.[7] He insists that to understand the 'event of image reception' we need to watch for multiple levels. In particular, we need to turn our attention to 'a disconnection of signifying order from intensity'.[8] He gives us a very different example of this bifurcation, which is nonetheless useful for our analysis of this image. The US president Ronald Regan conveyed a certain 'presidential quality'. He conjured 'up sovereignty by projecting confidence'.[9] Massumi claims that this projection was not filled with a determinate sense. It was not that the electorate knew exactly what Regan stood for and that he presented it in a way that would be affectively powerful. Instead, Regan 'was unqualified and without content'.[10] He bore a sort of incipience – he might develop in a number of different ways.

His speeches were filled with gestural flashes, veers and jerks. These veers were momentary, but Massumi argues that they operated like mime.

> Reagan politicized the power of mime. That power is in interruption. A mime decomposes movement, cuts its continuity into a potentially infinite series of sub-movements punctuated by jerks. At each jerk, at each cut into the movement, the potential is there for the movement to veer off in another direction, to become a different movement. Each jerk suspends the continuity of the movement, for just a flash, too quick really to perceive but decisively enough to suggest a veer.[11]

There was a bifurcation between what was being linguistically communicated and what Massumi calls 'asignifying intensities'. His 'every actual move and phrase' was doubled, and this doubling followed 'him like the shadow of a mime'.[12]

Regan was incipience. He was in the process of coming to meaning/affect. And this incipience meant that the different threads of his ragged ideas could draw different constituencies.

> Receiving apparatuses … selected one line of movement, one progression of meaning, to actualize and implant locally. That is why Reagan could be so many things to so many people; that is why the majority of the electorate could disagree with him on major issues but still vote for him. Because he was actualized, in their neighbourhood, as a movement and a meaning of their selection-or at least selected for them with their acquiescence.[13]

It was the disarticulation of the speech and the affective shadow that allowed these asignifying intensities to be filled in this way.

'Incipience' is an odd word to use for Ben Ali. He was a strong man who could facilitate the European neoliberal agenda in Tunisia (privatisation, 'free trade' zones, etc.) while trying to maintain the remnants of a socialised state. He ran an intense security state and was responsible for much brutality. But this image of 'Bouazizi's Bedside' is affectively incipient in the sense that it can draw its audiences to the fear and dread or the cautious hope or resignation. The image presents an affective bifurcation, but as Deborah Gould says, affect 'prepares the organism to respond to that which is impinging on it, *but in no predetermined direction*'.[14] For Massumi at least, the affective is not the ideologically encoded transmission of a message. The bifurcation opens both a signification *and* an immediate affective response. The key to this is to move beyond the image, to think about the event of its reception. It is not the visual construction of the image as such but the image as a surface from which affects flow. It can be seen there in the newspaper, it is on the computer or phone screen, it is on the TV. It affects the capacity of the bodies that it encounters, changing their capacity to act. They hold the newspaper with its front-page image, eyes flick to the screen as the image flashes up. The body is supposed to shudder with the cajoling promise that emanates from the image, alongside the anxiety of its threat. These resonate in each body touched by the image, rippling beneath the skin, as Fanon says.[15]

The image was meant to reach large swathes of the Tunisian populace. It was part of the dual strategy to offer concessions to those that would save the sovereign order and to crush those who would continue to revolt. But the intensity of the atmospheres that had grown in the squares, the affects which emanated from the other images of protest, the enthusiasm and excitement for a new order and ultimately the enmity that had developed for Ben Ali and his family proved far too powerful. The resonance of the streets and squares was 'an intensely bodily, spatial, political affair, materialized in the masses of bodies coming together in the streets'. People gathering, 'clashing with the police, temporarily dispersed by teargas and bullets, and regrouping again like a relentless swarm to reclaim the streets, push the police back, and saturate space with a collective effervescence'.[16] Writing in the very different Egyptian context, Gaston Gordillo almost trips over himself, trying to convey the sheer energy of this resonance: the 'words seem inadequate, partial, incomplete: enthusiasm, energy, passion, anger, contagion, electrifying, domino effect'.[17]

> Those who know it best, if intuitively, are the bodies that produce it in the streets. A 28-year-old protester told a reporter from *The Guardian* during the first days of clashes with the police, after showing him where the police had broken one of his ribs the day before: 'But I don't care – just look around you. The energy of the Egyptians is amazing. We're saying no to unemployment, no to police brutality, no to poverty'. Just look around you. You can see that 'amazing energy'.[18]

The resonance of Ben Ali's image is more subtle than that, seeking to play on the anxieties of those who gather with no idea of the future but who insist upon opening it up in all of its potentiality. There were no models and no warranties in Tunis, and this is precisely what the image seeks to play upon.

In these first three chapters we have taken three very different sites of sovereign affect. In the first, we saw the manner in which an affective atmosphere might stage sovereignty for those that make the pilgrimage to the national capital. It was the atmosphere of the space that gave the affective tone to the spatial and symbolic constitution of the space of the capital. The Jefferson Memorial stages an encounter with the calm majesty and authority of foundation. During the royal wedding, we saw the attempt to stage a sort of noisy, joyous heteronormative encounter with monogamous sovereignty. We focused on the dynamics of the ceremony – particularly the balcony scene – finding a symbolic order of glory and dignity being filled with the atmospheres of joy and happiness. The image of Bouazizi's bedside, on the other hand, is a surface through which sovereign dread and hope might be transferred. It was a surface of resonance and affect as it was printed in newspapers and light up on social media screens. The sovereign affects that emanate from Ben Ali's image are very different from the joyous affects of the royal wedding and from the resentful affects or the silent disco. Each of these spaces and sites is permeated with joy, love, hope; or they exude 'ugly' affects of dread, anxiety, paranoia, terror. They are produced as a key effect of any sovereign performance. The three scenes also differ in their context (a stable sovereign order and one that is about to topple) and in their form (atmospheres and images). We might also add on a different level that they differ in the way that I have theorised them: the materialist account of affect (which might also align with certain psychoanalytic and feminist accounts), the cultural theory account and the Deleuzian account. We will return to this question in the excursus at the end of this part, and again in the second half of the book when we begin to think about crowds and violence.

Notes

1 Sonja Foss, 'Theory of Visual Rhetoric' in Ken Smith, Sandra Moriarty, Gretchen Barbatsis, & Keith Kenney (Eds.), *Handbook of Visual Communication: Theory, Methods, and Media* (Routledge, 2011), 141.
2 Rania Said details the sensitivity of the regime to the cartoons of -Z-, a francophone political cartoonist. Ben Ali even complained that they were entering his nightmares (Rania Said, '-Z-: Flamingos, *Francophonie*, and the Arts of Urban Dissent in Tunis', 17.2 *Journal of Romance Studies* (2017), 215).
3 As Stacy Douglas pointed out, the image almost mirrors the double aesthetics of Jeff Wall's photography. His 'near documentary' photographs restage events from everyday life in a way that is reminiscent of still-life painting. The photos are carefully staged using full cinematographic scenes and actors, to restage quotidian events. Their photographic form gives them the uncanny, almost strained quality present in this photo.
4 Beatrice Hibou, *The Force of Obedience: The Political Economy of Repression in Tunisia* (London: Polity Press, 2011).
5 Ibid.
6 From the beginning of Ben Ali's regime – what became known as the 'blessed change' – he sought to claim the 'hearts and minds' of Tunisians by promising economic reforms, 'democracy, national reconciliation, and free elections'. Noureddine Jebnoun, N, 'Ben Ali's Tunisia: The Authoritarian Path of a Dystopian State' in Noureddine Jebnoun, Mehrdad Kia, Mimi Kirk, *Modern Middle East Authoritarianism: Roots, Ramifications and Crisis* (Routledge: 2013), 109.
7 Brian Massumi, *Parables for the Virtual: Movement, Affect, Sensation* (Durham: Duke University Press, 2004), 24.
8 Ibid.
9 Jon Beasley-Murray, *PostHegemony: Political Theory and Latin America* (University of Minnesota Press, 2010), 129, citing Massumi, *Parables for the Virtual*, 41.
10 Massumi, *Parables for the Virtual*, 41.
11 Ibid.
12 Ibid.
13 Ibid.
14 Gould, *Moving Politics*, 20 (emphasis in the original).
15 Fanon, *The Wretched of the Earth* (Grove Press, New York: 2004), 31.
16 Gaston Gordillo, 'Resonance and the Egyptian Revolution', *Critical Legal Thinking* (22/02/2011) http://criticallegalthinking.com/2011/02/22/resonance-and-the-egyptian-revolution/ (viewed on 27/02/2020).
17 Ibid.
18 Ibid.

4

THE GOVERNMENT OF TEMPER

In which we meet Ben Anderson and draw together the affective account of the last chapters – we see sovereignty as an apparatuses of perpetuation – we explore the government of affective life.

'The Situation Room' is one of the most extraordinary images of the presidency of Barak Obama. It captures the room in which Obama and his staff monitored the Seal Team 6 operation which killed Osama bin Laden in 2011. The image is suffused with tension. A study in intensity, as Pete Souza, the photographer, suggested.[1] The air seems still. Everyone holds their breath as they stare at an out-of-shot screen. 'Obama is leaning forward in his chair, jaw clenched, and Secretary Clinton is covering her mouth, appearing horrified by what is on the screen'.[2] Like the image of Bouazizi's bedside in the previous chapter, this image registers the affective resonance of sovereignty. But 'The Situation Room' is very different. Unlike 'Bouazizi's Bedside', 'The Situation Room' landed with its audience – it became a site of 'national investments in collective memory'.[3] It did this at least in part because of the way it resonated with the populace. 'The Situation Room' as an image could be invested with the emotions of Bin Laden's death, without portraying the gore of the scene or the mawkish gratuity of the dead body. It gave the public a pass into the situation room just after the sovereign decision had been made. Liam Kennedy underscores the 'reality effect' of the image. 'The "realism" of the scene accentuates the sense of glimpsing behind the facades of power to an intimate, unguarded moment when power is in play and our leaders appear vulnerable in relation to the unknown outcome, and so they become humanized, revealed as something more than figures of power'.[4] The audience is thrown into this feeling of tension, uncertainty and vulnerability. But the image itself was released to amplify feelings.[5]

FIGURE 4.1 Pete Souza, 'The Situation Room', 01 May 2011.

Over the last chapters we have seen the importance of sovereign affects. The sovereign is made to appear and to be made meaningful for the populace. We have seen this in radically different settings and using different sorts of affective and aesthetic analyses. But rather than continuing to fill an entire book with the scenes of sovereign affect, I want to use 'The Situation Room' to dive into a different aspect of this problem: the government of affective life. In a strange sense, 'The Situation Room' can be divided into two: the president and vice president sit to the left, they are worried and intense. The visual space around them is clear: the marbled wall is dappled and bright, fading to pure white light at the top. To the right, however, is a more crowded visual field. Officers, advisers and ministers gather closely behind those at the table. The image seems to delineate the sovereign from his government, while affirming that both are part of the same machine. The image shows us the *work* of the sovereign apparatus, which is undertaken by the governmental power. As we will see, the government (as *potestas*) signs for the sovereign (as *auctoritas*). But like the image of the regime conveyed in 'Bouazizi's Bedside', this image is also a part of that work of government. This image is an intervention in the morale of the populace in the 'war on terror'. The death of Bin Laden had important positive affects on domestic US morale, as well as on the morale of its forces in Afghanistan and its allies.[6] The image is an object of this morale boost, released to crystallise that set of feelings and desires. But rather than focusing once more on its intensity and reception, I want to use this image to refocus our analysis on what is affected. In particular, the chapter will explore Ben Anderson's idea of an apparatus which is designed to inscribe and manage the 'affective life' of the population. To grasp this, let us change wars.

There was a growing sense by mid-1941 that the US would (or should) be drawn into the Second World War. The US had seen the intensification of the conflict in the European and North African theatres. It had also observed that the affective life of the various domestic populations was a site of warfare. So in August of 1941, a large number of academics gathered at a symposium at the University of Chicago's Society for Social Research. Their task was to think through the affective dynamics of warfare. Their interdisciplinary reflections were focused on one term: morale. They worried that the US population's morale might collapse, leading to panic and social dissolution. A threat to morale was a threat to the national war effort. Published as a series of seventeen papers in the *American Journal of Sociology*, these analysts classify 'the multiple techniques that threaten the domestic population ... and demonstrate how the state imagines ways in which morale could be damaged and destroyed'.[7] It was essential that bad morale was secured against and that good morale was intensified to further the war effort.[8] The participants identified 'morale as a property of the population'.[9] It was imagined as the collective affective glue: 'Morale promises ... to enable bodies to keep going *despite the present*: a present in which morale is either targeted directly or threatens to break'.[10]

If morale was that element of shared spirit that would help people to continue even when all appeared to be lost, its opposite was panic. This was understood as a 'form of *dis*organisation. Panics ... are commonly understood as the dissolution of order emergent from disruptions or disturbances'.[11] In the context of total war: 'Destroying or damaging morale threatens to turn something interior and necessary to total mobilisation ... into a devastating, destructive force'.[12] Panic and morale are two poles. At one extreme, the population is imagined to succumb to an immanent panic; on the other, it remains hardy. 'Unlike the disordering panic, then, the promise of securing morale is that it enables bodies to coalesce despite the persistent presence of affections that may diminish or destroy bodies'.[13] Between the two extremes of immanent panic or total morale, there are ways of increasing or decreasing the productivity, intensity and inner strength of the population.

Anderson suggests that we think about 'morale' as an affective apparatus. An apparatus, for Foucault, only makes sense in relation to a target.[14] It has a 'dominant strategic function'.[15] The object-target of the apparatus orders 'a thoroughly heterogenous ensemble consisting of discourses, institutions, architectural forms, regulatory discourses, laws, administrative measures, scientific statements, philosophical, moral and philanthropic propositions'.[16] These heterogenous elements are drawn together, because they will help to deal with whatever the object-target of the apparatus may be.

> The apparatus itself is the system of relations that are established between these elements. ... In short, between these elements, whether discursive or

> non-discursive, there is a sort of interplay of shifts of position and modifications of function which has as its major function at a given historical moment of responding to an *urgent need*.[17]

The object-target orientates the apparatus allowing it to be gathered in the first place. At the same time, it is only by inscribing and subsequently acting upon the object-target that it is given its own existence. In the *Birth of Biopolitics* Foucault writes that the apparatus becomes something, but it is 'something however that continues *not* to exist'.[18]

> [W]hat I would like to show is not how an error … or an illusion could be born, but how a particular regime of truth, and therefore not an error, makes something that does not exist able to become something. It is not an illusion since it is precisely a set of practices, real practices, which established it and thus imperiously marks it out in reality.[19]

The apparatus is never simply something 'out there', independently existing in people's everyday lives. However, by identifying and constructing the object-target (imperiously marking it out in reality), the apparatus takes on a sort of existence.

'Morale' is the name that the government gives to that part of the affective life of the populace that is necessary to increase the capacity for war. Morale was inscribed as something crucial that should be tracked and acted upon. It was placed within a series of discursive dualities: morale and panic, productivity and disorganisation, government and chaos and ultimately the promise of victory and the risk of defeat. While morale might seem obvious to us today, given the familiarity with the questions involved, Anderson underlines the generativity of this analysis. Morale in these papers is 'something' *only insofar* as it is 'inscribed within reality'.[20] This is the case in two different senses. Firstly, the sense of morale is generated precisely in these discursive dualities. It is differentiated from things that are not morale (panic, disorganisation, etc.). But also in a more radical sense, the denomination of something called 'morale' creates a site of investigation and action. The very act of naming the affects constitutes an intervention. It identifies something to be measured and managed. Thus, the naming (and the discourse around it) is not an innocent denomination which is unconnected to the ends that the intervention seeks to achieve. Once the government begins to act upon the object-target that it has created, it becomes 'out there' as the 'discourses, institutions, buildings, laws, police measures, philosophical propositions'[21] that inscribe it gradually filter into social life. As 'morale', collective affective life is rendered knowable in particular ways and subject to particular interventions.

In the debate around the 1941 US affective interventions, the morale apparatus collected different discourses, psychological determinations, mass observations, media broadcasts, regulatory determinations, everyday personal communications and local collective action. This collection of linguistic and non-linguistic phenomena is in response to a threat and is organised by a dominant strategic function. Anderson finds it particularly interesting that these theorists of morale acknowledged that it could neither be seen nor influenced directly. Morale 'exceeds attempts to establish it as a thing in itself'.[22]

> For example, Major James Ulio discusses how techniques for maintaining morale in the military can be used in relation to civilians, but stresses morale's excessive qualities: 'It [morale] is like life itself, in that the moment you undertake to define it you begin to limit its meaning within the restrictive boundaries of mere language'. Instead, the focus for the state was on the 'conditions operative in morale formation' through a measurement and calculation of the actions of the population as an aggregate of sociobiological processes. Because morale is 'like life' and 'exceeds' as a 'something more', it must be tracked indirectly. With the exception of observational methods – such as the use of mass observation – morale was tracked through its various and varying traces. Traces which could be found throughout life. Any aspect of life could potentially reveal the presence or absence of morale, so techniques of knowledge must know all of life without limit or remainder. Morale is everywhere. In the UK, for example, morale was understood through the frequency, extent and duration of strikes, industrial output, convictions for drunkenness or drink-driving, crimes against property. In France 'bad morale' was known through '[p]olitical tension, public violence, repudiation of existing regime by large bodies of citizens, exaggerated individualism, general passivity, demographic factors, and susceptibility to panic and despair'. Whilst in China morale was known through: '[d]ependence on American and British aid, the relations of the "return to the coats" school with the "new hinterland" school, the price of grain, the absence of medical facilities, and the treatment of Manchurian troops by the central government'.[23]

Because morale is 'like life', it escapes definition. More than that, it escapes direct comprehension. Therefore, it 'does not offer a graspable hinge for action'.[24] It can 'be known only through its varied traces'.[25] The obscurity of affective life is one of the most important insights of these reflections on morale. We will come back to it over and again, because this obscurity and indeterminacy is precisely the problem for public order apparatuses. The affective life of the populace, at least insofar as it concerns the sovereign order, is always a risk to be managed.

In fact, a number of the interventions in the *American Journal of Sociology* frame morale as a matter of popular temper.[26] This temper is situated in the governmental analysis of the population. Anderson writes that the population 'is itself an affective structure'.[27] Famously, in *Security, Territory, Population* Foucault signals a series of shifts in modes of power between 'the state of justice of the Middle Ages [which] became the administrative state of the fifteenth and sixteenth centuries and was gradually governmentalized'.[28] One form of power did not simply replace the previous; instead there was a sort of accumulation of forms of power. Foucault describes this as an evolving triangular relation between 'sovereignty, discipline and governmental management'.[29] Mitchell Dean suggests that each successive phase evokes a new 'economy of power', whose dominant characteristics change in response to its object-targets.[30] The 'population' is a key site in the emergence of governmentality. Population 'is not a natural entity but the effect of particular forms of knowledge, the invention of new statistical techniques, sciences like demography, state policies on reproduction, health care, etc.'.[31] Like morale, the population is produced by the very fields of study which seek to study it. The emergence of the question of the population for Foucault signals a radical shift in the triangular relation between sovereignty, discipline and government, where governmentality as the 'conduct of conduct' takes pre-eminence.[32]

Here we might turn back to 'The Situation Room'. The image stages the relation between government and sovereign. The sovereign decision to kill Bin Laden is taken, what is left is the work of the government. The sovereign is left strangely depleted in the corner, anxious and consumed by the operation. The image claims to capture an event of death, and as it is released to the public it becomes a surface from which affects will flow. It is received with jubilation, as Berlant says it 'gets its shape from the way that it resonates strongly with previous episodes'.[33] In Anderson's register, it becomes a node in the massive apparatus of affective governmentality. Placing the question of morale into the broader analysis of governmentality is important. It helps us see the importance of the mediation of affective life: the governmental analysis and intentional intervention. What is more, this exercise also helps us to think about the opacity of affective life. Anderson points to the importance of displaced signals which stand for changes within the seething mass of life. The apparatus of morale seems to make the affective life of the populace knowable, but it can never be known. Even indirectly, affective life exceeds governmentality. It escapes from any given apparatus but is nonetheless impacted by them. This structure of opacity and excess is essential in the next part as we begin to explore 'public order' as an affective environment and as an affective apparatus. Where morale concerns the unity, efficacy and efficiency of the population in its war effort, public order concerns the temper of the populace. It describes their state of peace and quiet, and the governmental structures designed to maintain that state.

Notes

1 Alan Siverleib, 'Obama on Sunday: A Photo for the Ages?' CNN (04/05/2011) https://edition.cnn.com/2011/POLITICS/05/03/iconic.obama.photo/index.html (viewed on 28/02/2020).

2 Megan McFarlane, 'Visualising the Rhetorical Presidency: Barak Obama in the Situation Room', 23.1 *Visual Communication Quarterly* (2016), 3.

3 Liam Kennedy, 'Seeing and Believing: On Photography and the War on Terror, 24.2 *Public Culture* (2012), 266.

4 Ibid., 268.
5 In 'Affect in the End Times', Jordan Greenwald asks Lauren Berlant to comment on the images of Bin Laden's assassination that 'elicited an upsurge in public emotions, most of them positive – elation, vindication, 'closure', relief – despite the common acknowledgment that this victory was largely, if not completely symbolic' (Lauren Berlant and Jordan Greenwald, 'Affect in the End Times: A Conversation with Lauren Berlant', 20.2 *Qui Parle* (2012), 71–72). Berlant responds initially by underlining the relation between episode, situation and event in her work: 'An *episode* is a perturbation in the ordinary's ongoingness that raises to consciousness a *situation* that follows from something without bringing with it conventions or prophecies about what its ultimate shape as event will be' (Ibid. 72). That unassembled structure, then, gathers articulations with previous episodes which generate familiarity. 'A situation usually gets its shape from the way that it resonates strongly with previous episodes, such as, in the case you offer [of Bin Laden's death], state-induced assassination, state- and media-orchestrated collective experience, popular imperialist revenge/repair fantasies, politicized erotophobia and so on. Insofar as it can be read through these other frames, the episode becomes part of a series and its danger to normative epistemology and affective habits (intuitions) is diminished, and people don't have to be too anxious or creative in their processing of it. In contrast, if a situation arises that feels like a massively genre-breaking one, then the situation can become the kind of event whose enigmatic shape repels being governed by the foreclosure of what has happened before' (Ibid.). Bin Laden's death and 'The Situation Room' are scenes that resonate with the episodes of the 'war on terror'. Like a snowball, they collect meaning in ways that mean the perturbation of the affective life is reduced. But what surprises Berlant in Greenwald's question is that the death has 'had such little staying power. … It was an episode that arose, raised some poll numbers that then sank, and evaporated. It will be available in the election season when Obama is reminding us that he was an authoritarian sovereign after all while he was also presiding over the intensified chaos of economic and culture wars. So its becoming-event remains open. That's in the nature of all events: they become dormant but remain resources in potential. Bin Laden's assassination had a place on a checklist of delayed retributive satisfactions that is now checked off, and we have moved on to other anti-authoritarian spectacles' (Ibid. 74).
6 The European Union's ambassador to Afghanistan, Vygaudas Usackas, commented that 'It could be a game changer in boosting the morale and confidence of the US and international community that the efforts and sacrifices of almost the past 10 years of involvement in Afghanistan and in the region are not in vain' (Sam Jones and Ben Quinn 'Osama Bin Laden dead: Aftermath', *The Guardian* (02/05/2011) https://www.theguardian.com/world/2011/may/02/osama-bin-laden-death-live (viewed on 28/02/2020). Foreign Policy insisted: 'In war, the issue of morale is critical. To break the enemy is to break his morale. The killing of Osama bin Laden by U.S. Special Operations forces in a firefight north of the Pakistani capital of Islamabad delivered a pivotal boost to American morale and a blow to the morale of al Qaeda, with repercussions that are being felt worldwide' (Suzanne Merkelson 'Osama's Dead, but How Much Does It Matter?' *Foreign Policy* (02/05/2011) https://foreignpolicy.com/2011/05/02/osamas-dead-but-how-much-does-it-matter-2/ (viewed on 28/02/2020).
7 Ben Anderson, *Encountering Affect: Capacities, Apparatuses, Conditions* (Ashgate, 2014), 39.
8 Arthur Pope, who created the Committee for National Morale in 1940, argued that: 'Morale wins wars, solves crises, is an indispensable condition of a vigorous national life and equally essential to the maximum achievement of the individual'. Ibid. 23–24.
9 Ibid., 42.
10 Ibid., 41.
11 Ibid.

12 Ibid., 42, citing Jackie Orr, *Panic Diaries: A Genealogy of Panic Disorder* (Duke University Press, 2006).
13 Ibid., 42, citing Orr, *Panic Diaries.*
14 Staf Callewaert, 'Foucault's Concept of Dispositif' in 1–2 *Praktiske Grunde* (2017), 29.
15 Michel Foucault, *Power/Knowledge: Selected Interviews & Other Writings, 1972-1977* (Pantheon: New York, 1980), 195.
16 Ibid., 194.
17 Ibid., 195.
18 Michel Foucault, *The Birth of Biopolitics: Lectures at the College de France 1978-1979* (Palgrave MacMillan, London, 2008), 19.
19 Ibid.
20 Anderson, *Encountering Affect*, 37.
21 Giorgio Agamben, *What Is an Apparatus? And Other Essays* (Stanford University Press, 2009), 3.
22 Anderson, *Encountering Affect*, 44.
23 Ibid. Quoting Henry Durant, 'Morale and its Measurement', 43.7 *American Journal of Sociology* 1941: 408–412.
24 Anderson, Encountering Affect, 45.
25 Ibid.
26 Lindeman formulates it as the 'collective temper of a people' and the 'public temper' (Eduard Lindeman, 'Recreation and Morale', 47.3 *American Journal of Sociology* (1941), 397 and 398). Hocking talks about a 'group temper', others talk about temperament and other aspects of temper (Ernest Hocking, 'The Nature of Morale', 47.3 *American Journal of Sociology* (1941), 302).
27 Anderson, *Encountering Affect*, 40
28 Foucault, *Security, Territory, Population*, 108–109.
29 Ibid. 107–108 quoted in Mitchell Dean, *The Signature of power* (Sage, 2013), 46.
30 Dean, *Signature of Power*, 46.
31 William Walters, *Governmentality: Critical Encounters* (Routledge, 2012), 16.
32 See Nicholas Rose, Pat O'Malley and Marianna Valverde, 'Governmentality', *Annual Review of Law and Social Science,* Vol. 2, pp. 83–104, 200. For a critical legal approach, see Bal Sokhi Bulley, *Governing Through Rights: Human Rights in Perspective* (Oxford: Hart Publishing, 2016).
33 Berlant and Greenwald, 'Affect in the End Times', 72.

5

EXCURSUS 1

Affective life

An excursus steps out of the flow of a book. Standing aside in this way, it is possible to reflect on what has passed. But an excursus is also a diversion; it focuses on a subject which is not addressed by the flow of the book. I will use the book's four excurses to examine ideas which run in parallel to the main topic under consideration. They will focus on theoretical questions which have not been directly developed in the preceding part. This first excursus is therefore fairly straightforward. In the first part we have overwhelmingly used an aesthetic idea of sovereignty to understand affective dynamics. The four scenes of sovereign affect that we have seen in the last four chapters have underscored the manner in which we might think through sovereign affect. All of this sets that first argument of the book in motion: to be meaningful, sovereignty must be performed. But it also takes us beyond the question of performance. These instances help us to develop a vocabulary for *sovereign encounters*, the affective encounters that give sovereignty its meaning.[1] These were moments which resonate as sovereignty for the populace. Beneath these encounters, however, have been competing theorisations of affect. I have brought them to bear upon the particular constellations of sovereign affects to introduce these different ways of thinking about affects. Let me sharpen the distinctions here before we move on.

Perhaps most important has been Anderson's deployment of the idea of 'affective life', which will be used throughout this book. I take it not to name any particular set of affects but rather to point to the affective circulation which occurs throughout the populace (and beyond). In affective life affects take hold, change, flow, resonate, dampen and excite.[2] By talking about affective life, rather than, perhaps, an affective field,[3] Anderson points to the manner in which affect is incorporated, moving through bodies. Human bodies respond to these affects (in the sense of endocrine, neurological or dermal changes) in ways that might evince particular feelings or emotions.[4] The affective changes might simmer just below the consciousness, affecting one's response to various events through mood but without reaching the level of perception. Or again, the affective changes might sensitise bodies to particular images or narratives which resonate. These affective forces operate to shape the capacity of the body to act. This does not mean that the body *must* do or think or feel something because it is affected in a certain way. Affect gives inclinations; it gives intensity, charge or valence to particular activities or inactivites, to images, things or spaces. Philippopoulos-Mihalopoulos suggests that we might think about affect as a force which shapes our desires.[5] In this way someone might always 'go against the flow'. Some affective forces are quite intense, and certain places have specific atmospheres, for instance. But we also have terms for less intense and more diffuse affective constellations: ambience, public sentiment, national mood, social feeling or zeitgeist.

For Teresa Brennan (as we saw in Chapter 1) and Brian Massumi (Chapter 3) affect is im-mediate. It changes the body before being captured by language, emotion or consciousness. For these theorists, affect is more or less autonomous. Massumi, in particular, insists that it is entirely autonomous, requiring a sort of radical ontology to begin to understand the manner in which it operates. In this view, affects are a direct material co-mingling of bodies without any need for language, history or any other mediation. Emotions are social, but affect is pre-personal. In her influential critique of Massumi and Tomkins, Ruth Leys summarises:

> affects must be viewed as independent of, and in an important sense prior to, ideology – that is, prior to intentions, meanings, reasons, and beliefs – because they are nonsignifying, autonomic processes that take place below the threshold of conscious awareness and meaning. For ... [these] theorists ... affects are 'inhuman', 'pre-subjective', 'visceral' forces and intensities that influence our thinking and judgments but are separate from these.[6]

Massumi insists upon the 'autonomy' of affect, its independence from cognition and signification. Affect circulates between bodies (human and inhuman) without the need for perception, cognition or signification. Cognition *always* comes late. It arrives micro seconds after the moment and then 'makes sense' of what has occurred, as though it was always the driving force. Similarly, language captures the vibrancy of affect: it 're-register[s] an already felt state, for the skin is faster than the word'.[7] But affect remains 'independent of signification and meaning'.[8] In 'making sense' of affect, Massumi claims that two things happen: the emotional response captures and closes the affect, reducing its potentiality to something calcified and dead, and that even with this apparent capture, the affect has already escaped.[9]

This pure immediacy of affect can be contrasted with the work of Ruth Leys and William Mazzarella, who both seek to refute the autonomy thesis. Leys suggests that the autonomy of affect is neither a credible reading of the biological literature nor a theoretically coherent position.[10] 'The problem', she writes, 'is not the idea that many bodily (and mental) processes take place subliminally, below the threshold of awareness. Who would dream of doubting that they do?'[11] The problem is that Massumi and others insist upon the primacy of affect and its absolute autonomy. In this way, Leys argues that it is possible that affects may operate autonomously, but they may also be interspersed with language, ideology and emotion. Where Leys approaches the question from the philosophy of science, Mazzarella works with the history of social theory. In particular, he returns to the clash between the early sociologists Emile Durkheim and Gabriel Tarde in the early twentieth century. Non-representational theories of affect tend to draw heavily on Tarde's immanent forms of imitation. Mazzarella rejects Tarde's account of society, and instead he proposes Durkheim's theory of social forces. In particular, he suggests that the affective mediation of 'resonance' can explain the same phenomena, but without the autonomy of affect. In both Leys and Mazzarella, beings are affected, energy and excitement is contagious, but this happens both in language and in materiality at the same time. Or at least neither the bodily nor the symbolic have an ultimate function in determining the affective significance of a matter.

In parallel to this ontological debate, we have seen glimpses of the cultural studies approach of Lauren Berlant (Chapter 1) and the political theories of Bonnie Honig and Elizabeth Anker (Chapter 2). These approaches are less concerned with the ontological wellsprings of affect and, instead, insist upon tracing out its impact on cultural and political phenomena. Berlant, in particular, remains ambivalent about the autonomy debate. She keeps a significant position for mediation in her idea of affect, as can be seen in her reflection on the relation of affect studies to ideology critique. In *Cruel Optimism* Berlant comments that 'at least since Althusser, ideology theory has been the place to which critical theory has gone for explanations of affective realism, of how people's desires become mediated through attachments to modes of life to which they rarely remember consenting, at least initially'.[12] Althusser shifts ideology critique 'from a *cognitive* to an *affective* theory'.[13] Therefore, Berlant claims that 'affect theory is another phase in the history of ideology theory; the moment of the affective turn brings us back to the encounter of what is sensed with what is known and what has impact in a new but also recognisable way'.[14] Berlant's identification of Althusser is important. She points to his understanding of the materiality of ideology: 'Viewed sociologically, [ideology] consists of a range of material practices or rituals (voting, saluting, genuflecting and so on) which are always embedded in material institutions'.[15] Berlant points to intuition 'as the process of dynamic sensual data-gathering through which affect takes shape in forms whose job it is to make reliable sense of life. … At the same time … the visceral response is a trained thing, not just an autonomic activity. Intuition is where affect meets history, in all its chaos, normative ideology, and embodied practices of discipline and adjustment'.[16] Gould develops this further, arguing that the 'focus on affect can help us to understand the workings of ideology'.[17] She continues:

> our affective states are what temper and intensify our attentions, affiliations, investments, and attachments: they help us to solidify some of our ideas and beliefs and attenuate others. Affect, then, greases the wheels of ideology, but it also gums them up. As a result, attending to affect can illuminate how hegemony is effected but also why it is never all-encompassing.[18]

Power operates through affect.

Finally, we have seen Ben Anderson's idea of affective mediation (Chapter 4). Anderson is more explicit than Anker and Berlant in one sense. He retains the autonomy of affect, while simultaneously insisting that this does not change the importance of affective mediation. In the final chapter of *Encountering Affect*, Anderson glosses an epigraph from Raymond Williams.[19] He draws out a double sense of mediation:

> First affective life is always-already 'in the midst of' relations and processes and inseparable from those relations and processes. Second, processes of mediation are active in the sense that affective life differs as it is mediated. Differences are not a secondary reaction or response to the specific forms, types and channels of organization that produce patterns of affective life. Instead differences in affects, feelings, emotions, structures of feeling and atmospheres emerge through processes of ordering.[20]

Anderson insists that his analytic of affect remains faithful to the non-representational quality of affect, while drawing our eye to the manners in which affects can be culturally mediated or governmentally managed.

The aim of this excursus is to draw out some of the basic commitments of the approaches to affect. This book is interested in those parts of the affective life of the populace that concern their relation to the sovereign and their governability. The four chapters in this part have sought to identify four interventions in the affective life of the populace. The first three were attempts to manage the affects which flow to the sovereign – the last of them was specifically about a government of their temper. These affective questions will come back into play in Parts III and IV, as we return to the question of crowds and unrest. But before we get to that, we must turn our attention to the primary apparatus that aims at unrest. We must begin to explore public order and the sovereign's peace.

Notes

1 Although it is not a vocabulary that she uses, I have found Stacy Douglas's *Curating Community: Museums, Constitutionalism and the Taming of the Political* (Ann Arbor: University of Michigan Press, 2017) remarkably useful to think about the mediation and framing of sovereignty for a popular audience.

2 This is never the singular 'life as we know it' that Sara Ahmed analyses so carefully in *The Cultural Politics of Emotion,* 101–141. Even as it partially resolves in feelings enmity

(as we see in the final part) it can never become that idealisation, which then exerts a normalising force.

3 Gould, *Moving Politics,* 33.
4 Silvan Tomkins, in Eve Sedgwick, *Shame and Its Sisters: A Silvan Tomkins Reader* (Duke University Press: 1995).
5 Philippopoulos-Mihalopoulos, *Spatial Justice.*
6 Ruth Leys, 'The Turn to Affect: A Critique', *Critical Inquiry,* 37(3) (2011): 437.
7 Massumi, *Parables for the Virtual,* 25.
8 Leys, 'The Turn to Affect', 443.
9 Massumi, *Parables for the Virtual,* 35.
10 Leys 'The Turn to Affect'.
11 Ibid., 456.
12 Lauren Berlant, *Cruel Optimism* (Duke University Press, 2011), 52.
13 Terry Eagleton, *Ideology: An Introduction* (Verso, 2007),19.
14 Berlant, Cruel Optimism, 53 (my emphasis).
15 Eagleton, *Ideology,* 149.
16 Berlant *Cruel Optimism,* 52.
17 Gould, *Moving Politics,* 27.
18 Ibid.
19 'All active relations between different types of beings and consciousness are inevitably mediated, and this process is not a separable agency – a "medium" – but intrinsic to the properties of the related kinds. … Thus mediation is a positive process in social reality, rather than a process added to it by way of projection, disguise, or interpretation' (Raymond Williams, *Marxism and Literature* (Oxford: Oxford University Press, 1977) 98–99).
20 Anderson, *Encountering Affect,* 163.

PART II

The apparatus of public order

In *State of Exception*, Giorgio Agamben points out that the archetype of the modern state of exception is the Roman proclamation of the *iustitium* – a sort of legal standstill or 'suspension of the law'. He explains briefly that prior to the proclamation of the *iustitium*, there first had to be a recognition of the existence of a state of *tumultus*. While a *tumultus* might arise from news of a war, it was nonetheless irreducibly different from the war itself. Instead he writes, 'the term technically designates the state of disorder or unrest ... that arises in Rome as a result of' an external war, or 'from an internal insurrection or civil war'.[1] In short, Agamben argues that the *tumultus* that gives rise to the suspension of law is not the state of war, as such, but the *affective state of unrest of the populace* of Rome. Everyday threats might need emergency measures, but the state of unrest requires something far more exceptional. It requires the full suspension of law.

When Agamben discusses the state of unrest, he does so to explicate the *iustitium*. He moves quickly from the state of unrest to the state of exception. But what if we paused on the state of unrest? As Agamben underlines, the state of unrest is not some minor hiccup; it is the affective state of the populace in the moment that the state deploys its exceptionality. Pausing on the tumult requires a certain re-situation of the question of exceptionality. Lingering on it in a modern context produces a distinct script, not inimical to Agamben's analyses of exception but nonetheless different. In the affective unrest of the modern tumult, the script includes the growing swelling feeling of discontent and undulating waves of disruption, occupation and resistance. The unrest is not a quasi-natural event that befalls the people of Rome because of a surprise war, and to which the sovereign then declares the suspension of law. Today, unrest happens because of crowds and crisis, streets full of placards and tents. Today, unrest occupies squares and parks, it marches through streets. It smells like tear gas and sweat, and sounds like a chorus and a party. Today, unrest is made up of the police, militias and thugs. It is armed with batons, sound cannons, tear gas, stun grenades, personnel carriers, water cannons and an armoury of automatic weapons. It emerges because of problems with austerity, representation, police violence, climate, repression, rights and refusals. In the affective unrest of the modern tumult, the sovereign sets loose its exceptionality entwined with the 'norm'. The force of law is deployed to re-establish its 'peace'.

'Public order' is the name given to the apparatus gathered to manage this tumult. It is quite different to the apparatuses that gather around the 'war on terror' and the various recent 'border crises', in which Agamben's theory of exception has found its most avid contemporary applications and challenges.[2] Like them, public order requires a massive development of techniques that might 'manage' its object-target. But unlike the camps of the war on terror and the border crises, the exceptionality of public order is sporadic. There is no permanent border wall, no remote site of torture that looms large in people's imaginaries. Instead, the violence is situated in exactly the spaces of everyday life. The police on horseback charge down protestors in the same city square that they cross to go to work.[3] Public order management produces exceptionality with a different type of immanence, more sporadic and involving much larger swathes of the populace. Turning theories of the 'state of exception' onto the problem of unrest neither simply reconfirms Agamben's core thesis nor overturns particular aspects of it. But it does underline the critique which has been growing since the first publication of the *Homo Sacer* book series: that Agamben occludes histories of race and colonialism. The structures and strategies deployed around the world against moments of popular discontent and unrest are overwhelmingly colonial in their development. The police govern from the background, holding their latent exceptionality over the populace. When they deploy force, it comes in complex forms of psycho-affective violence. The exceptionality which is developed in the colony returns. It boomerangs.

In one sense, this part is a genealogy of contemporary British public order – which is sometimes perceived to be one of the more consensual models.[4] It identifies moments of torsion where the mechanisms which manage the temper of the populace are rearticulated.[5] Crucial to this genealogy is the emergence and the development of the colonial police. These were the forces whose primary function was the 'management' of the populace of the colony. In this sense, the first chapter is the exception. It discusses the waxing and waning of the doctrine of the sovereign's peace across a large span of time. After that the focus narrows. The second chapter explores the colonial extension of the sovereign peace, and the emergence of a key instability. The third chapter moves to the emergence of the public order police in Ireland, and the spread of this form of ordering around the expanding British Empire. The fourth explores a step change in colonial public order policing that occurred in Hong Kong in the late 1950s and 1960s. Finally, the fifth chapter explores the moment this colonial public order knowledge returned to the UK. Each chapter explores important shifts in the nature of the public order apparatus, tracing both the significance of the changes and the manner in which the changes circulate globally. However, beneath each of the chapters in this part lies the question of how the sovereign order knows and manages the temper of the populace. As we will see, the 'state of unrest' is key in each major shift in the apparatus of public order.

The Foucauldian concept of an 'apparatus' that was introduced in Chapter 4 is a linchpin for this part. The apparatus, you will recall, is a 'heterogenous ensemble consisting of discourses, institutions, architectural forms, regulatory decisions, laws, administrative measures, scientific statements, philosophical, moral and philanthropic propositions – in short, the said as much as the unsaid'.[6] It is gathered to deal with 'an *urgent need*', and this 'dominant strategic function' allows the apparatus to articulate and rearticulate itself in different forms.[7] The state of unrest is the 'urgent need' of public order. The dominant strategic function of public order is to maintain a 'peaceful' populace and to supress or manage them when they grow restive. In the UK, as we will see, the sovereign's peace is a part of an *oikonomic* or governmental power. Agamben helps us to understand that public order names a way in which sovereignty and government (as *auctoritas* and *potestas,* or *polis* and *oikonomia*) are different but also drawn together.[8] Public order is a sign of the sovereign. But at the same time, the sovereign is unable to directly manage the affective life of its populace. It requires an *oikonomic* or governmental management. And in this deployment, the government signs for the sovereign order, it gives it meaning and form. After the late eighteenth century, in the UK and its colonies the apparatus of 'public order' often articulates with what Foucault calls 'the general apparatus of governmentality'.[9] For instance, as we will see in Ireland, public order management is often part of a broader pattern of biopolitical experimentation. Throughout the part we will trace the shifting sense of 'public order' through the sovereign's minor offices and agents, their interventions and interdictions. Most importantly, we will see the emergence of a field of knowledge that aims to respond to the popular temper. These offices respond to (real or imaginary) perturbations in the affective life of the populace, constructing the problem of unrest and their response to it. In this way, public order appears to name a social sentiment of peace and calm, but it is also the apparatus aimed at preventing or managing tumult and unrest.

Notes

1 Giorgio Agamben, *State of Exception* (University of Chicago Press, 2005), 42.

2 Richard Bailey, 'Up Against the Wall: Bare Life and Resistance in Australian Immigration Detention', 20 *Law and Critique* (2009), 113; Dag Tuastad, '"State of Exception" or "State in Exile"? The Fallacy of Appropriating Agamben on Palestinian Refugee Camps', 38.9 *Third World Quarterly* (2017), 2159; Adam Ramadan, 'Spatialising the Refugee Camp', 38.1 *Transactions of the Institute of British Geographers* (2013), 65; Patricia Owens, 'Reclaiming "Bare Life"?: Against Agamben on Refugees', 23.4 *International Relations* (2009), 567; Bulent Diken, 'From Refugee Camps to Gated Communities: Biopolitics and the End of the City', 8.1 *Citizenship Studies* (2004), 83; Prem Kumar Rajaram and Carl Grundy-Warr, 'The Irregular Migrant as Homo Sacer: Migration and Detention in Australis, Malaysia

and Thailand', 42.1 *International Migration* (2004), 33; Sheila Nair, 'Sovereignty, Security and the Exception: Towards Situating Postcolonial *Homo Sacer*', in Gerard Delanty and Stephen Turner *Routledge International Handbook of Contemporary Social and Political Theory* (Abingdon: Routledge, 2011), 386; Stuart Elden, 'Terror and Territory', 39.5 *Antipode* (2007), 821; Patricia Owens, 'Beyond "Bare Life": Refugees and the "Right to have Rights"' in Alexander Betts and Gill Loescher (eds) *Refugees in International Relations* (Oxford University Press, 2011), 133; Claudia Aradau, Rens van Munster, 'Exceptionalism and the "War on Terror, Criminology meets International Relations', 49.5 *The British Journal of Criminology* (2009), 686; Anthony Downey, 'Zones of Indistinction: Giorgio Agamben's "Bare Life" and the Politics of Aesthetics', 23.2 *Third Text* (2009), 109; Fiona Jenkins 'Bare Life: Asylum-Seekers, Australian Politics and Agamben's Critique of Violence', 10.1 *Australian Journal of Human Rights* (2004), 79; John Lechte and Saul Newman, *Agamben and the Politics of Human Rights: Statelessness, Images, Violence* (Edinburgh University Press, 2013).

3 There is an interesting piece of site-specific art developed after the Egyptian revolution by Kaya Behkalam which underlines this overlay of spaces of exceptionality and everyday life. 'Augmented Archive' is a geo-locating app which can be downloaded to your smartphone. The app directs you to specific places around Cairo. You are encouraged to look around the space as it is now, before switching to your phone which gives you a 360 degree view of the space during the revolution. In this way, Behkalam seeks to temporally dislocate, drawing on the spirit of optimism which suffused those moments, and breaking the contemporary domination of public space. See Kaya Behkalam's personal website http://kayabehkalam.net (viewed 30/03/2020)) and the project page (Kaya Behkalam, 'Augmented Archive' http://augmented-archive.net (viewed 30/03/2020)).

4 Didier Fassin, *Enforcing Order: An Ethnography of Urban Policing* (London: Polity Press, 2013), 216.

5 It is important to note at this stage that of course there are different (overlapping) genealogies of public order that are centred through France, Germany, the US or other post-imperial states. These have different actors, and different temporalities, but in many ways they resemble each other in the sense that they require a paramilitary force capable of crushing unrest, they require the emergence of a psycho-affective analysis which helps them focus on the crowd. And they require a series of apparatuses, capable of gathering knowledge and reproducing them as training across the full extent of the force.

6 Foucault, *Power/Knowledge*, 194.

7 Ibid., 195.

8 Mitchell Dean explains: 'Both the concept and practice of power are caught between two poles, which might be expressed in terms of one or more of the following apparent antinomies: the ontological and the pragmatic; the sovereign and the governmental; the juridical and the economic; the theological and the secular; providence and fate; political theology and economic theology; reign and government, and so on' (*The Signature of Power*, 193).

9 Foucault, *The Birth of Biopolitics*, 70.

6

THE SOVEREIGN PEACE

In which we examine public order as a sovereign relationality – the English doctrine of the king/Queen's peace – the role of the peace in establishing sovereign metaphysics – and public order as an aesthetic/affective structure.

Public order is a *particular* order. It is not something natural and obvious. It is a spatial and affective order whose primary aim is the construction of 'lawful normality'. This is traditionally identified as a key element of the sovereign order. As Blackstone wrote, the peace 'is the very end and foundation of civil society'[1] and the sovereign is the 'fountain of justice and general conservator of the peace of the kingdom'.[2] In Britain, the nexus between the sovereign and public order is given in the very name of the doctrine. Depending on who is on the throne, public order is the king's or Queen's peace. In other words, at least in the UK, that calm, measured, good order that you (hopefully) find when you go out into the street in a few hours' time is directly attributable to the sovereign. It belongs to the Queen, and she is its conservator. Public order is, or at least is claimed as, a form of sovereign relationality.[3] This then gives rise to two entwined dynamics that this chapter will sketch: the peace is articulated in the transcendent terrain of sovereign metaphysics, and it is a terrene practice borne by a variety of the sovereign's knight, officers and agents, who must make that order present to the populace. I suggest that the metaphysical pronouncements (like the king is everywhere present by his dignity) cause changes in the deployment of sovereign force, and the needs of the officers and agents lead to shifts in their metaphysical justifications. The doctrine of the sovereign's peace provided a keystone for the development of the early modern British state. It would be part of the metaphysical and terrene foundation of the power of the state in every local community for over five hundred years. In this chapter we will trace this centrality, but we will also see the manner in which the significance of the sovereign's peace would begin to wane once its work had been done, after the sixteenth century.

Sir Carleton Kemp Allen suggests that to understand the sovereign's peace we must begin in pre-conquest Britain, where:

> there was not yet any established, comprehensive peace of the whole realm. While we think of wrongdoing as a breach of *the* peace, our ancestors thought of it as a breach of *a* peace. Each man carried with him a personal shield against unwarranted attack … and [the nature of this shield] varied greatly according to his social rank.[4]

This symbolic shield varied from the lowliest to the greatest of men, and there were none greater than the king himself. The king's peace was a particular order. It was not a generalised mode of ordering. It seems to signify the calm (or at least lack of physical violence) that should surround the sovereign's body. The king's peace did not originate in the general majesty of the Crown. Rather, in Anglo-Saxon law, the peace belonged to the order of the king's household. 'In the sanctity of the homestead', Pollock and Maitland claim, 'we have one of the earliest securities for order; and it is one of the foundations, if not the chief foundation', of the king's peace.[5] The king's household in Anglo-Saxon law did not refer to the king's home, to this or that castle. Rather, the king's household was a mobile sphere, a bubble that surrounded the king as he moved around his kingdom.[6] This bubble that formed around the king's body was called the 'verge'. It had a radius of 10 km, meaning,[7] in effect, that anyone who came within this bubble surrounding the king's body was subjected to different economic obligations and a different security regime (to use deeply anachronistic terms). The 'peace powers' were *oikonomic* or household powers. Where law imagined itself to be a reasoned use of principle and authority, the household power was without generality, focusing on particular responses to deal with particular problems.

Beyond his verge, the king's peace was extended to those on the king's business (holders of writs) and projected into particular spatially and temporally constrained zones. Pollock and Maitland quote from the compilation *Laws of Edward the Confessor* (circa 1130), identifying particular spaces where the king's peace takes hold. In particular, it names 'the four roads: namely Watling Street, Foss, Hikenild Street, Erming Street, whereof two traverse the kingdom in length, the others in breadth. Another belongs to the waters, whereon provisions are shipped … to cities and boroughs'.[8] Particular periods were also covered by a more general king's peace: the day of the king's coronation and the week that followed, a week at Easter, Christmas and Whitsunday. The king could also give a special peace locally at particular times: 'we find in [the] Domesday [book] that Dover had it from Michaelmas to St Andrew's day', for instance.[9] In this sense, the Anglo-Saxon king's peace is a particular form of order. It is spatially and temporally limited – a way of constructing particular places at particular times, giving them special protection. Through it, events and agents could represent the king's body like a mirror,[10] generating different forms of more exceptional control.[11]

Following the Norman Conquest, the king's peace was increasingly synthesised in the emergent hybrid legal order. Pollock and Maitland show that 'the various forms in which the king's special protection had been given disappear or rather merge in his general protection and authority'.[12] This terse statement hides the complexity of the dynamics of this change. The spatially limited zone began to creep outwards. Initially, the king's peace extended to roads which intersect with the four traversal highways, gradually extending outwards through all spaces of circulation to become all-pervasive in public space. By the start of the twelfth century, McBain notes that the king's peace was formally extended throughout the realm, 'the inevitable result of William I's requirement in 1086 that all subjects acknowledged his sovereignty or overlordship'.[13] But a gap remained between the formal declaration of subjection ('that the king is everywhere present')[14] and the material reality. Almost a century later, Glanvill would discuss the special peace that the king might distribute to his favourites or to particular places and times, suggesting that William I's universalisation of the peace did not equate in a simple way to the actual immanent control.

When Henry III died in 1272, his son Edward was in Palestine on the eighth crusade and there were simmering fears of revolt. It took Edward two years to get back to be crowned. However, given that the king's peace was initially associated with the physical body of the king, the 'great men' of the court feared disorder. This was perhaps not an unreasonable fear as it was reported that upon the death of Henry I in 1135, 'there was tribulation … in the land for everyman that could forthwith robbed another'.[15] Pollack explains:

> It was intolerable that there should be no way of enforcing the king's peace till the king had come back to be crowned: and the great men of the realm, by a wise audacity took upon them to issue a proclamation of the peace in the new king's name forthwith. This good precedent being once made, the doctrine of the king's peace being in suspense was never afterwards heard of.[16]

The king was dead and with him went the possibility of guaranteeing public order by his personal dignity. A new order of peace had to be inaugurated even before the new king's inauguration. And so they proclaimed: 'The King is dead, long live the King!'[17] The peace was to continue because while the king might not yet have been inaugurated, the peace might be associated with the office – in the Crown. We can see now that this is an essential moment in the emergence of the doctrine of the king's two bodies.[18] It continued and amplified the disarticulation of the sovereign's natural body (this particular king) from the super-natural body of sovereignty (kingship) which rests in a particular natural body at any given moment. As the natural and transcendent body of the king was increasingly disassociated, and as this distinction took on an increasing significance in British constitutional history, the status of the peace and its officers grew increasingly murky.[19]

We can see the metaphysics of this extension of the king's body in an example given by Peter Goodrich. It was a warm May morning in 1318. You might picture it, if you wish. A man stands on Fleet Street in medieval London; he is urinating on the prostrate body of William de Thorp. We might imagine the flow of urine, the gasps from onlookers, but this is mere projection. All we know for certain is that de Thorp was beaten and humiliated as he walked from the Inns of Court to the Court at Westminster, where he was the king's sworn clerk. Thomas Mackerel pissed upon the man as he lay in the dirt of Fleet Street and trampled him. The sworn clerk was the bearer of the king's dignity. Mackerel's charge 'stated that the defendant was in contempt of the King and his Court … and further that this contempt was committed in the presence of the court'.[20] By insulting de Thorpe, Mackerel committed an act of violence on the dignity of the Crown, and the peace of the king. As Goodrich explains,

> When William de Thorp was attacked it was only coincidentally a natural person who was injured. The real subject of the contempt was the dignity …, symbolic presence, or office of law. What was attacked was not a simple body but rather an image or sign of law's other body, the other scene of its presence and place.[21]

The king's sworn clerk was a bearer of the king's peace, which here operated as a special protection. When violated, it resulted in a more serious charge against Mackerel. But we can reverse the perspective here, thinking less in terms of individual quasi-criminal responsibility and more in terms of the structural function of officers bearing the peace. As these men moved around the kingdom, they carried this special protection; they were extensions of the sovereign's *oikonomic* power. They brought this administrative power to the populace.

It is in the emergence of specific officers of the peace that the sovereign's peace genuinely takes on a gravity of its own. As Agamben insists, it is not the God-figure of the sovereign that effectuates his order but 'the angels, messengers and the functionaries that appear to represent it'.[22] The justices of the peace find their first expression in Richard I's 1198 identification of particular keepers of his peace, but it was with the collapse of the feudal order in the mid-fourteenth century that their office would be transformed. The Black Death wiped out between 40% and 60% of the British population in 1348–1349. This catastrophe resulted in a mobile underclass, capable of demanding higher wages.[23] In response, the Statute of Labourers (1351) was deployed to cap wages at their level prior to the plague. Local commissioners of labour were appointed to police this regulation. At the same time, the powers of the keepers of the peace were expanded.[24] The feudal order was increasingly frayed and torn in this context. The commons and the Crown struggled to maintain order. In the spring and summer of 1360 soldiers began to return from France following the end of the first phase of the Hundred Years' War. The Crown and the commons agreed that these former soldiers presented a significant danger to the delicate balance of forces in the polity. On top of a new outbreak of the plague (which would kill roughly another 20% of the British population in the 1361–1362) and fearing widespread disorder that had just occurred in France during the 'Jacqueries' of 1358 and that would be seen twenty years later in the Peasants revolt (1380), they created the office of the *Justice* of the Peace.[25] Ostensibly, the role of this new class of functionaries was the local management of offenders, rioters and barraters (brawlers). Crucially, however, the justices of the peace would become the key form of juridical-administrative power through which the sovereign order would be made present to the populace until the emergence of the police in the nineteenth century.[26] They would extend the order of the sovereign's dignity through the realm in a new way. At least until the Civil War, they functioned as a form of mediation between the king's sovereign order and the local customary order.[27]

This is not the place to investigate the shifting nature of the office of the justices of the peace, but it is important to note that as the office overtakes the old feudal structures of control to become the primary mode of management of the populace, a complex and nuanced juridical-administrative knowledge about the sovereign's peace begins to be gathered for them. Agamben suggests that this is a non-epistemic form of knowledge, which does not need Right but operates instead upon the question of its own effectiveness. In Chapters 8, 9 and 10 we will trace this knowledge as an archive of affective analysis of the temper of the people. For now, we can note that this began as a series of manuals aimed at explaining the role of these minor state functionaries.[28] Fitzherbert's *New Boke of Justices of the Peas* (1538) was the first of these, then Lambarde's *Eirenarchia* (1581), which was named after the Ancient Greek officer of the peace. In the early seventeenth century, Dalton's *The Countrey Justice* (1619) also proved extremely popular. Each of these texts recycled similar ideas about the nature of the peace and the role of its officers to maintain social order. Indeed, Blackstone relied heavily upon these texts at various points.[29] Jones comments that this type of manual was aimed at facilitating 'the extension of a networked territoriality to all parts of England and Wales'.[30] They were a key site in the development of the sovereign peace as a stable unitary order, increasingly less subject to local differences or customs.

For all of this, between the end of the sixteenth and eighteenth centuries, the question of the sovereign's peace begins to disappear as a unitary object of knowledge. The reason for this is threefold: to begin with, the feeling that the sovereign was responsible for the calm, good order of their realm had become entirely hegemonic; secondly, the bundle of concepts it connected had begun to break apart; and thirdly, we increasingly see the emergence of a distinct field of what we now call 'public order law'. Let us take each of these in turn. Firstly, between the eleventh and the eighteenth century, the sovereign's peace became the way in which order was made and maintained. From a situation pre-conquest, where it was a local bubble around the king's body, to the complex structure of the late sixteenth century, which extended and preserved the sovereign order in each locality, we might say that the sovereign's peace became the *only* show in town. It began to develop a sense of naturalness by way of its exclusion of other modes of ordering. The sovereign's peace was made as *the* peace. Paradoxically, however, because this affective sense of the sovereign order was *everywhere*, its perceptibility began to grow faint to those who lived within it. In this, its natural quality made it difficult, if not impossible, to imagine an order that was not simply the sovereign's. Even in revolutionary movements, the sovereign held the key to this ordering. The sovereign's peace became the way of modulating the necessity of the sovereign order. In the context of the collapse of the strong sense of divine authorisation, this was particularly important.

Secondly, the bundle of concepts that it had held loosely together at least since the fourteenth century began to break apart. The constitutive parts of the peace became divided into distinct fields of knowledge. So, for instance, McBain notes that within this period the peace increasingly became associated with Pleas of the Crown, to the extent that by the seventeenth century, it had become entirely synonymous with the criminal law. In this, the sovereign's peace takes on a sort of double liminality. It was both a symbolic foundation of criminal law without any identifiable power *and* an undefined power without distinct limits. With regard to the first of these limits, as Blackstone explains:

> All offenses are either against the king's peace, or his crown and dignity; and are so laid in every indictment. For, though in their consequences they generally seem (except in the case of treason and a very few others) to be rather offenses against the kingdom than the king; yet, as the public, which is an invisible body, has delegated all its power and rights, with regard to the execution of the laws, to one visible magistrate, all affronts to that power, and breaches of those rights, are immediately offenses against him, to whom they are so delegated by the public. He is therefore the proper person to prosecute for all public offenses and breaches of the peace, being the person injured in the eye of the law.[31]

As the king's peace becomes increasingly attributed to the criminal law, a central part of the sovereign order loses its resolution. The peace is still a matter of sovereignty but now simply the ground from which criminal law grows. Instead of extensive tracts on the structures and forms of the peace, we increasingly see reflections on criminal law. The actual meaning of the sovereign's peace, which held a great deal of significance when the nature of the peace was still in question, is now hollowed out so that it has no significance beyond a form of words.

At the same time that the sovereign's peace becomes this foundation without force, we see a second sense emerge as well. Glanville Williams explained this in the twentieth century: 'Every crime is a breach of the royal peace, *but the notion of crimes involving a breach of the peace is a specific one*'.[32] A 'breach of the peace' is a civil action against someone for actions which disturb the peace of His Majesty, the majesty which is spread across the realm. It is an ill-defined form of action that is not of the criminal law. At the same time, it does not match other forms of law. If the general sense of the Queen's peace is a form of power without substance, then the 'breach of the peace' is power without form.[33] It empowers anyone (but today, particularly the police) to intervene or detain anyone who may have or may be about to breach the peace. Despite various attempts to either abolish or define this power, it remains relatively amorphous.[34] Thus, the Queen's peace became liminal to the legal system in two ways: a symbolic form without substantive power and substantive power without a formal structure.

The third reason that the sovereign's peace begins to disappear is that in the sixteenth century we see the emergence of a distinctive field that would become public order management. This was lead initially by the legislature and would give birth to ever new types of officers with responsibility for the identification and suppression of the disorderly. While there is a longstanding common law offence of riot,[35] the first series of *Riot Acts* (1549, 1553, 1559) created a

> sliding scale of riotous offences. The legislation assessed the gravity of riotous offences according to the following criteria: the number of people involved in gatherings; their intent; whether they had been commanded by a magistrate to depart; the longevity of the disturbance; and the seriousness of the threat represented by the riot.[36]

These Acts were allowed to lapse upon the death of Elizabeth I (1603). Only to return over a century later in 1715 with the *Riot Act* (1715) that would remain in force in the UK until 1973. As Shoemaker shows, the period between the Civil War and the Gordon riots (1780) marks a 'long process in which the political elite lost control of popular disturbances in London'.[37] Between 1780 and the Peterloo massacre in 1819, public order law was reconstituted. Michael Lobban points to a re-articulation of public order law in response to Peterloo, where seditious libel (the prosecution of choice until the turn of the nineteenth century) was overtaken by the prosecution of unlawful assemblies.[38]

At the same time as public order *law* was reformulated, new modalities of population *management* were emerging. As Panu Minikkinen puts it, law was increasingly 'a "rationality" that is annexed to technologies and mechanisms of power'.[39] In the nineteenth century these other mechanisms become increasingly essential as far as public order is concerned. Where the Peterloo massacre generates a distinctly *legal* controversy, once the police are introduced more broadly in Britain by the middle of the century, public order management was radically reframed. Instead, as a unity of law and sovereignty, law becomes a tactic to be deployed to ensure the particular end, in this case public order. Foucault says that it is no longer a matter 'of imposing a law on men, but of the disposition of things, that is to say, of employing tactics rather than laws, or, of as far as possible employing laws as tactics'.[40] Ben Golder explains: 'To employ law as a tactic is to approach it not as a substantive ideal or a normative system binding to all, but rather as an assemblage of power-knowledge available for appropriation by various social actors that can be, and is put to varying uses'.[41] In this sense, after the eighteenth century, the question is less the sovereign's peace, as much as the government's management of public order. However, we will come back to this in Chapter 8.

The peace is the ground upon which the interiority of the modern state is built.[42] It names the sense of control of territory, the exclusion of counter-powers and the ability of the sovereign apparatus to demand allegiance of its populace. From its outset, in the UK at least, it emerges as an *oikonomic* power. It is a power modelled on the management of the home. But at the same time, the peace is increasingly mixed and confused with the sovereign majesty and dignity. In other words, the peace operates both through law and beyond it in the field of government. What we see in this period can be categorised in Foucauldian terms as a distinctly sovereign formation of power. The reliance in particular on legality and the office of the Justice of the Peace is important. In the next chapter we will turn to the beginning and end of the American revolutionary war, in order to explore what happens as the sovereign order is challenged through the peace. The state of unrest which we see being excited and tempered reveals precisely the operation of the modern sovereign apparatus. In its dysfunction, the collapse of public order shows us how the sovereign apparatus was supposed to work and how it might be reinstituted after the revolution.

Notes

1 William Blackstone, *Commentaries on the Laws of England*, Book I, Chapter 9. For instance as Burke would comment three years later, 'Peace is the great End of *all* Governments' (08/03/1769, *The Writings and Speeches of Edmund Burke Volume II*, 225, emphasis in the original).
2 Blackstone, *Commentaries*, Book I, Chapter 7.
3 It is important to note here that 'public order' is not historically an English formulation, as Townshend makes very clear (Charles Townshend, *Making the Peace* (OUP, 1993), 4–5).
4 Carelton Kemp Allen, *The Queen's Peace* (Stevens and Sons, 1953), 10.
5 Frederick Pollock and William Maitland, *The History of English Law before the time of Edward I, Vol I* (Cambridge: Little, Brown & Co, 1895), 70.
6 Entitled *seu Commentarius juris Anglicani*. Ironically, likely called the *Fleta* because its author was imprisoned '*in Fleta*', the Fleet street prison.
7 The circle had a circumference of twelve leagues (66 km). *Fleta*, Book 2, Selden Reports, Vol 73 (1953), 109.
8 Pollock and Maitland, *The History of English Law before the time of Edward I*, 75.
9 Ibid., 79.
10 This is exactly the language that Blackstone will use in the eighteenth century. In the *Commentaries* he writes: 'A CONSEQUENCE of this prerogative [to prosecute all breaches of the peace in the king's name] is the legal *ubiquity* of the king. His majesty, in the eye of the law, is always present in all his courts, though he cannot personally distribute justice. His judges are the mirror by which the king's image is reflected. It is the regal office, and not the royal person, that is always present in court, always ready to undertake prosecutions, or pronounce judgment, for the benefit and protection of the subject' (Blackstone, *Commentaries*, Book I, Chapter 7).

11 This is important in that it disrupts some of the myth-making in the long history of the UK police force by the likes of David Ascoll, *The Queen's Peace: Origins and Development of the Metropolitan Police 1829-1979* (Hamish Hamilton, London: 1979), 9–25.
12 Pollock and Maitland, *The History of English Law before the time of Edward I*, 87. There is some dispute about whether the language of universal peace predated conquest. In 'The Pig and the Peace' Lisa Ford cites Margaret Kelly's unpublished doctoral thesis entitled 'King and Crown: An Examination of the Legal Foundation of the British King' (Macquarie University, 1998, 55–63) to suggest that it can be dated to the tenth century (Lisa Ford, 'The Pig and the Peace' in Shaunnagh Dorsett', and Ian Hunter, *Law and Politics in British Colonial Thought: Transpositions of Empire* (Palgrave McMillan, 2010), 171).
13 Graham McBain, 'Modernising the Law: Breaches of the Peace & Justices of the Peace', *Journal of Politics and Law*, 8.3 (2015): 172.
14 Pollock and Maitland, *The History of English Law before the time of Edward I*, 87.
15 Ibid.
16 Ibid., 88. For an instance of someone being released because they committed their act during the interregnum, see *Annon v Howelle* in 1316m and Jack Weber's discussion of this in 'The King's Peace: A Comparative Study', 10.2, *The Journal of Legal History* (1989): 135.
17 It is worth noting that this move was not entirely new. In many ways it was no more than the practical confirmation of Bracton's earlier argument that 'things pertaining to the king's peace and jurisdiction were "things quasi-holy" [*res quasi sacrae*] … existing for some common utility of the realm … Bracton held that those things belong to the Crown as a royal privilege' (Ernst Kantorowitcz, *The Kings Two Bodies: A Study in Medieval Political Theology* (Princeton University Press, 1957), 168)..
18 Ibid.
19 The association of the king's peace with the king's physical body remained even after the creation of the fiction of the king's two bodies. Boyd cites the former Lord Advocate George McKenzie who wrote at the end of the seventeenth century that the Justice of the Peace's commission 'may be said to expire with the King and parliament who gave it'. Robert Boyd, *The Office, Powers and Jurisdiction of His Majesty's Justices of the Peace and Commissioners of Supply* (E Balfour, Edinburgh: 1787), 5–6. We can also point to a line of thinking, from Blackstone to contemporary commentators that associates the Crown with the peace. Loughlin observes: 'the presence of majesty itself operated as an ordering force' (Martin Loughlin, 'The State, The Crown and the Law', in Maurice Sunkin and Sebastian Payne (eds) *The Nature of the Crown: A Legal and Political Analysis* (OUP, 1999), 41). We will see more of this conflation later.
20 Peter Goodrich, 'Specula Laws: Image, Aesthetic and Common Law', 2, *Law and Critique* (1991): 239.
21 Peter Goodrich, *Oedipus Lex Psychoanalysis, History, Law* (University of California Press, 1995), 9.
22 Giorgio Agamben, 'K' in Justin Clemens, Nicholas Heron and Alex Murray (eds), *The Work of Giorgio Agamben: Law, Literature, Life* (Edinburgh University Press, 2008), 25.
23 Neocelous identifies the emergence of the police with the collapse of the feudal order. Mark Neocleous, *The Fabrication of Social Order: A Critical Theory of Police Power* (Pluto Press, 2000), 2.
24 Bertha Haven Putnam, 'The Transformation of the Keepers of the Peace into the Justices of the Peace 1327-1380', 12, *Transactions of the Royal Historical Society* (1929), 12–48.
25 *Justices of the Peace Act* 34 Edw 3 (1361).
26 In 1929 Prof. Bertha Putnam demonstrated that it was the commons rather than the king that developed the office of the keepers of the peace in the fourteenth century: 'the commons in the reign of Edward III seem … to have shown considerable

initiative and to have formulated a definite policy for local government; and thus to have played a large part in the development of the justices of the peace ... the traditional view that the justices represented *primarily* the interests of the Crown against the feudal lords does not seem to me sound, for the fourteenth century. ... In the reign of Edward III ... there is plenty of evidence to show that the Crown preferred to rely on the feudal lords, the magnates, rather than on the local gentry [the justices of the peace], in its fight for suppressing disorder. In other words, it was the commons, rather than the central government, who first recognised the value of the "pivot" of the English constitution' (Putnam, 'The Transformation of the Keepers of the Peace into the Justices of the Peace 1327-1380', 48).

27 This came to a particular head before the Civil War with 'Charles's semi-conscious assault on local autonomy and his insistence on obedience to the letter of the statute law'. John Morrill, *Revolt in the Provinces: The People of England and the Tragedies of War, 1630–1648* (London, Routledge, 1999), 35. For a fuller discussion of this see Christopher Tomlins, *Freedom Bound: Law Labour and Civic Identity in Colonizing English America, 1580-1865* (Cambridge University Press: 2010), 212–215.

28 Bertha Haven Putnam, *Early Treatises on the Practice of the Justices of the Peace in the Fifteenth and Sixteenth Centuries* (Oxford: Clarendon Press, 1924).

29 So, for instance, Blackstone writes: 'The king's majesty is, by his office and dignity royal, the principal conservator of the peace within all his dominions; and may give authority to any other to see the peace kept, and to punish such as break it; hence it is usually called the King's peace' (Blackstone, *Commentaries*, quoted in Frederick Pollock *Oxford Lectures, and Other Discourses*, MacMillan and Co: London, 1890, 90). He complains that the order of the household is the true origin of the peace, rather than the king's 'majesty and dignity royal'. But Blackstone's words appear to have been drawn directly from Dalton's explanation in *The Countrey Justice* (1619): 'the king's majesty (by his dignity royal) is the principal conservator of the peace within his dominions'. (See McBain 'Modernising the Law' 180 and 182.)

30 Rhys Jones, *Peoples, States, Territories: The Political Geographies of British State Transformation* (Royal Geographical Society Book Series, Blackwell, 2007).

31 Blackstone, *Commentaries*, Book I, Chapter 7.

32 Glanvlle Williams, *Criminal Law: The General Part* (2nd edition, Stevens and Sons, 1961), 715, my emphasis.

33 Police may charge subjects with a 'breach of the peace', such a charge would not be a part of the police's statutory or criminal powers. Indeed, someone arraigned on a breach of the peace is held by the police on a civil suit.

34 The 'breach of the peace' remains an incredibly powerful tool in the armoury of the police, a form of power that can be deployed in a preventative manner, without statutory restraint, and with a 'complex' common law history. The amorphous nature of the breach of the peace power means that even when detention is challenged in the courts, police will have a better than normal chance of having their decisions upheld. What's more, even where the operational decision is struck down by the courts, the power has served its function by detaining someone in advance or during the public order situation. In this sense it presents a 'win/win' situation for the police.

35 This was defined as 'three or more persons assemble in a violent and tumultuous fashion, under their own authority, with the mutual intent of committing a breach of the peace'. Andy Wood, *Riot, Rebellion and Popular Politics in Early Modern England* (Palgrave 2002), 41.

36 Wood, *Riot, Rebellion and Popular Politics in Early Modern England*, 40.

37 'Whereas the London riots that helped precipitate the Civil War involved "a strong element of political direction and discipline", in 1780 the Gordon Riots, the most violent and destructive riots in London history, had the quality of 'an assault on symbols of authority'. Robert Shoemaker, 'The London "Mob" in the Early Eighteen Century' in Peter Borsay (ed) *The Eighteenth-Century Town, A Reader in English Urban History, 1688-1820* (Routledge, 1990), 221.

38 Seditious libel had become increasingly difficult to deploy as it required juries to consider the political nature of the speech. This opened the door to sympathetic juries reading the speech in question in ways that prevent conviction. Lobban explains that public order law shifted focus to unlawful assembly. While this was not a new charge, 'by taking a new set of facts – the collective behaviour of political crowds – and putting them into different technical forms, the courts were able to consider new questions, and thereby to determine new types of political crime not used hitherto' (Ibid.).

39 Panu Minikkinen, *Sovereignty, Knowledge, Law* (Abingdon: Routledge, 2009), 96.

40 Foucault, *Security, Territory, Population*, 99.

41 Golder, *Foucault and the Politics of Rights*, 117.

42 As Gilbert Leung puts it, historically 'to breach the peace literally … means to strike at sovereign pacification'. Gilbert Leung, 'Breach of the Peace, or Violence and/of Silence' in Elena Loizidou, *Disobedience: Concept and Practice* (Abingdon: Routledge, 2013), 37.

7

SIGNS TAKEN FOR SOVEREIGNTY

In which we explore the process of breaking the sovereign peace in the name of another order – signature is a way of thinking about the relation between government and sovereign – the temper of the people can be excited, but it can also be calmed in a new order.

In 1768 the commissioners of the Port of Boston had excited the 'temper of the people'. Various acts of the government had garnered the ire of a significant proportion of the populace. They expressed this displeasure directly against the officers, agents and symbols of the governor. In one of the most notable of these minor acts of disobedience, when the commissioners of the Port tried to seize John Hancock's ship, the *Liberty*, a large crowd had gathered. They broke windows and burned one of the commissioner's pleasure boats under the liberty tree. Among other acts of disobedience that year, a seized cargo of molasses was 'rescued' from the Crown authorities and distributed. The colonists challenged the *management* of the colony, all the while insisting upon the authority of the Crown. Lisa Ford points out this was a process of doubling of the sovereign's peace. The colonists simultaneously refused to act in accordance with the king's peace as determined by the governor, but they did so in the name of a different public order. The governor of Boston wrote to London, worrying about the 'humour of the people' and explaining that 'we are not without a Government, only it is in the Hands of the People of the Town, & not those deputed by the king, or under his authority'.[1] In this sense, we can construct the problem from two angles. The governor saw a basic continuity between the authority of the Crown (colonial sovereignty) and his management of the colony (government); the colonists on the other hand saw a discontinuity. They claimed to uphold the king's peace against the mismanagement by the governor. They claimed, initially at least, to act for the king against this local maladministration.

As Ford explains for the governor: 'The only thing worse than a riot in a town where "the authority of Government and the magistracy … have been continually insulted" was the suggestion that the peace was not the King's to keep'.[2] Ford connects a series of events over the next five years which repeated the same basic form – agents of the Crown sought to enforce the law; their legitimacy was challenged and a crowd gathered to ensure the initial decision could not be enforced. In this way, she underlines the manner in which the basic structure of the colonial sovereign order was being subverted in the run up to the revolution. The king's peace could not be enforced, but the result was not anarchy. Alongside the disorder of the crowd's subversion of the sovereign order, something else was beginning to emerge. 'Bostonians challenged metropolitan innovations in the imperial constitution by disrupting the peace but also by closely defining it, and bounding it'.[3] In other words, the colonists sought to maintain social order in the name of the king, even as they prevented the governor's exercise of power. In those years, another order was emerging, a different structure of loyalty, another form of life. In time, this new order would demand a different form of government. Crucially, the sovereign's peace was the modality of emergence.

> Leaving aside the endless pontifications of the men who sought to recreate the constitution of empire, the king's colonial peace was the main game. It was central not only because urban riot chipped away at the politics of deference, turning peaceable shoemakers into rebel leaders. Crowd action was also central because, as Maier demonstrated, Whig ideology carved out a special place for the public, and through it, the crowd. It was central because breaches of the peace daily performed the untenable limits (legal, ideological and practical) bounding executive authority in the colonial Northeast. Ultimately, disorder in Boston demonstrated that colonial subjects had refused their medieval obligation as free men to keep the peace on behalf of the king.[4]

In this, the sovereign's peace comes to the foreground as a substantive subject of analysis. In the last chapter we saw it with an almost natural aura. It appeared to develop in Britain with a certain inevitability. But in the colonists' disorder, the everyday nature of the peace dissipates. Instead, public order becomes the very mode of the political struggle. The colonists were creating another, parallel order that would sit alongside the delegated structure of sovereign power, represented by the governor. The American Revolution, Ford hints, can be seen as a process of re-staging public order.

We can think about this in a slightly different way. The governor of the Crown colony of Massachusetts was the conservator of the king's peace, which meant simultaneously that he possessed the Crown's authority and that he made the sovereign present in the colonial space through his officers and men (his government). We might say in the most banal of senses that the governor signed for the Crown. But this sense of 'signature' also carries a more complex relation as well. In Agamben's work, a signature is not simply a word or name that might be read as other words are. The signature relates one field to another. A 'signature does not merely express a semiotic relation between a *signans* and a *signatum*; rather, it is what … displaces and moves it into another domain, thus positioning it in a new network of pragmatic and hermeneutic relations'.[5] He gives the example of a coin which bears the signature of its value:

> the signature has no substantial relation with the small circular metal object that we hold in our hands. It adds no real properties to it at all. Yet once again, the signature decisively changes our relation to the object as well as its function in society. Just as the signature, without altering in any way the materiality of Titian's painting inscribes it in the complex network of relations of 'authority', here it transforms a piece of metal into a coin, producing it as money.[6]

The signature is not read, Jenny Doussan explains; it is *recognised*.[7] It moves and displaces 'concepts and signs from one field to another … without redefining them semantically'.[8] In the Crown colony of Massachusetts, the governor signed for the sovereign.[9]

However, order was not maintained by signature alone. It was also necessary for the populace to uphold the sovereign order. By the middle of the eighteenth century, 'the colonials saw the king as a caring figure who expressed his affections to them in royal proclamations, in political rites and in his behaviour as reported by the colonial newspapers'.[10] Indeed, Brendan McConville talks about a 'cult of monarchy that had muscled its way to the centre of public life' by the 1730s.[11] There was significant prestige and esteem for the king in Boston immediately before the revolution:

> after the Hanoverian succession, agents of the crown in the colonies started a cultural campaign to bolster the popularity of its singularly uncharismatic German kings at home and abroad. King's holidays and anti-Catholic parades tethered his name with fetes and holidays. Eighteenth-century consumer culture enabled a certain class of Americans to pursue status by purchasing metropolitan fashion and learning metropolitan manners. Lowbrow anglophilia made a much wider section of the community consumers of the king's symbols. Mugs bore his mug. Pubs sported his arms. Towns like Boston were covered with the king.[12]

With veneration being produced by the populace, and effective government of their temper by the governor, the colonial sovereign machine was fully operative. It signalled one simple system, a loop whereby the governor signed for the sovereign, whose authority was confirmed by immanent veneration.

What Ford describes emerging in Boston around 1768 is a fundamental rupture in this sovereign apparatus. The king remained as the apogee of authority.

But as McConville says, he was becoming institutionally unfixed, and an 'institutionally unfixed king could be all things to all people'.[13] McConville details the manner in which violence erupted in the middle of the century as subjects deployed their projections of kingship *against* the institutional structures of the king's authority. The people of Boston began to sign for the king, as they imagined themselves keeping the king's peace.[14] But their peace was defined against what they saw to be, or at least claimed to be, the excesses of the governor. In this sense, a parallel public order began to emerge, one that was increasingly unsutured from the governor as the sign of the sovereign's body. Ford's essay underlines the increasing enculturation in *this plural* sense of the king's peace which leads up to the revolution. The peace was doubled, which is to say that its natural status became contested. A wedge was driven between the *auctoritas* (authority or sovereignty) and *potestas* (power, government or *oikonomia*). We might return to the commissioner of the Port's sign of the sovereign order. Because when this sign was delivered to the populace, it was *not* a sign taken for sovereignty. They took it to be maladministration. Instead, the colonists began to sign *for* the king, displacing his actual governmental structures with their own protean self-governance – the keeping of order. By the time it became apparent to them that the governor and the king were in agreement, it was too late. This realisation was experienced as a sense of betrayal of his people by the king. The bond had been broken and a new sense of (the people's) *order* had begun to emerge. Taking this question of the people's (or public's) order, we can switch our attention from Boston in 1768, twenty years later to post-revolutionary Philadelphia. Because there is a beautiful symmetry between the old sovereign's loss of control of public order and the new sovereign's practices of generating it.

On the 4 July 1788, a large silent crowd moved calmly through the streets of Philadelphia. They stretched out for over three miles, and the city fell silent at the dignity of the throng. The physician and political theorist Benjamin Rush wrote: 'A solemn silence reigned both in the streets and at the windows of the houses. This must be ascribed to the sublimity of the sight, and the pleasure it excited in every mind; for sublime objects and intense pleasure never fail at producing silence!'[15] The explicit purpose of the procession was to venerate the new federal constitution. It was the bottom-up acclamation necessary to glorify the new sovereign apparatus.[16] But the substantial procession of 17,000 people also underlined the possibility of a new federal people: a calm, orderly and restrained popular sovereign whose sublimity and dignity were entwined. In the self-discipline, we find both majesty and dignity. 'It was very remarkable', Rush wrote, 'that every countenance wore an air of *dignity* as well as pleasure'.[17] He explained that this dignity stemmed from the mutual respect and elevated feeling of even the most lowly of worker, as they processed through the city. Rush compared the demeanour of the procession to 'the splendid processions of coronations in Europe'.[18] This was a sovereign majesty and dignity being staged. But it was a specifically republican formation where the aesthetics of dignity and majesty were put in play in the generation of a new sovereign aesthetics.

A major concern after the revolutionary war was the cultivation of 'a spirit of subordination and obedience to government'.[19] The fervour of revolution was inconsistent with the republican government. As Jason Frank comments in *Constituent Moments*, there was an 'excess of democracy'.[20] Because the temper of the people had been sustained for an extended period during the revolution, the people were dangerously sensitive to insults and failures of government to account to their interests. In this sense, Rush's political project was to alter the temper of the people. 'Republican citizens had to be habituated into a capacity for virtuous self-government', because republicanism was not just a 'form of government' but a 'form of life'.[21] In 1792 Adam Ferguson, who had been Professor of Pneumatics and Moral Philosophy at Edinburgh, finally published the fruits of the lecture courses that he had delivered until his resignation in 1785. The *Principles of Moral and Political Science* is helpful for our purposes because it draws out precisely the dynamics to which Rush points.[22] In particular, Ferguson helps us think about habituation. 'Habit', he argues, 'is a source of inclination'.[23] Gradually a person acclimatises to an action, an idea or a certain situation. Ferguson gives habit a crucial role of social relations, wondering 'whether any thing be so fixt in the nature of man, as that habit or custom cannot change it or remove it?'[24] Habits establish 'affection or temper of the mind',[25] which gives a certain valence to things. Ferguson comments that the government, in particular, is subject to these affective dynamics:

> The authority of government itself, under every political establishment, rests on the habits of thinking, which prevail among the people. … [I]n republics, which admit every order of the people some share in the government of their country, the object of respect is conceived in the state itself, and the law by which it is governed.[26]

This sense of respect should not be understood as a rational 'consent'. His point throughout is that habituation is the process whereby a feeling becomes habitual. The authority of a government rests upon habitual relations. In relation to sovereignty, he identifies an 'implicit faith':

> In ordinary times, the pretensions of sovereignty are received with implicit faith. Unnecessary applications, whether of force, or even of argument, in support of those pretensions, do but endanger the shaking of a habit of thinking, which might otherwise remain unmoved.[27]

In ordinary times habit renders sovereignty's authority implicit and the government of temper is imperceptible. In the case of the new American republic, the sovereign order was still raw; the people were still sensitive to it. The new public order needed to be imperceptible or an-aesthetic.[28]

The question for Rush was how to regain that sense of obviousness that had been shaken by the events of the revolution – how to anaesthetise the populace.

They were sensitised to government, they were suffering under a 'species of insanity' that he called '*anarchia*'. This was 'brought on by "the dissolution of civil government"'.[29] The populace needed to be desensitised. To do this Rush developed a republican practice of the collective cultivation of moral sentiments. In Ferguson's words, Rush sought to be the 'artificer' of the people's nature.[30]

> This moral cultivation would target not only the citizenry's corrupted principles, but more importantly for Rush, their corporeal habits and dispositions. ... 'A physical regimen should as necessarily accompany a moral precept, as directions with respect to air – exercise – and diet, generally accompany prescriptions for the consumption and the gout'. What is needed 'is the proper direction of those great principles of human conduct: sensibility, habit, imitation and association'.[31]

Rush identified a number of key sites of intervention. He developed educational principles to be taught to school masters. These would cascade through the population as students passed through their schools. He developed directions for the media and legislature, which were designed to shepherd the popular sentiments of the people. Editors had an important role in shaping the feelings of the public sphere and prison governors in shifting the habits and tendencies of the corrupted. In this way, the temper of the people might be cured of its disease of *anarchia*.

Thus we come back to the federal procession in Philadelphia in 1788, where the populace manifests itself but in calm and orderly form. This is crowded sovereignty, but it is not tumultuous. Instead it glorifies the new sovereign order. It gives everyone an experience of the people that is not riotous. Bracketing the American revolutionary war in this way is useful because it helps us see the way in which tempers might begin to fray and at the same time the practices which might provide a balm to these tempers. What emerges, I suggest, is an idea of the sovereign apparatus as a series of affective movements or flows. From the sovereign, there is an excitement of affects of loyalty or consent. At the same time, the governmental power signs for the sovereign, actually managing the popular temper. Finally, there is a popular practice of the peace. This may take the form of veneration and acclamation, but it can also be found in the calm everyday sense of 'peace'. To reduce it to something pithy, we might say: the sovereign appears, the government signs for it and the populace habitually accepts it.

Sovereignty (qua peace) is at its greatest when no one has to think about it. The events in Boston in 1768 are important because they bring out the instability within the peace. The events in Philadelphia in 1788 are important because they bring out the practices of stabilisation necessary to recreate the peace. The long lineage of the king's peace that we traced in the last chapter lends this all an air of permanence, but in fact 'the sovereign peace' names a particular weakness in sovereign order. It is this fault line that every protesting crowd understands implicitly. Against every liberal and conservative that asks, 'what is the point of protest?', it is necessary to insist that on a metaphysical level, as well as a practical level, sovereignty relies upon the peace and calm of social relations. There is nothing more dangerous to sovereignty than a state of unrest!

Notes

1 Quoted in Lisa Ford, 'The King's peace and the Imperial Constitution: Boston 1764-1770' (unpublished work, manuscript with the author), 2.
2 Ibid.3, quoting a letter from Governor Bernard to Hillsborough, 30 June 1768, T1/465, part II.
3 Ibid., 21.
4 Ibid.
5 Giorgio Agamben, *The Signature of All Things* (Zone Books, 2009), 40.
6 Ibid.
7 Jenny Doussan, *Time, Language, and Visuality in Agamben's Philosophy* (Palgrave/MacMillan, 2013), 135.
8 Agamben, *The Kingdom and the Glory*, 4.
9 For Agamben, the signature helps us identify the political theology that lies beneath practices of sovereignty, but this is fraught with dangers as Alberto Toscano shows. He warns of a danger with a simple adoption of this idea of signature. He writes that Agamben's idea of the signature 'means that there is no need to actually gauge the mechanisms that allow for the transition from one discursive field to another, since the very presence of the signature *immanently* refers us back to an origin in the theological field' (Alberto Toscano, 'Divine Management: Critical Remarks on Giorgio Agamben's *The Kingdom and the Glory*', 12.3 *Angelaki: Journal of the Theoretical Humanities* (2011), 128). The effect of this, he argues, is to delegitimate the political concepts. 'Political economy, for example, is reduced to a "social rationalisation of providential *oikonomia*". The "theory" of signatures thus seems to engage in what we could call a *reductivist idealism*, a mirror-image of sorts of the much-maligned Marxian reduction of ideal structures to social relations' (Toscano, 'Divine Management', 128). In this chapter, instead of a reduction of sovereignty and government to the political or economic theology, I use signature to bring attention to the juncture between sovereignty and government. In the coming chapters, we will explore precisely in techniques of government and police which make the sovereign present, and which manage the populace in its affective life.
10 Brendan McConville, *The King's Three Faces: The Rise and Fall of Royal America* University of North Carolina Press, 2006), 108.
11 Ibid., 145.
12 Ford, 'The Kings Peace and the Imperial Constitution', citing Richard Bushman, *The Refinement of America: Persons, Houses, Cities* (Vintage Books, 1993) and McConville, *The King's Three Faces.*
13 McConville, *The King's Three Faces*, 170.
14 Ford, 'The Kings Peace and the Imperial Constitution'.
15 Benjamin Rush, in *Letters of Benjamin Rush, Vol I* (Butterfield, L H (ed), Princeton University Press 1951), 471, quoted in Jason Frank, *Constituent Moments: Enacting the People in Postrevolutionary America* (Duke University Press, 2010), 102–103.
16 For further discussion on the relations of the political and constitutional power of acclamation, veneration and glory, see Agamben, *The Kingdom and the Glory*, or Dean, *The Signature of Power*, 200–211.
17 Rush, *Letters of Benjamin Rush*, 472 (emphasis in the original).
18 Ibid., 470.
19 George Washington, *Circular to State Governments* (1783), quoted in Frank *Constituent Moments*, 68.

20 Frank *Constituent Moments*, 113.
21 Ibid.
22 Rush had also met Ferguson in London and refers positively to his work more generally. Benjamin Rush, *Benjamin Rush's Lectures of the Mind* (American Philosophical Society, Philadelphia, 1981), 409–412.
23 Adam Ferguson, *Principles of Moral and Political Science* (Strahan, 1792), 209.
24 Ibid., 223.
25 Ibid., 224.
26 Ibid., 215.
27 Ibid., 215–216.
28 Terry Eagleton, *The Ideology of the Aesthetic* (Blackwell, 1990), 58.
29 Frank Constituent Moments, 116.
30 Ferguson, *Principles of Moral and Political Science*, 227.
31 Frank, *Constituent Moments*, 118. As Eagleton writes in a different context: 'The ultimate binding force of the bourgeois social order … will be habits, pieties, sentiments and affections. And this is equivalent to saying that power in such an order has been *aestheticized*. It is at one with the body's spontaneous impulses, entwined with sensibility and the affections, lived out in unreflective custom' (*The Ideology of the Aesthetic* 20).

8

THE STATE OF UNREST

In which we explore the force deployed by the colonial police – the manner in which the Irish police emerge – we see the development and circulation of a form of knowledge of public order.

In parliament in 1831 the great Irish emancipator Daniel O'Connell complained that the 'effects of the establishment of the police has been, that whenever the populace resist the police they are put to death by them. In England resisting the police was a misdemeanour but in Ireland it was punished with death'.[1] The police were 'a force armed with deadly weapons, which they were reckless in using on very slight occasions'. He underlined:

> four times more men fell at the hands of the police than by the hand of the executioner. Thus four times more men were shot to punish rioters than to punish all other crimes. The land was red with blood spilt by police.[2]

The colonial police deployed a brutal de-socialised force against the Irish populace in the name of keeping the sovereign order. Colonial public order was a mode of exceptionality, a suspension of ordinary legality that could be deployed when the state of unrest appeared to emerge. Half a century later Jenny Marx would sharpen this analysis. Writing in 1870 against Gladstone's redeployment of the *Peace Preservation (Ireland) Act*, she explained: 'Theoretical fiction has it that constitutional liberty is the rule and its suspension an exception, but the whole history of English rule in Ireland shows that a state of emergency is the rule that the application of the constitution is the exception'.[3] This chapter is not simply about the brutality and exceptionality of colonial public order management in the nineteenth century. It is important to see that with the creation of a new public order apparatus in Ireland the affective life of the populace became an object-target. In other words, with the creation of the police it was possible to reconstitute the field of sovereign affects in a new way. This meant the generation of new practices of efficient suppression of disorder and new forms of knowledge that could habituate the police to these powers. These had become so effective that when the British began to think about the management of their colonies in the mid-nineteenth century, they turned not to the unarmed police of London but to the paramilitary Royal Irish Constabulary (RIC). Each British colonial police force trained in Dublin (or after Irish independence in Belfast and ultimately Palestine) and so 'for a hundred years, Ireland became a base for an enormous training operation controlled from London'.[4] In the nineteenth and early twentieth centuries, Irish officers travelled the world giving basic training, while 'officers who needed advanced training for promotion returned to Ireland'.[5] In this chapter I want to explore the emergence of these new practices of suppression. The aim is not to detail strategy, because at this stage it remains somewhat inchoate, but rather to focus on the nature of the force being practised.

To begin to understand the micro-practices of colonial government, we need to cast back to Robert Peel's introduction of the peace preservation force in 1814. In the early nineteenth century, Ireland became a social laboratory. It was a site of experimentation for new modes of government that would prove crucial as the pace of British colonial expansion increased.[6] These experiments were based around one problem: Ireland's populace was restive and social relations were opaque to the government in Dublin Castle. The Irish populace was often perceived to be ungovernable. When the extraordinarily young Irish secretary Robert Peel was appointed in 1812, he was convinced of the need for a new approach. Among other things, he gradually settled upon a radical reconfiguration of the modes of control that would be exercised in Ireland. Thus, in 1814 Peel introduced the *Peace Preservation Act* which created a new breed of public order officers. There would be 'stipendiary magistrates with authority to override local justices' of the peace and a 'permanent force of special constables'[7] specifically trained as 'outrage specialists'.[8] In effect these constables were a riot squad who could be deployed anywhere in the country to put down unrest.[9] They mimicked the magistrate/constable structure but were actually the beginnings of a very different form of power.

The colonial administration in Dublin Castle had long worried that the populace was becoming opaque to the civil authorities. This was brought to the point of crisis by the secret societies, bound by oaths, local traditions and allegiances that had formed the basis of the United Irishmen's revolution sixteen years before in 1798. Where in England, as Edmund Burke identified, tradition was 'a stabilizing principle', in Ireland 'tradition was a disruptive force, drawing attention to the successive phases of confiscation and bloodshed perpetrated by colonial conquest'.[10] The affective–aesthetic order (of affect, habit, tradition, language) pulled against the colonial allegiance to the sovereign. As Eagleton points out, the United Irishmen had deployed this aesthetic resistance based on the 'irreducible state of being impenetrable to all alien Enlightenment rationality'.[11] The system of colonial control before the peace preservation force was introduced was built on aristocratic magistrates living locally and enmeshed within the local social fabric; however, their network of informers and spies was patchy. The army were feared and despised for the sheer violence of their interactions.[12] But outside of Dublin, the extant structures had proved utterly useless in response to this new revolutionary aesthetics of 1798.

From his arrival, Peel 'maintained that Ireland could not be governed as if it were England, for there was a difference in the character and spirit of the governed'.[13] He identified a difference in the affective life of the populace, a difference in temper and temperament, related to a deeper racial element. He wrote, 'the Irishman's natural predilection is for outrage and a lawless life which I believe nothing can control'.[14] This fundamental difference would require a new type of solution, one that did not rely upon immanent control through disdainful (but intimate) knowledge of the social fabric. The delinquency required a fundamental reordering of the civil 'apparatus of surveillance, control and punishment'.[15] Peel revived the *Insurrection Act* (1814), an explicit piece of emergency legislation, designed to allow the suspension of law in the name of suppression of an insurgent populace. The act had been instrumental in the suppression of the 1798 United Irishmen uprising and rooting out the remnants of the secret societies.[16] But it was allowed to lapse in 1810. In its amended form, this gave the Lord Lieutenant the power to declare a state of emergency and to take direct military control of the territory upon the request of a special session of the justices of the peace (i.e. seven magistrates).[17] In effect, Peel was insisting that he was willing to employ war powers to subject insurrections, but he also made clear that this would not be the first resort. In March of 1815 (after Napoleon's escape from Elba), Dublin Castle received four requests to apply the *Insurrection Act*. Rejecting each one, the administration instead offered to apply the *Peace Preservation Act*.[18] Peel wrote, 'We are determined to reserve this strongest and last remedy for occasions of great emergency. … Depend upon it, however, that nothing will be half so effectual as an active stipendiary magistrate [peace preservation force] patrolling by night with thirty or forty mounted constables. … The *Insurrection Act* itself would not be half so useful'.[19] Peel sought to displace the simple turn to pure military force. There were a number of contingent reasons for this; the government could not afford military deployments in Ireland due to the continuing War of 1812 in America and the Napoleonic Wars on the continent and because there was a fairly deep uncertainty about the reliability of the military, much of which was drawn from the ranks of the Irish. However, Peel also had a more significant, far-reaching purpose.

He sought to displace the pre-eminence of the Magistracy in the containment of popular unrest. The peace preservation force would become a new machine for *transforming* the affective life of the populace. At stake was nothing less than a new wave of the 'civilisation' of the lawless Irish temper, he wrote. 'By the operation of such measures the enterprise of the rich and the industry of the poor will be encouraged, those shameful excesses which are the obstacle to all improvement will be punished and repressed, and the foundations will be laid on which at some future period permanent good order and tranquillity may be established'.[20] As David Nally underlines in 'The Coming Storm', the British government in Ireland introduced a series of major biopolitical and disciplinary institutions in Ireland in this period, from the asylums to dispensaries, and from workhouse reform to schooling.[21] The public order police was therefore only one element of the transformation of Irish society. However, it remained a particularly important site of intervention. Walter Benjamin, of all people, helps us understand the particular importance of this institution.

In the 'Critique of Violence', Benjamin distinguished law-founding (*recthsetzende*) and law-preserving (*rechtserhaltende*) violence.[22] Law-preserving violence was the violence used to protect and preserve the state order. Law-founding violence, on the other hand, was the violence associated with the revolutionary or colonial foundation of the state. In the liberal paradigm, the police are understood to simply enforce the law, remaining distinctly law-preserving in their application of force. Benjamin insisted, however, that law-founding violence did not simply occur in a single period of foundation but was *continually manifested within the constituted order* as the state rearticulated itself in ever new forms. Achille Mbembe also deploys the language of a law-founding violence. He writes that colonial sovereignty

> helped to create the space over which [force] was exercised; one might say that it presupposed its own existence … [and the colonial power] regarded itself as the sole power to judge its laws – whence its one-sidedness, especially as … its supreme right was (by its capacity to assume the act of destroying) simultaneously the supreme denial of right.[23]

In other words, what is at stake in the law-founding violence of the colony is not so much that actual violence but the (pure, unadulterated, unsupported) assertion of the sole right to exercise violence as (legitimated) force.

By the nineteenth century in Ireland there had been so many 'law-founding' moments that it might seem strange to frame Peel's public order police in these terms. However, that is precisely what is at stake in the development of the Irish constabulary. Peel reconstituted the normative space in which colonial power could be exercised, by reconfiguring the state's right to force. The introduction and development of this new type of officer shifted the management of the affective life of the populace. He supplanted the military with a mobile paramilitary force of police constables under the civil control of the Irish secretary, capable of employing brutal force or regulating the minutiae of the lives of the colonised[24] – a central civil authority with its own force for 'order' and 'civilisation'. Rather than the dichotomy of juridical and military power, Peel sought to introduce an intermediate stage. The magistrate and his men were the first response to a single outrage; then the new colonial police force would intervene upon the emergence of a more general state of unrest in the locality. Only after the spread of the unrest would the army be deployed, following the declaration of insurrection.[25] This 'intermediary' phase, in fact, synthesised the other two forms of power, at once capable of the extreme force of the military but at the same time civil and 'peaceable' in its function. However, this is not as simple a synthesis as it might seem.

In the 'Critique of Violence', Benjamin notes this mixture of force. 'In contrast to law, which has a place and time of decision, policing operates as a ghostly, diffuse, amorphous presence'.[26] It breaks down the distinction between law-preserving and law-founding violence. The police, especially in the colonial formation now under consideration, were 'emancipated from both conditions'.[27] Benjamin writes:

> The assertion that the ends of police violence are always identical or even connected to those of general law is entirely untrue. Rather, the 'law' of the police really marks the point at which the state, whether from impotence or because of the immanent connections within any legal system, can no longer guarantee through the legal system the empirical ends that it desires at any prince to attain. Therefore, the police intervene 'for security reasons' in countless cases where no clear legal situation exists.[28]

The police identify certain types of security reasons, such as a public order situation where the sovereign's right to rule, the economic obligations or later the life of the populace is at stake. These situations grant the police (as the newly minted guardians of the sovereign order) a terrifying and ill-defined zone of activity.[29] When Peel introduces the police to Ireland, he exercises a law-founding violence, rearticulating the modality of social control. But the violence that emerges from this law-founding is neither simply law-founding nor law-preserving, but an indistinction between the two. This type of argument is more complex today as we will see in coming chapters, but it could not be more evident than in the case of the 'peace preservation force' and its colonial policing successors.

The formation of these 'outrage specialists' proved immensely useful for the British colonial project. In essence, it was a key part of the intensification of *oikonomic* forms of power over the traditionally legal/sovereign powers. The 'Irish model' which was exported around the British imperial world had two key dynamics which constituted the nature of its force. Firstly, the police should not be 'of' the society they sought to police. The aim was to de-socialise the force. They were not allowed to serve in any area where they had familial relations; they were housed in barracks separate from society; and they could not serve in an area where they held land or had other employment. Hawkins suggests that the RIC often described themselves as 'Ishmaels'. For them, this was a biblical reference to the child of Abraham who was sent away with his mother, only to be lost in the desert, founding a martial people (associated with 'the Arabs' in nineteenth-century Ireland) there.[30] The act of being cast out from their home, to a space where they had no bonds of fealty and received little sympathy from the populace, was designed to harden them. This strategy was simultaneously a 'liberation' of the police officers' bonds with home and the establishment of a *spirit de corps* among the ranks. It meant that, unlike the magistracy, which was entwined with local habits and customs, the police would exercise an unfathomable force, one that was neither connected by nor mediated through local ideas, beliefs, habits or customs. In short, in response to the emergence of the secret societies that rendered Irish social relations opaque to the colonial eye, Peel created a force that would respond with an equally opaque force.

The second key element is the reliance upon military style of training, and drill in particular. The aim here was to create a disciplined and self-controlled body of men who would be capable of acting with calm resolve when faced with disordered crowds. The activities of the six-month officer training program in 1908 are instructive. It combined the individual self-discipline of gymnastics and jujitsu; the collective discipline of drill and command; and the more familiar modern civil functions of the police.[31] Sinclair comments on the constant worry in the British colonies in Africa that the RIC were becoming 'domesticated'. They feared that focusing more on civil policing of weights and measures, detection techniques or the niceties of evidence gathering, rather than on drill, command and musketry, devalued the training by reducing the time given to the 'essential' public order training.[32] It is sometimes easy to get lost in the hard coercive force of the colonial police. But what interested the colonial police in this training was the drill – the movements of bodies that could stop and break up the hard mass of the crowd. The movement of police bodies is something trained to the point of instinct, each body knowing without thought where it should be in the deployment. In this, command is not an instruction but a cue to move collectively from one mass shape to another. The drill enjoins a bodily memory. It instils collective movement at the level of instinct and habit. In the drilling of instinctual responses, we find a crucial dynamic in the emergence of an affective management of colonial populaces.

Over the nineteenth and early twentieth century, this drill training began to develop a new specificity in the hands of the police. In particular, officers began to redraw the training processes for public order situations rather than the infantry's battlefield for which it had originally been designed. New analyses of disorder, colonial mentality and the crowd's temper began to enter the knowledge, as we will see in the next chapter. Agamben explains that alongside management as the form of power: '*Oikonomia* designates a practice and a non-epistemic knowledge that should be assessed only in the context of the aims that they pursue'.[33] The public order police force developed new forms of public order training, all aimed at the object-target of the affective life of the colonised populace as it expressed its dissent. Peel's invention of the Irish colonial police more than anything else generated a site from which a new force could be developed and deployed. This force increasingly took aim at the affective life of the populace.

Notes

1 Ellison and Smyth, *The Crowned Harp,* 14, quoting Daniel O'Connell.
2 Daniel O'Connell, 'On the Motion for Defraying the Charge of the Yeomanry and Volunteer Corps for Great Britain and Ireland', Hansard: HC Deb 27 June 1831 vol. 4 cc388-402.
3 Jenny Marx-Longuet, 'Articles on the Irish Question', available at https://www.marxists.org/archive/marx/bio/family/jenny/1870-ire.htm (viewed on 27/02/2020).
4 Gerry Northam, *Shooting in the Dark: Riot Police in Britain* (Faber and Faber, 1989), 128.
5 Ibid., 128.
6 David Nally's, '"The Coming Storm": The Irish Poor Law, Colonial Biopolitics and The Great Famine' is a brilliant exposition of precisely this idea of colonial experimentation. Nally uses the anthropologist Ann Stoler and historian Gyan Prakash to identify the call for 'scholars of colonialism to examine Europe's colonies less as 'sites of exploitation' than as 'laboratories of modernity' (98.3 *Annals of the Association of American Geographers* (2008) 719). Nally details the broad biopolitical aims of the nineteenth-century interventions in Ireland: 'In fact, from the beginning "the laboratory" was much more than an experiment in sectarian restructuring. Centralized political administration, a unified police force, paid magistrates, public dispensaries, a unified and regulated network of lunatic asylums, and state-backed elementary schooling – this was a massive undertaking requiring a new "biopolitical" regime of calculation and surveillance' (Nally, 'The Coming Storm' 720).
7 The cost of these officers of the colonial peace was to be levied upon 'each disaffected area where its services might be required' (Ascoll, *The Queen's Peace,* 68).
8 Galen Broeker, *Rural Disorder and Police Reform in Ireland: 1812-36* (Routledge, 1970), 93.
9 Graham Ellison and Jim Smyth, *The Crowned Harp: Policing in Northern Ireland* (Pluto Press, 2000) 7–8, 13.
10 Luke Gibbons, *Edmund Burke and Ireland: Aesthetics, Politics and the Colonial Sublime* (Cambridge University Press, 2009), 14.
11 Eagleton, 'Nationalism: Irony and Commitment', 32.
12 In fact, the growth of secret societies in rural Ireland led to ever growing paranoia – although without the overarching structure of the defeated United Irishmen these were perhaps not particularly dangerous to British rule on the Island. But the 'authorities were [nonetheless] totally mystified by the activities of the rural secret societies. Even when arrested and charged, people maintained a wall of silence' (Ellison and Smyth, *The Crowned Harp,* 9). This worried Dublin Castle – the seat of colonial administration in Ireland – because it was precisely the failure of the informant network in Wexford that meant the Army was ill-prepared to defeat the 1798 uprising before it began, as they had so successfully in Dublin.
13 Broeker, *Rural Disorder and police Reform in Ireland,* 60. It is interesting here to contrast the unrest in Ireland in the latter eighteen tens with the events in Manchester in 1819 when the Yeomen and Hussars were set loose on a reform meeting in St Peter's field. The Peterloo massacre was far more significant in scale than the events in Ireland in the preceding decade. However, the response in London was to reaffirm the rules around unlawful assembly and to valorise the magistrates and troops. As Lord Chancellor Lord Eldon summarised in the House of Lords: 'number constituted force, and force terror, and terror illegality' (quoted in Nadine El-Enany, '"Innocence Charged with Guilt": The Criminalisation of Protest from Peterloo to Millbank', in Francis Pakes and David Pritchard (eds.) *Riot: Unrest and Protest on the Global Stage* (Palgrave Macmillan, 2014).
14 Ellison and Smyth, *The Crowned Harp,* 9.
15 Ibid., 2

16 As Ellison and Smyth note: 'The Rebellion of 1798 shocked the British government for a number of reasons: its egalitarian republican ideology, the participation of Presbyterians on the side of the United Irishmen and the intervention of France. More lives were lost – about 30,000 – than during the French Revolution' (Ibid. 7–8).
17 For a full discussion of these provisions see Broeker, *Rural Disorder and Police Reform in Ireland*.
18 Ibid., 80–81.
19 Robert Peel, 'Letter to James Daly Esq.' (18/01/1816) in *Sir Robert Peel from his Private Papers Vol. 1* (John Murray, 1891), 206.
20 Peel, R, 'Letter to the High Sheriff for County Wicklow' (22/03/1816), in *Sir Robert Peel from His Private Papers*, 232.
21 Nally, 'The Coming Storm', 720.
22 See Hamacher for the translation of 'positing': Werner Hamacher, 'Afformative, Strike, Benjamin's "Critique of Violence"', in Andrew Benjamin and Peter Osborne, *Destruction & Experience* (Clinamen Press, Manchester, 2000),, 108.
23 Achille Mbembe, *On the Postcolony* (University of California Press, 2001), 25.
24 This approach would later be confirmed by General Sir Charles James Napier, who put down Scinde (now Pakistan) in 1842–1843 but whose military career spanned the colonial hotspots of the day: 'Rendering civil power dependent upon the military for protection in ordinary cases is of all evils the greatest. I speak from nearly 50 years' experience. I saw it in Ireland in 1798, and again in 1803. I saw it in the Ionian Islands. I saw it in the Northern Districts. I saw it in Scinde' (quoted in Ellison and Smyth, *The Crowned Harp*, 8).
25 See Broeker, *Rural Disorder and Police Reform in Ireland*, 231.
26 Andrew Robinson, 'Walter Benjamin: Critique of Violence', *Ceasefire Magazine* (21/12/2013), https://ceasefiremagazine.co.uk/walter-benjamin-critique-state/ (viewed on 30/03/2020).
27 Benjamin, 'Critique of Violence', 243.
28 Ibid.
29 As Mbembe comments: 'the security state can be seen to feed on a *state of insecurity*, which it participates in fomenting and to which it claims to be the solution. If the security state is a structure, the state of insecurity is instead a kind of passion, or rather an affect, a condition, or a force of desire. In other words, the state of insecurity is the condition upon which the functioning of the security state relies in so far as the latter is ultimately a structure charged with the task of investing, organising and diverting the constitutive drives of contemporary human life'. Achille Mbembe, 'The Society of Enmity', 200 *Radical Philosophy* (2016).
30 Hawkins, 'The 'Irish Model' and the Empire'. 26. Contrast this with the sense of Ishmael signifying slavery (Anne Kane, *Constructing Irish National Identity* (Palgrave McMillian, 2011), 129).
31 'The course included instruction in the following: gymnastics, jujitsu, riding, swimming, life-saving, tropical hygiene and sanitation, fire drill, ambulance drill, discipline, drill and command, musketry, fingerprint identification, police duties, court procedures, duties of a public prosecutor, law of evidence, and elements of criminal law. The course also laid particular emphasis on the R.I.C. code and use of its manual'. Georgina Sinclair, 'The "Irish" Policeman and Empire: influencing the policing of the British Empire-Commonwealth', 36.142 *Irish Historical Studies* (2008), 179.
32 Ibid., 180.
33 Agamben, *The Kingdom and the Glory*, 19.

9

PSYCHO-AFFECTIVE PUBLIC ORDER

In which public order policing meets crowd psychology – we see Hong Kong's crucial experiments with structure and nature of public order policing in the late 1950s – the role of Le Bon's crowd theory in the development of police thinking – and the complexity of the public order apparatus intensifies.

Public order is an affective apparatus. It is a network of 'discourses, institutions, buildings, laws, police measures, philosophical propositions, and so on'[1] which aims at the management of the affective life of the populace. Public order techniques are deployed to preclude unrest, or when disorder breaks out the apparatus seeks its minimisation, suppression or exhaustion. In the last chapter we saw the emergence of the Irish colonial police and the hard exceptional force that they would deploy to maintain this order. This chapter takes a closer look at the types of public order knowledge that began to emerge in the British Colonies before and after the Second World War. In particular, it identifies a major shift in Hong Kong in the late fifties which would shape British public order practice to the present day. To understand the novelty of Hong Kong's new structure, we need step back, connecting it with the last chapter's consideration of the RIC's late-nineteenth-century public order training and the more sophisticated model that emerged in the inter-war years, what Martin Thomas calls 'a new repressive consensus'.[2]

To begin with, it is necessary to place the very particular problem of the colony in the foreground. Colonial public order required a constant police operation precisely because the affective structure of the colonial society (its violence, racial dynamics, hierarchical organisation and overseas subjection) was unsustainable without it. For those colonial societies that had not wiped out the colonised population, the problem was of an often massive populace that resented the very fact of colonial sovereignty. The absence of consent in the colony is one way of thinking about this. But consent can also mislead us. It seems to suggest a conscious dichotomy between wilful consent and resistance. In the mid-nineteenth century, John Austin and Jeremy Bentham posited the idea that sovereignty should be defined by the populace's habitual obedience.[3] Bentham wrote:

> A *habit* is but an assemblage of *acts:* under which name I would also include, for the present, *voluntary forbearances.* A *habit of obedience* then is an assemblage of *acts of obedience.* An *act of obedience* is any act done in pursuance of an *expression of will* on the part of some *superior.*[4]

For Bentham, habits of obedience are merely a pattern of *acts* and restraints that are done because a superior has willed them. Initially, this seems simply to reframe the question of consent from a subjective conscious decision to objective acts. But in fact by shifting the terrain from consciousness to habitual action Austin and Bentham contemplate ways in which the populace might express the outward habits of obedience, while harbouring affects of resentment, disdain and contempt. In this sense the acts of obedience might be suffused with affects other than willing consent. Contemporary analysis of habit is more compelling than Bentham's brief exposition. Caroline Pedwell's work in particular is exemplary.[5] She renders habit 'as evolving psychic and somatic relationships between bodies and their environments, habits constitute an "organism's subconscious predisposition to transact with its physical, social, political and natural worlds in particular ways"'.[6]

No longer simply acts and forbearances of obedience, habit is a subconscious and affective patterning of activity. Colonial sovereignty's 'peace' was a pattern of obedience in the subjected populace. It was a certain docility that might or might not bear the beliefs and desires of loyalty or consent. The colonial administrations needed to keep control of populace that was temporarily docile, but that would always be at risk of spilling over into disorder. This meant that the colony was a key site for the development of the techniques of affective management. The aim of these techniques was never to simply disperse a particular crowd but to use that moment of disorder to defeat whatever broader movement it manifested. In the inter-war years, Thomas underlines the emergence of a 'new repressive consensus' which mostly eschewed extreme force.[7] Coming towards the end of the period, British Guiana's *Riot Manual* (1944) and *Drill Manual* (1945) are exemplary of this approach.[8] In the late nineteen forties, these were considered the height of sophistication by the Colonial Office. The British Guiana riot manual primarily focuses upon the legal powers of the colonial police, before moving to consider how the police should conduct themselves when faced with a 'felonious crowd'.[9] The manual first notes that 'good temper' among the police is a good way to manage native crowds. 'The tactful but firm handling of a situation may, by instilling confidence in the forces of law and order in law-abiding persons, prevent disorder spreading. … At the same time weakness must not be displayed in enforcing the law'.[10] The manual then shifts to briefly focus on *force*: 'Firing should only be resorted to when other means such as the use of batons has failed or when the situation is so desperate or the force of the Police is so small that felonious outrage cannot otherwise be prevented'.[11] There is a certain restraint here, but it is followed by a blank cheque: 'Every member of the Forces may be assured that whatever is honestly done by him in the execution of his duty to suppress a riot will be supported and justified by the Common Law'.[12] As if to emphasise the requirement to intervene at any cost to 'native' life, the manual continues: 'Every member of the Force should understand and learn by heart the following order':

> Every member of the Force is required to do all that in him lies for the suppression of a riot and each has authority to command all other subjects of the King to assist him. If persons and property are in danger and Occasion demands immediate action and I cannot get orders from a Superior or from a Magistrate it is my duty to act for myself. If some felonious outrage such as murder, arson, robbery or dangerous violence cannot otherwise be prevented or if when engaged in apprehending a rioter I cannot otherwise protect myself or overcome resistance I am entitled to fire or order those under me to fire to save the persons or property in danger, or in self-protection.[13]

It is of the utmost importance that officers are instructed to *learn this off by heart.* This paragraph was to provide a sort of valorising mantra that should return to the colonial police when they interact with the colonised in these intense moments. This mantra makes present to the officers their *duty* to beat and shoot. It drills this into them, becoming instinctual.

The *Riot Manual* must be read alongside the *Drill Manual* (1945).[14] Like the RIC manual discussed in the previous chapter, the British Guiana *Drill Manual* underlines the importance of the habituation of police bodies to forms of collective movement.[15] Police Commissioner Orrett, the author, explains that squad and arms drills were adapted from military manuals,[16] aimed at generating a military *spirit du corps*. But the baton and riot drills were specifically designed for riotous situations. They include various precise corporeal directions (point batons, right/left cut, upward/downward cut, right/left/head guard, etc.) that instruct the platoon how to individually move their bodies as they hold, brandish and move the baton. On the training field, these would have been performed in unison giving a sense of unity and collective strength. Other commands direct the platoon to undertake complex movements as a whole ('lock batons', for instance, describes a manoeuvre where a platoon uses their batons to form a sort of road block). In the baton and riot drill, the manual is limited to a small number of positions for blocking a road, diamond and square advancing shapes, charging and firing positions. Both the *Riot* and *Drill Manual* present the colonial police with a small number of options. Without reducing it terribly we might say that these were simply charm, intimidate, charge or open fire.

When the intense civil unrest broke out in Hong Kong in 1956, the colonial police would have been trained with something approaching the British Guiana manuals. While the disorder was suppressed, there was a broad perception among the police and government that their training and weaponry were inadequate for a more serious and sustained campaign. Inspectors John Lees and Leslie Guyatt were tasked with investigating reform of the 'internal security' structures of the Hong Kong police force. The proposals they brought forward were far-reaching and radical. They suggested that the entire force should be seen as a civil police force, *but* at the same time it should always be ready to be deployed as territory-wide paramilitary force.[17] This suggestion was made against the backdrop of the 1948 Home Office review of the forty-three constituent forces that made up the Colonial Police Service. The review had proposed using the 'counter-insurgency policing used in Malaya during the "Emergency"'[18] as a model for colonial police forces.[19] The simple structure of a 'paramilitary gendarmerie was thought inappropriate for Hong Kong. In the heightened atmosphere of the times, all arms of the colonial government had to appear impartial and politically neutral to avoid providing China or Taiwan with any excuse for intervention'.[20] Instead, the conventional structure where police were deployed in pairs on their beat would be maintained, keeping the paramilitary function dormant until such time as disorder broke out. This latency was important because the paramilitary form of the police only existed virtually, as a sort of training exercise. The entire force would be drilled extensively and continually as paramilitary units. But to the populace, the police would retain the air of normalcy. The possibility of manifesting the exceptional mode of organisation (and the exceptional force that comes with it) would remain in the background until such time as a major crisis emerged. Then, the police would rapidly switch from neighbourhood officers to paramilitary collectives, capable of responding to the scale of the unrest. The great benefit of this structure of latency is that the police force could simultaneously operate through their civil function in government of bodies *and* as an exceptional counter-insurgency force. It could seek to win 'hearts and minds' with a velvet glove,[21] while also being capable of drawing down a crashing fist on a restive populace. In this sense, Lees and Guyatt drew on the traditions of Robert Peel's Irish experiment, refining and intensifying the affective dynamics of colonial police. They could create this double structure precisely because for a substantial part of the Hong Kong populace, the colonial regime was broadly supported, or at least not openly resisted.[22]

To sustain this latency, Lees and Guyatt proposed a highly trained internal security unit that would simultaneously have the initial responsibility for public order operations *and* for training the rest of the police force in case of general mobilisation.[23] With the support of senior management of the Hong Kong police, the new 'Police Training Contingent' (PTC) set about improving the 'technology of repression, by implementing changes to systems of command and control, purchasing communications equipment, restyling police riot control uniforms, producing a force riot manual, and buying more modern types of armoured vehicles road-tested in other colonial insurgencies'.[24] As Roy Henry, Hong Kong's Police Commissioner from 1978–1984 explained these reforms represented the culmination of British colonial policing knowledge-production. It was a systematisation of the 'internal security mechanisms of past colonies such as Malaya, Borneo, Kenya and Cyprus' that had begun over 150 years before in Ireland.[25] The way that the PTC combined a sort of practical 'research' and experimentation with teaching, training and manual writing proved highly effective. It meant that the specialist officers were always watching for new ways to subdue crowds, and their practical successes and observations from the front line could be tested, repeated and then rapidly rolled out to the entire Hong Kong police force. What is more, this experimentation would inform the gradual collection of tactics and techniques in the secretive Hong Kong training manual. In essence, the PTC (and its later successor the Police Tactical Unit (PTU)) would become a key site of colonial experimentation.[26] As Deane-Drummond would write in a different context, this built up 'a fund of empirical and practical knowledge on how to deal with crowds. This knowledge is constantly changing and adjusting itself in line with political conditions and the developing experience of the police'.[27]

These structural changes would have had very little impact, had they not been coupled with the gradual mainstreaming of psychological theories of the crowd. The step-change in the police's public order analysis in Hong Kong came from the identification of the psycho-affective life of the crowd as the object–target of intervention. Instead of the efficient and disciplined application of force on the bodies of the colonised, public order intervention would become about psycho-affective techniques of popular management. With some fanfare in 1959, the University of Hong Kong's Extra-Mural Studies department launched an annual short course aimed at police officers:

> The course, lasting for two weeks with 24 HKP officers, was designed to put crime, law and punishment in a broader psychological, social and cultural context. Lectures included: the conflict between Chinese attitude and British law; problems of youth; *psychological aspects of crime-crowd behaviour*; psychiatric aspects of crime; reliability of witnesses; public and police; and treatment of offenders.[28]

The course proved essential to the development of the public order manual – introducing an elementary understanding of crowd theory to the colonial police.[29] As Jones and Vagg suggest, after the 1966/67 riots, these short courses increasingly introduced 'theories such as Le Bon's "the psychology of the crowd" and the social and psychological aspects of crime'.[30] Between these external modules at Hong Kong University and the PTU's training programme, Le Bon's analysis of crowds was woven into the fabric of public order training in the colony. He provided police theorists and trainers with an easy way to grasp the psycho-affective dynamics of 'the crowd' as a trans-historical and trans-cultural actor.

While the lecture materials of these courses are unavailable, we might surmise their content by thinking about what might be strategically useful in Le Bon's writings and by tracing the contours of his thought in subsequent police manuals. Le Bon identified three key factors that determine crowd dynamics: number, contagion and suggestibility. Number is both the gateway to the crowded state – the 'psychological crowd' – but it also has a substantial effect within the crowd. Large numbers of people, gathered together gives rise to 'a sentiment of invincible power'.[31] Number valorises the crowd's sense of itself and its power. The feeling of being at one with a great sea of humanity gives the feeling of strength. This is matched with the sense of anonymity through which people feel their acts are substitutable: at once theirs but also belonging to the great swell of the crowd. In the crowd 'ideas, sentiments, emotions and beliefs possess … a contagious power as intense as that of microbes'.[32] Every sentiment and act is contagious, meaning that it may move like wild fire through the crowd.

The flipside of contagion is suggestibility. The crowd may be directed with ease, according to Le Bon.

> We see, then, that the disappearance of the conscious personality, the predominance of the unconscious personality, the turning by means of suggestion and contagion of feelings and ideas in an identical direction, the tendency immediately to transform the suggested ideas into acts; these we see are the principal characteristics of the individual forming part of the crowd.[33]

As Fournier had suggested, the collective unconscious state was the result of the influence of the spinal cord, rather than the brain.[34] Suggestibility comes with the suspension of individuality that Le Bon claimed came in the crowd. 'Those elements of the human personality which control the usually latent but nonetheless powerful feelings of aggression, which in ordinary language we term "conscience" and "discipline", are weakened and, if excited by oratory, by rumours injected into the crowd, by fear, by voices from unofficial leaders within the crowds, may be violently released'.[35] People within the crowd are easily moved.

Leaders tend to be drawn from the crowd, particularly from those on the edges of madness, Le Bon says. These are the 'strong-willed men' to whom the crowd listens. These leaders start from the mass but break away by their fixation upon an idea. The idea 'has taken possession of him to such a degree that everything outside it vanishes, and that every contrary opinion appears to him an error or a superstition'.[36] The leader uses the crowd instrumentally, certainly, but they are not in control of their desires. Instead it is the idea which possesses the new leaders that has become sovereign. Their possession by the idea (a madness according to Le Bon) generates a crowd that is rabid. Crucially, the crowd become an expression of the leader's unconsciousness. From Le Bon, the colonial educators appear to have borrowed the relation between the suggestible crowd and the agitator. As Simpson puts it, '"ringleaders", "troublemakers", "agitators", "subversives" and the like ... occupied a special place in the demonology of colonialism, as corrupters of the basic loyalty of colonial subjects'.[37] Le Bon helped the police to think about the ways in which an 'inhuman' crowd could co-exist with an otherwise reasonable populace that was 'being civilised' by Western colonial intervention. He provided a racialised account of crowded 'savagery' which neatly fitted into oriental projections.

The analyses of number, contagion and suggestibility gave the police a new object–target. No longer was the populace to be returned to habitual obedience by beating or killing some of their number. Instead, the police began to think about intervening in the psycho-affective dynamics of the crowd. In his survey of international public order practice, Major Anthony Dean-Drummond observes the importance of this distinction, he writes that in 'its simplest and most brutal form [the quelling of riots] can be done by the application of [extreme] force'.[38] He contrasts this quelling of riots, with riot *control.*[39] Riot control is more complex because it must avert and defuse 'riotous situations if they develop'.[40] For the police, 'riot control' names the period in which they are able to avert a riot without deploying lethal force.[41] In this stage the police can apply psycho-affective techniques or non-lethal force on the crowd in order to defuse the situation, divide or disperse the crowd. By identifying crowd psychology, they could begin to try to control the situation more directly. They could intervene to prevent the gathering of great numbers, to interrupt contagion, to snatch emergent leaders from the crowd. They could also make use of suggestibility and try to change the affective atmosphere to nullify the potential of the crowds. As Yung and Chau explain, by the early eighties:

> Public order policing [in Hong Kong] reflected a concept of the crowd as irrational and therefore easily influenced by undesirable elements. This in turn was associated with a strategic emphasis on the removal, containment, or the disruption of agitators through the use of force, lest they manifest their ability to hijack the crowd. When it was not possible to achieve this, then a strategic and tactical shift toward the use of force against crowds as a whole was evident.[42]

Le Bon's insights were initially introduced to the PTC in the early sixties, and they began the work of synthesising those insights with their own practices. This process only intensified after the riots of 1966–1967.

The idea of the Hong Kong police was to govern through 'normality'. The government aimed at the subjected people's hearts and minds, convincing them of the fairness of the system. But beneath this the latent exceptionality provided a sort of elasticity within the fabric of normality. When the populace grew sufficiently restive, the police could deploy their new public order management tactics, new weapons and armour,[43] and their new types of knowledge and techniques. They could do it in small highly trained specialist groups (that could constantly innovate new techniques), or through the entire police force as a paramilitary unit. This is a sort of affective meta-structure, an attempt to maintain that fine balance of keeping the subjected populace sufficiently on side, keeping the interests of the communists and nationalists sufficiently at bay and maintaining colonial rule. But the shift from quelling riots to crowd control is *essential* to understand contemporary public order. The introduction of social psychology presents an important development by opening a new field upon which police could exercise force. The new model of public order management is therefore a crucial in explicitly introducing and intensifying the focus on the psycho-affective dynamics of protest, and indeed on the broader populace.

Notes

1 Agamben, *What is an Apparatus?*, 3.
2 Martin Thomas, '"Paying the Butchers Bill": Policing British Colonial Protest After 1918', 15.2 *Crime, History and Societies* (2011), 57.
3 John Austin, *Lectures on Jurisprudence or The Philosophy of Positive Law* (London: John Murray, 1869).
4 Jeremy Bentham, *A fragment on Government* (The Lawbook Exchange, New Jersey, 2001), 138 (emphasis in the original).
5 Caroline Pedwell, 'Transforming Habit: Revolution, Routine and Social Change', 31.1 *Cultural Studies* (2016): 93.
6 Caroline Pedwell, *Transforming Habit: Affect, Assemblage and Change in a Minor Key* (pre-publication draft), 4, quoting Shannon Sullivan, *Revealing Whiteness: The Unconscious Habits of Racial Privilege* (Bloomington and Indianapolis: Indiana University Press 2006), 23.
7 As Thomas explains: 'This "repressive consensus" rarely broke down in the British Empire between the wars. Spectacular instances of such breakdown – as, for example, over the Amritsar massacre in 1919 or quarrels over the recruitment of Jewish police auxiliaries during the Arab rebellion in Palestine after 1936 – were exceptions rather than the rule' (Thomas, 'Paying the Butcher's Bill', 56–57).
8 The National Archives of the UK, CO 111/796/6.
9 While the manual emphasises that a felonious crowd might be intent on murder, arson or property damage, the manual underlined just a few pages before how a magistrate might render *any* crowd felonious by deploying S.312 of the Criminal Law (Offences) Ordinance ('making a proclamation to rioters to disperse'). This declaration required magistrates to get as near as possible to the crowd in question before making the following declaration: 'Our Sovereign Lord the King chargeth and commandeth all persons being assembled immediately to disperse themselves, and peaceable to resort to their habituations or to their lawful business, upon pain of being guilty of an offence, on conviction for which they may be sentenced to penal servitude for life. GOD SAVE THE KING' (British Guiana, *Riot Manual* 13, The National Archives of the UK, CO 111/796/6, 8-9). Those who remained 'to the number of twelve or more ... then within fifteen minutes ... shall be guilty of a felony' (ibid. 9). The provisions then place a duty on the justice or mayor to discourse the crowd and indemnifies them and their agents for any injury or death that occurs while they are dispersing the crowd.
10 Ibid., 13.
11 Ibid., 14.

12 Ibid.
13 Ibid., 14–15.
14 British Guiana, *Drill Manual* (1945), The National Archives of the UK, CO 111/796/6.
15 Sir Frederick Sayers commented that the main reason for the success of use of lathis/long batons by various Indian police forces in maintaining public order 'is training, training and then more training. All armed and unarmed men are trained continuously and the subject is regarded as the most important one in drill to count for efficiency. The reason for this is that the training gives the men – even in small numbers – absolute confidence in themselves and their weapons. … The only advice I could give is to train all policemen in baton drill and its practical application until the men attain sure confidence in themselves and get an enthusiasm for attack, when necessary, which ought to carry any trained squad supported by fresh waves, through any unarmed mob' (The National Archives of the UK, CO 968/146/4).
16 British Guiana, *Drill Manual*, preface.
17 Hong Kong Police, 'History: Police Training Institutions' (available: https://www.police.gov.hk/info/doc/history/chapter06_en.pdf), viewed on 22/07/2019.
18 Carol Jones and Jon Vagg, *Criminal Justice in Hong Kong* (London: Routledge, 2007), 307.
19 WC Johnson, police advisor to the secretary of state for the colonies, 28 December 1949 CP3/214/50, reported in Jones and Vagg, *Criminal Justice in Hong Kong*, 320.
20 Jones and Vagg, *Criminal Justice in Hong Kongi* 308.
21 Ibid., 310–313.
22 Gary Ka-wai Cheung, *Hong Kong's Watershed: The 1967 Riots* (Hong Kong: Hong Kong University Press, 2009), 133.
23 Hong Kong Police, 'History: The Modern Era 1945-1967' (available: https://www.police.gov.hk/info/doc/history/chapter02_en.pdf), viewed on 22/07/2019.
24 Jones and Vagg, *Criminal Justice in Hong Kong*, 308–309.
25 Northam, *Shooting in the Dark*, 135, quoting interview with Roy Henry
26 To be clear, I am claiming that Hong Kong's combination of a 'hearts and minds' tactics and paramilitary tactics should be understood as a *development* and *intensification* of the colonial model. It is a new phase in colonial public order policing. It remains precisely a *colonial* mode of policing rather than being understood as a 'hybrid of old *colonial* and *civil* police practices', i.e. of colonial and non-colonial modes of policing (cf. Sinclair *At the End of the Line,* 173).
27 Deane-Drummond, *Riot Control*, 18.
28 Kam C Wong, *Policing in Hong Kong: Research and Practice* (Palgrave MacMillan, 2015), 6 (my emphasis).
29 Thomas insists that it is a 'reasonable supposition that most politicians with security responsibilities in Paris and London had some acquaintance with Gustave Le Bon's ideas. … Even those who never encountered their writings directly were bound to do so indirectly when reading the police manuals and colonial government instructions that dealt with police responses to protest and crowd violence' (Thomas *Violence and Colonial order*, 71).
30 Jones and Vagg, *Criminal Justice in Hong Kong*, 520.
31 Le Bon, *The Crowd*, 33.
32 Ibid., 143.
33 Ibid., 35–36.
34 Henry Fournial had called crowds 'spinal creatures' as Ernesto Laclau points out in *On Populist Reason* (Verso, 2005), 41. Le Bon continues: 'In this respect a crowd is closely akin to quite primitive beings. … A crowd is at the mercy of all external exciting causes, and reflects their incessant variations. It is the slave of the impulses which it receives' (Le Bon, *The Crowd*, 41).
35 Deane-Drummond, *Riot Control,* 19.
36 Le Bon, *The Crowd*, 134.

37 Brian Simpson, *Human Rights and the End of Empire* (Oxford University Press, 2004), 836, quoted in Jones and Vagg, *Criminal Justice in Hong Kong*, 314.

38 Anthony Deane-Drummond, *Riot Control* (Royal United Services Institute for Defence Studies: London, 1975), 18.

39 Ibid.

40 Ibid.

41 As the UK Public Order Steering Group's 'Suggested Draft Introduction' insists: 'In any attempt to resolve or regulate conflict or clashes of interest by the use of force it is not always necessary or desirable to rely on directly applied restraints. The threat of force to compel, or evidence of that capability is frequently quite sufficient constraint. We mainly exist in that civilized state. Even when actual violence in the strategy of force is used it can and should be highly selective to illustrate and amplify a still greater capability to cam or to contain and/or cut out the principal cause of the conflict or friction. The latter has the greatest inherent risk of escalating the violence' (Public Order Steering Group, 'Suggested Draft Introduction' The National Archives of the UK, HO 325/524).

42 Wing Kwong Yung and Sandy Chai, 'Paradigm Shift in Hong Kong Public Order Policing' in John Eterno, Arvind Verma, Aiedeo Das and Dilip Das, *Global Issues in Contemporary Policing* (CRC Press, 2019), 166.

43 We must remember here that the 'rubber bullet' that is so central to all public order management today was first created in Hong Kong. It was initially a teak (timber) baton round, imagined initially as an extension of the batons carried by the police themselves. In a *Time* article, Nate Jones claims that, these were initially made from 'modified broom handles' before the police began to manufacture 'wooden bullets made out of teak' (Nate Jones, 'A Brief History of Riot Control', *Time Magazine* (06/08/2010) http://content.time.com/time/world/article/0,8599,2009006,00.html, viewed on 07/08/2019).

10

THE COLONIALITY THAT REMAINS

We investigate one 'boomerang' movement whereby colonial violence returns to the metropole – we explore contemporary public order management – we see the affective management of the populace through the moments of its crowded protest – the relations between coloniality and exceptionality are explored.

In very quick succession in the early 1950s, Hannah Arendt and Aimee Césaire described the 'boomerang effect' of colonial violence.[1] The violence of subjection could not be isolated in the colonial peripheries; it infected the metropole. Césaire wrote, for instance, that

> colonization ... dehumanizes even the most civilized man; that colonial activity, colonial enterprise, colonial conquest, which is based on contempt for the native and justified by that contempt, inevitably tends to change him who undertakes it; that the colonizer, who in order to ease his conscience gets into the habit of seeing the other man as an animal accustoms himself to treating him like an animal, and tends objectively to transform himself into an animal. It is this result, this boomerang effect of colonization that I wanted to point out.[2]

The colonial endeavour affected those who bore that order, brutalisation changed the way the colonised and coloniser saw the world. This 'moral re-education' could not be kept in the colony but seeped back to the metropole. At the same time the specific techniques of subjection – the colonial knowledges and their epistemology – also returned to the metropoles. The boomerang effect took the specific techniques developed against populaces that never consented to the colonial state and returned them to the metropoles. The public order laboratories of Ireland, Malaya and Hong Kong (among others) were sites of knowledge production, and once these techniques became available in manuals and training programmes, they would prove impossible to contain. This chapter will focus on the remains of colonialism, arguing that we can see contemporary public order in terms of a continuing coloniality. This means that the police conceive of their role in terms of the latent exceptionality that we saw in the last chapter. The chapter explores the 'boomerang moment' in the UK, looking closely at the psycho-affective techniques of public order policing introduced in the 1980s. But it also moves beyond that period to understand contemporary public order management, exploring what the remnants of colonialism mean today.

On the 3rd of September 1981, in the small English city of Preston, the UK Association of Chief Police Officers (ACPO) held its autumn conference. Its focus was to be on public order. The assembled Chiefs and Deputy Chiefs of Police heard presentations from the Royal Ulster Constabulary about operations in Derry and Belfast; the London Metropolitan force provided initial analyses of the Brixton riots that had occurred four months before; and finally, Richard Quine, the director of operations for the Royal Hong Kong Police, presented key elements of their public order training manual. The Hong Kong manual was radically different from the approach to public order that had become settled on the island of Britain in the previous seventy five years. Unlike Hong Kong's 'shadow police', the British police claimed to employ a consent-based policing strategy. However, with growing racial and industrial unrest, there was a general perception that this approach was in crisis. ACPO were deeply impressed by Hong Kong's approach, precisely because it maintained consent-based policing on the surface, while building a deep paramilitary structure beneath.

Over the next two years the British police explored the manual in a succession of working groups, before rolling out a massive training programme to over 20,000 police officers. Police officers were drilled in the new techniques and their commanders were taught the strategies behind the deployment of particular tactics. What is remarkable about this process is the secrecy with which it was achieved. Because while the sight of riot-clad police officers, deploying dogs and horse charges is relatively familiar to us today, we must not forget that this was a radical shift in both the symbolic and material practices of the British police of the time. Gerry Northam unpacks this well: the mythology of the British force was that they could only operate because the people they policed consented. Former chief of police for Greater Manchester, John Anderton, explained this in *Brass Tacks,* a BBC documentary:

> You need the consent of the people to police effectively. If you don't carry the people with you, your policemen will lose confidence in the public and begin to turn in on themselves. They will become alienated. They will in fact, become a minority just like other minorities, and only by sticking together and using their force and power will they feel safe.[3]

Anderton's argument is that the latent exceptionality adopted from Hong Kong changes the policing of disorder. But he also appears to have seen something like Césaire's boomerang. The latent exceptionality also infects the practice of 'consent-based' policing itself. Sir Lawrence Byford, chief inspector of Constabulary, celebrated that 'even the rural policeman can be armed in riot gear one day and the next be required to return to his benevolent "Evening all" attitude'.[4] But Northam shows that it was impossible to keep these two forms of power separate, something a Metropolitan Police firearms officer specifically commented on in a BBC interview. He said: 'We can't pat kids on the head one day and then shoot plastic bullets the next'.[5] The roles bleed into one another. For the populace and the police, the hard edge of exceptionality can be felt beneath the soft finish of 'consent'.

On the 18th of June 1984, the 'new' British police tactics and training were deployed for the first time. The colliery town of Orgreave would become a byword for the latent exceptionality of this newly imported public order violence. The town was home to a coking works which converted coal into coke to be used in steel production in Scunthorpe. Striking miners targeted the coking plant with a mass picket, hoping to prevent deliveries of coal. At the time these practices of mass picketing and secondary actions were legal. But the police force that was deployed on that warm day in June to prevent the success of the picket, was unlike anything that had been seen in Britain since the military had last been used to crush strikes during the 'great unrest' of 1909–1912.[6] What struck both observers and the miners on the day was the sheer level of aggression, the police willingness to escalate the violence and their unrelenting desire not just to disperse the mass picket but to destroy it. In Orgreave and in the subsequent police deployments against the racialised urban populace, striking workers and new age travellers, we see a deeply colonial form of power being deployed against the populace. Many who write on this subject decry the sheer aggression of the police, focusing on particular instances of violence – a baton blow, a horse trampling, a crush caused by a police cordon. However, these analyses miss the crucial element of coloniality at play here. The aim is not simply to damage particular bodies that present themselves in public space, representing demands that the system cannot or will not accept. Colonial public order management is about using these moments to damage and defeat broader movements. The aim is to exhaust movements, smothering their momentum frustrating their desire for change and thereby pacify the populace.

To understand this we must engage with the specific techniques adopted from Hong Kong. As we have seen in the last chapter, the Hong Kong police moved beyond the old colonial approach of beating or shooting at a crowd until it dispersed. Instead the police intervention sought to affect the psychology of crowded protest and thereby get to the affective life of the populace. At the heart of what ACPO adopted were a series of affective techniques aimed at shifting the affects and atmospheres upon which crowd psychology emerged. The ACPO manual aims to change the capacity to act of the protestors and the police, by changing their bodily conditions. The policing strategy was to deploy high levels of aggression to strike fear through the crowds. To do this, the manual introduced a series of comparatively linear progressions which were designed to increase aggression levels through a series of step-changes: once there was disorder which required the deployment of the public order police; the police arrive in a 'show of force'; if the disorder did not dissipate, then the police would deploy increasing levels of physical force to disperse those present.[7] Aggression marks the police desire to shift the affective atmosphere from the very outset. The police arrive with a 'show of force':

> To use the 'show of force' to the greatest advantage, officers should make a formidable appearance. Officers should assemble at some point beyond the sight of the crowd. … When the unit is in formation, it should be marched smartly into view at a reasonably safe distance from the crowd, thus giving the impression of being well organized and highly disciplined. … The show of force must convince the crowd that the police are determined to control the situation and are in a position to do so.[8]

The police's deployment should manifest their *control* from the outset. If the fear projected from the sheer numbers of police did not lead to the crowd's flight, the police would begin to underline a terrific power. The problem of crowded scenes was that the sheer number of bodies (police and protestors) frustrated the police desire to deploy force. So the police were intensively trained to deploy force efficiently. They learnt how to drum their batons rhythmically against shields to project high levels of aggression and to underline their coherence and strength; they learnt techniques to allow baton officers to move through a shield line that was suddenly porous or ways of breaking a shield line for a horse charge; there were techniques for driving police cars and vans at a crowd in a zigzag pattern to simulate high speed, as well as forms of dog handling that would evince fear, shame and worry amongst protestors. The police sought to project their strength of numbers and to efficiently deploy their latent exceptionality. These techniques were not simply aimed at the specific crowd in their moment of protest, strike or unrest. The affective deployment of aggression-fear was supposed to seep out from the protest zone, signalling that the police could 'manage' the unrest that any movement might produce.[9] The police would deploy exceptional force in order to suppress dissent that was deemed too dangerous. The various public order battles in the UK in the eighties and early nineties were designed to signal this reassertion of control. They were designed to convey the feeling that popular 'threats' could be 'managed'.

The question of coloniality arises here not simply because of the colonial context from which these techniques emerge. The police deployment at the battle of Orgreave or the battle of the Beanfield would represent a coloniality of power irrespective of whether it came from expertise developed in Hong Kong or from France and the US.[10] This is because 'coloniality' describes a structure of power rather than simply a colonial lineage. This more radical sense of coloniality comes from the theorists of the 'decolonial turn'. Anibal Quijano, Walter Mignolo, Nelson Maldonado-Torres and others use the term 'coloniality' to identify the way in which (over hundreds of years) the structures of colonialism could assemble a broad epistemology. Mignolo suggests that coloniality should be understood as a 'colonial matrix of power', 'a structure of management (composed of domains, levels and flows) that controls and touches upon all aspects and trajectories of our lives'.[11] Coloniality does not name an association with this or that colonial regime but one with a structure of power. It is a network of ways of knowing, of taxonomies and of subject-constructions. It is not simply what occurred in the late nineteenth and early twentieth centuries. Instead it is a structure of power that continues in re-modulated forms.

Stephen Morton has suggested that contemporary states of emergency require that we 'turn back to the colonial archive of violence and repression, to records and narratives of the colonial formations of sovereignty, policing, and surveillance'.[12] He argues that colonialism is a condition of possibility for contemporary states of exception. In public order, this insight is particularly important. By thinking about exceptionality as an iteration of coloniality, different aspects of the paradigm begin to emerge. One particularly important instance of this is Alexander Weheliye's exploration of Giorgio Agamben's work. Weheliye takes Agamben's argument that the camp is the paradigm of Western modernity but points out that as a form, the concentration camp emerged from colonial experimentation. It emerges from the Indian resettlement camps in the US, the German camps in Southwest Africa, or the British variants during the Boer war.[13] The camp was *first* a racialised site of bare life. It was the space of 'racial slavery, colonialism and indigenous genocide'.[14] However, rather than simply renouncing Agamben for his silencing of colonial histories, Weheliye further radicalises his argument. Following Agamben, he agrees that the camp is the nomos of Western modernity but focuses on the racialised and racialising nature of the colonial camp. Thus, he says that racism, slavery, and colonial suppression are the 'nomoi of modern politics'.[15] Mbembe makes a similar point in *Necropolitics*, arguing that 'Far from leading to democracy's spread across the planet, [colonialism] … opened onto a new law (*nomos*) of the Earth, the main characteristic of which was to establish war and race as history's two privileged sacraments'.[16] This goes beyond Morton or Shenhav's arguments that imperialism 'provided the main arena in which the state of exception was practiced most vigorously, systematically and violently'.[17] Emergency and exception are not just techniques that were particularly developed in the colonial context. Instead, as Weheliye makes clear, there is a fundamental relation between colonialism and exceptionality. Mbembe explains: 'Little by little, a terror that is molecular in essence and allegedly defensive is seeking legitimation by blurring the relations between violence, murder and the law, faith, commandment, and obedience, the norm and the exception, and even freedom, tracking and security'.[18]

Coloniality is imprinted in the latent exceptionality of contemporary public order management.[19] Latent exceptionality remains at the heart of UK public order management. But like all apparatuses, the different elements are constantly in flux. After the policing failures of the poll tax riot (1990), and the public backlash against the extremity of the police's violence, the police began to shift away from the sheer aggression of the Hong Kong model. Instead they began to use the powers to enforce conditions on public processions and assemblies in sections 12–14 of the *Public Order Act* (1986) to force early negotiations with protest organisers. They began to frame their interventions as cooperative planning of events, using organisers to self-police their own actions and even engaging trained negotiators who could seek out an agreement with the various groups.[20] However, this shift should not be understood as an elimination of latent exceptionality. This 'negotiated management' approach to protest merely postpones the deployment of the techniques of coloniality. I suggest that instead of thinking about different 'models' of public order policing as some do, we can instead see this as the public order apparatus multiplying the ways in which it approaches its object-target.[21] This was not because the police suddenly decided that protestors deserved a modicum of respect but in response to the shifting affective life of the populace. Thus, after the defeat of organised labour and the collapse of an organised radical left in the UK, the nature of the 'threat' presented by the populace had changed. During the nineties, aside from the poll tax riots, public order policing was primarily concerned with illegal raves, road protests and 'reclaim the streets' parties. In the absence of large-scale racial or industrial unrest, the public order apparatus could reconfigure itself. Police could dial back the level of aggression to fit the scale of the perceived threat. At the end of the nineties, however, a new global network would begin to emerge and the apparatus would again reconfigure itself. Police would dust off their colonial tools, drawing from around the world once more to intensify their psycho-affective techniques.

Like Orgreave in the UK, the 'Battle of Seattle' in 1999 marks the emergence of a new model of public order management.[22] After Seattle, police forces around the world began to adopt new tactics to deal with the anti-globalisation movement, a model termed 'strategic incapacitation' by analysts.[23] Tactics included the arrest of key organisers both before and during protests (decapitation) and the zonal management of protests, where the police might confine protestors to 'free speech zones', exclude them from a particular zone or 'contain' a moving crowd.[24] In the UK, however, it is the adoption of the tactic of 'containment' that has been the most instructive about the nature of power being deployed. Known colloquially as 'kettling', containment is the technique where police form a cordon around protestors, holding them in one place for a period of time.[25] The critical literature is useful to understand the dynamics of the kettle. In particular, in 'Capturing Protests in an Urban Environment', Alan Neal, Sven Opitz and Chris Zebrowski underline that:

> tactics of protesting twist the rules of particular places: they turn sites of traffic into sceneries for symbolic mass spectacles and centers of commerce into venues for political assembly. In so doing, they often challenge, circumvent or divert modes of spatial control – and the police adjust their operational protocols accordingly. … [T]he strategy of kettling has been devised to counter emergent forms of dispersed and disruptive protest.[26]

Kettling is a spatial control which holds the crowd in place, to undermine its rearticulation of space. Neal et al. explain that this holding of the crowd in place leads to an affective acceleration and deceleration.

The kettle is a technique of differentiation. It is an attempt to divide the violent elements from the peaceful.[27] The kettle is a tool for purifying mixtures. The police kettle ramps up the pressure by forcing the crowd to remain static. 'Containment of the public can generate great anxiety and frustration', as the review of public order tactics by Her Majesty's Inspectorate of Policing remarked in 2009.[28] But this acceleration or intensification is not an accidental side effect. As Dibyesh Anand explains: containment 'is not a strategy that prevents disorder, contrary to the police claims, for it encourages more anger, fear and exasperation amongst those "contained". During the [UK student] protests [of 2011], it was clear that peaceful resistance became less so only after police started kettling'.[29] The kettle gets the crowd to their boiling point. This intensity of atmosphere pushes some to express that anger at the police lines, under the glare of surveillance cameras.[30] In this way the crowd can be refined. People infuriated in the kettle are taken to have always been 'violent elements', even if it is the kettle that has driven them to confrontation. The flipside of the intensification or acceleration of the crowd is its exhaustion or deceleration. The kettle must always hold the participants just too long. The containment operates then to 'allow' the crowd to take place, intensifying energies so that the crowd burns itself out. The police then release the participants in slow orderly streams, often requiring that they identify themselves so they can be added to the surveillance database or later prosecuted. But the aim is ultimately to ensure that the crowded subjectivities do not re-form. The police fear that the release of the kettled crowd will lead to sparks of anger drifting around the tinderbox of the city, fanning flames at multiple sites. In this sense, exhaustion is essential.

Neal et al. point out that the kettle 'hollows out liberal space' by excising 'small bits of terrain from the realm of free movement'.[31] They frame this through the logic of exceptionality.

> The kettle does not enact an exclusionary ban from the city comparable to the expulsion of the medieval leper or, to choose a contemporary example, the area bans issued on selected population groups [here the authors refer to Beckett and Herbert's work on policing 'unwanted populations']. It rather produces an inner outside that usually lasts for several hours at a location that is not predetermined or fixed – as if highly malleable city walls were

> erected inside the city on an ad hoc basis. ... It carves out a temporary zone of abandonment, putting those contained into what Giorgio Agamben has once termed a 'relation with the nonrelational'. This particular form of unrelatedness is epitomized by the scene of policemen standing at the fringe of the kettle and not responding to any requests from inside – be it for using a toilet, receiving nutrition or accessing medical service.[32]

This exceptionality is crucial because it allows the police to reach beyond this particular crowd, to the movement or cause beyond. The crowd is rendered in this violent space, not only without the protection of law but subject to the threat that the lines will open and horses or vehicles will roar in.

Unlike the tactics deployed by British forces in the eighties, the kettle is not borrowed directly from colonial public order policing. However, by understanding it through the history of colonial public order we can see it in a different light. The exceptionality deployed is a form of power used to keep the populace in order, to frustrate social change and exhaust movements. Understanding exceptionality through coloniality helps to displace and supplement the theologico-political genealogy that Agamben develops. The characters and dynamics of exceptionality change. Interestingly, it does not necessarily lead to a radically different place: the logics of rule and exception are still blurred; there are zones of indistinction, spaces of exceptionality; government and sovereignty are distinct but connected. Yet at the same time we are not trapped in the same folds that Agamben wraps us in, searching for a form-of-life developed by Franciscans, watching for bare life and the desubjectified non-subject that might emerge. By framing public order in terms of coloniality a different horizon emerges: that of *decolonisation*. Public order names the way that the contemporary sovereign order understands the affective life of its people. Decolonising public order means decolonising the affective relation between the state and its populace. It means radically reshaping social, political, economic and legal ordering.

Notes

1 Aimé Césaire, *Discourse on Colonialism* (New York University Press, 2000), Hannah Arendt, *The Origins of Totalitarianism* (New York: Meridian Books, 1958).
2 Césaire, *Discourse on Colonialism*, 41.
3 Quoted in Northam, *Shooting in the Dark*.
4 Ibid., 63.
5 Quoted in Ibid., 64; BBC, *The Queen's Peace* (1986).
6 See Martin Thomas, *Violence and Colonial Order: Police, Workers and Protests in the European Colonial Empires, 1918-40* (Cambridge University Press: 2012), 66–67, citing Barbara Weinberger, *Keeping the Peace? Policing Strikes in Britain 1906-1926* (Oxford: Berg Publishers, 1990).
7 In the US this increased to the level of deploying live fire, but in the UK both the police and the secretary of state, Willie Whitelaw, agreed that this would be unacceptable. The army would have to be deployed before that stage was reached.
8 Northam, *Shooting in the Dark*, 185. The similarity to the US idea of a show of force is worth noting. In *Riot Control: Materiel and Techniques* (Stackpole Books, 1969) Rex

Applegate writes: 'The Show-of-Force can be based on either the surprise appearance of a large unit of riot-equipped police officers in a formation, or by using the saturation technique, massing large numbers of personnel at a given point in full view of the mob. To crowds, the psychological impact of witnessing the arrival of large numbers of police emerging from patrol cars, special riot vans, police helicopters, etc. can be very great' (Applegate, *Riot Control*, 35–36).

9 For a discussion of the affective dynamics of the deployment of riot police, see Carolina Olarte's discussion of 'robots announcing the state', in 'From Territorial Peace to Territorial Pacification: Anti-Riot Police Powers and Socio-Environmental Dissent in the Implementation of Colombia's Peace Agreement', 67 *Revista de Estudios Sociales* (2018), 26.

10 The UK had explicitly reached out to its 'international partners' when it was exploring the possible reforms to public order models in the early 1980s. In particular, the UK was curious about the threat monitoring systems in use. The responses to these requests, contained in the British Archives at Kew, are interesting for their paucity. The Netherlands proved most forthcoming, donating a public order manual in Dutch. The US gave a glossy booklet on 'community relations' which included an interesting discussion of a rumour control centre. Germany offered a meeting with Herr Schöttler of *Referat P13*, the police department that dealt with public order which included detailed discussion of the various measures. France didn't answer the specific questions asked by the British Embassy and instead gave a terse summary of their public order threat detection structures (The National Archives of the UK, HO 325/517).

11 Walter Mignolo, 'Coloniality is far from over and so must be decoloniality', 43 *Afterall* (2017), 40.

12 Stephen Morton, *States of Emergency, Colonialism, Literature and Law* (Liverpool University Press 2013), 4.

13 Alexander Weheliye, *Habeas Viscus: Racialising Assemblages, Biopolitics and Black Feminist Theories of the Human* (Duke University Press, 2014), 31–36.

14 Ibid., 36.

15 Ibid.

16 Mbembe, *Necropolitics*, 6.

17 Yehouda Shenhav, 'Imperialism, Exceptionalism and the Contemporary World', in Marcelo Svirsky, and Simone Bignall (eds), *Agamben and Colonialism* (Edinburgh University Press, 2012), 19.

18 Mbembe, *Necropolitics*, 7.

19 For an extraordinary ethnography of this coloniality (although it is not a word that he uses), see Fassin *Enforcing Order.*

20 This model too had a deployment of psycho-affective force, but it emphasised individual pre-engagement rather than in-the-moment collective might. We might think of the failure of the anti-Iraq war demonstrations to effectuate any change in government policy as a huge success for 'negotiated management' tactics.

21 Patrick Gillham, 'Securitizing America: Strategic Incapacitation and the Policing of Protest since the 11 September 2001 Terrorist Attacks' *Sociology* (2011), 12.

22 Lesley Wood, *Crisis and Control: The Militarization of Protest Policing* (London: Pluto Press, 2014).

23 Patrick Gillham, Bob Edwards and John Noakes, 'Strategic Incapacitation and the Policing of the Occupy Wall Street Protests in New York City, 2011', 23.1 *Policing and Society* (2013), 82.

24 Paul Passavant, 'Policing Protest in the Post-Fordist City' 2.1 *Amsterdam Law Forum* (2009), 93.

25 The UK 2010 manual, 'Keeping the Peace' explained that 'containment' was a 'contingency tactic to be used when alternative tactics to prevent serious disorder, serious injury or loss of life have failed or are expected to fail' (ACPO 'Keeping the Peace', 110). This very narrow construction of the tactic should be understood in light of the

fact that the 2010 manual was the first UK manual to be written in the knowledge that it would be made public. Previous manuals were written in secret, and only became publicly available after a leak or by operation of the Freedom of Information Act.

26 Andrew Neal, Sven Opitz and Chris Zebrowski, 'Capturing Protest in Urban Environments: The 'Police Kettle' as a Territorial Strategy', 37.6 *Environment and Planning D: Society and Space* (2019), 1047.

27 UK College of Policing, *Public Order: Tactical Options*, https://www.app.college.police.uk/app-content/public-order/planning-and-deployment/tactical-options/#containment (viewed on 03/04/2020); Organisation for Security and Cooperation in Europe, *Human Rights Handbook on Policing Assemblies*, (Office for Democratic Institutions and Human Rights, Warsaw) https://www.osce.org/odihr/226981?download=true (viewed on 03/04/2020).

28 Her Majesty's Inspectorate of Policing, *Adapting to Protest* (London: HMIC, 2009) (https://www.justiceinspectorates.gov.uk/hmicfrs/media/adapting-to-protest-20090705.pdf (Viewed on 04/04/2020).

29 Dibesh Anand, 'The Violent Vocabulary of Policing', *Critical Legal Thinking* (13/12/2010) http://criticallegalthinking.com/2010/12/13/the-violent-vocabulary-of-policing/ (Viewed on 04/04/2020), See also Neal, Opitz, and Zebrowski, 'Capturing protest in urban environments', 1055.

30 Amedeo Policante, 'Of Cameras and Balaclavas: Violence, Myth and the Convulsive Kettle', 8.4 *Globalizations* (2011), 457.

31 Neal, Opitz, and Zebrowski, 'Capturing protest in urban environments', 1054.

32 Ibid., 1053–1054.

11

EXCURSUS 2

An affective theory of public order

In a widely cited police case from 1930, Justice McCardie makes a useful observation about the nature of public order. He explains that 'order' is the condition established by the state, upon which (what he calls) the 'honest citizens' 'may go about their affairs in peace'.[1] Public order is understood as the condition on which everyday life can subsist. There is a certain calm or orderliness, which is difficult to identify precisely because when undisturbed it is nothing but the background of everyday activity. Public order is precisely what fades into the background, becoming hidden from sense perception.[2] Arthur G. Keech (the inspector in charge of training the Kent County Constabulary) gives us a different way into the same question. He explains the importance of building a feeling of security for the populace at the very end of a short pocket book aimed at a police audience. This is done, he argues, in a police officer's minute interactions on the beat, on the street corner or outside the school gates. 'This is the man who has built up the feeling which, on the part of the public, means *security*'.[3] Keech meant to leave the police who would be reading this pocketbook with that warm and fuzzy feeling. They could rely on the general public for support and cooperation, just as the public could rely upon them for security. The police officer should radiate this feeling, leaving his affective trace as he moved through the populace. As the guardian of the sovereign's order, the police officer had to understand the affective fug through which he moved and act upon it. While Justice McCardie's observation zooms us out, providing a god's eye view of public order, Keech's police officers were in the midst of this affective life.

In his Hamlyn Lectures of 1953, Sir Carelton Allen briefly underscores the affective structure of this sense of public order. He writes:

> The 'peace of our Sovereign Lady the Queen' [public order] has been described by. … Maitland, as an 'all-embracing atmosphere' in our law,

> and, we may add, in our whole social life. We could not breathe in any other atmosphere, and we take it for granted as if it were part of the order of nature.[4]

Allen gives thanks to the sovereign for creating a sort of biosphere, an affective atmosphere of peace that facilitates human life. '[E]ach of us is a trustee of that "peace-and-quiet" which is all men's desire', he says.[5] This sense of atmosphere is something which we have seen throughout this part and which we will return to in the next from the perspective of the crowd. But Allen also underlines an anaesthetic function which was hinted at by Keech and McCardie. He writes: 'we take it for granted as if it were part of the order of nature'. His point is that this atmosphere is not 'natural' order; it is not just found out there in the world. It has to be *produced*. But when it is produced effectively, we attune to it. The populace is not supposed to feel it because it works affectively, shifting their bodily reactions.

I say that the populace is not supposed to feel it, but actually this is not exactly correct. If we return to Justice McCardie's formulation, we can see an important delineation. If public order is sound and secure, the 'honest citizen' can go about his own business, moving through the smoothed space of the public sphere. However, within this is the implication of certain 'others' – the not-so-honest citizens, the suspect populations for whom public space is striated.[6] For them, public order cannot fade into the background. When Eric Garner died in Brooklyn insisting that he could not breathe beneath the chokehold of the police officer, his final words seemed to crystallise a sense of a public order that renders certain bodies 'suspect'.[7] He could not breathe beneath the intense police discipline; he could not breathe as a black man; he could not breathe and it killed him. In the claustrophobia of public order, the atmosphere itself was hostile. Racialised discipline, police power, these are modes of asphyxia. When Allen writes that public order is an atmosphere where 'we' can breathe, and that 'we' take for granted, he invisibilises those suspect populations. They are not part of his 'we'.

Allen misses what the old critical legal theorists used to call 'tilt'. Thinking about public order as a tilted affective field draws us away from the familiar knots of disagreement, where these questions can be reduced to bad police officers or a mud-slinging contest about whether some offence might have occurred before the police arrived on the scene. Public order is a tilted affective field; it is tilted in a systematic way.[8] The atmospheres of public order are not neutral and inert. They are one of the ways in which the sovereign's order can enhance the capacity of the 'honest citizen' to undertake an almost infinite variety of acts in public, but it also must diminish the capacity to act of suspect populations.[9] This is the crack from which the latent exceptionality of public order seeps out into the everyday. Crucially, these suspect populations cannot afford to take the benignness of public order for granted. There are no anaesthetics for these bodies; they must be affectively hypersensitive.

When disorder breaks out, the suspicion begins to spread. The state apparatus focuses in on the protest organisers and organisations. The state of enmity that existed for the suspect populations is extended to those who now enact their dissent. The difference, however, is that the generalisation of disorder begins to tear the fabric of normality wherein the populace is anaethetised to the affective order of sovereignty. The temper of the populace is excited. Irritated and angry, people come to the streets. Their force of numbers builds new atmospheres, which then seep out into the streets. In other words, the calm order of sovereignty is increasingly in question. Both protests and their policing are focused upon the affects of the disorderly scene. The state of unrest names the point in time where sovereign affects no longer dominate the affective life of the populace and desires and beliefs around new forms of sovereignty begin to emerge.

Notes

1 McCardie J. in *Fisher v. Oldham Corporation* [1930] 2 KB 364.
2 Illan rua Wall, 'Law's Ordinary Affects', *Law Culture and the Humanities* (forthcoming).
3 Arthur Keech, *Public Order* (Jordan and Sons Ltd: London, 1952), 46. The police create a feeling of security, but as we have seen in Benjamin, it is exactly the question of a 'security situation' that allows police to deploy their exceptional force. For an intriguing analysis of security atmospherics, see Peter Adey, 'Security Atmospheres or the Crystallisation of Worlds', 32, *Environment and Planning D: Society and Space* (2014), 834.
4 Sir Carelton Kemp Allen, *The Queens Peace* (Stevens and Sons Ltd, 1953), 3. I am extremely grateful to Nina Power for this reference!
5 Allen *The Queen's Peace*, 183.
6 Darren Ellis, Ian Tucker and David Harper underline the role of surveillance in this type of striation. See Darren Ellis, Ian Tucker and David Harper, 'The Affective Atmosphere of Surveillance', 23.6 *Theory and Psychology* (2013), 716.
7 For a full account of Garner's death see Matt Tabbi, *I Can't Breathe: A Killing on Bay Street* (New York: Spiegel & Grau, 2017). For a specifically atmospheric account of breath, see Marijn Nieuwenhuis 'Breathing Materially: Aerial Violence at a Time of Atmospheric Politics', 9.3 *Critical Studies on Terrorism* (2016), 513. Kashif Jerome Powell, 'Making #BlackLivesMatter: Michael Brown, Eric Garner, and the Spectres of Black Life – Towards a Hauntology of *Blackness*', 16.3 *Cultural Studies – Critical Methodologies* (2016), 253.
8 Tabbi, *I Can't Breathe*, 136, 300. Paul Passavant, 'I Can't Breathe: Heeding the Call of Justice', 11.3 *Law, Culture and the Humanities* (2015), 330.
9 Alison Young writes: 'What is the secret that is obscured in our cities? It is the secret of everyday violence, raining down upon individuals as they attempt to move through everyday life' (Alison Young, Arrested Mobilities: Affective Encounters and Crime Scenes in the City', *Law Culture and the Humanities* (forthcoming), 17).

PART III
The crowd and the people

The people appears to arrive on the scene just in time. The crowds have been gathering, protesting the manifest injustice of the political order. They have been calling themselves the people, calling for others to join their collective political body. But the people only arrives at that liminal moment when the political order finally collapses. It arrives in a flash – confirmed by the turning of the sovereign orders – a revolution. The people confirms that it had been there all along, that even the small crowds that gathered weeks ago were the foreshadow, the aura of its glory. If the crowd's revolt had been suppressed then this moment of confirmation would never occur. The crowd's claim to have been the people would be falsified; it could be construed by the legal order as a mere mob with pretensions to glory. In the successful revolution, however, the people is the crowning glory of the crowd. There is a mysterious dynamic to revolutions, an alchemy where the leaden substance of the crowd turns to the gilded people. However, every political crowd that calls itself the people holds the possibility of this confirmation.

This is the paradox of constituent power.[1] In the moment of revolt the crowds are identified as seditious by the constitutional structure. They seem to reach out into the future, to a time when their acts will have been foundational. But in the moment, their legitimacy is still to come. In the critical theory of constituent power we find this relation between the crowd and the people carefully theorised: from the left populism of Ernesto Laclau who suggests that the people is an empty signifier, claimed from below in the moment of revolt,[2] to Derrida's deconstruction of the US Declaration of Independence, where the signatories sign for a people who only comes to existence by their signature,[3] to the quasi-autonomism of Michael Hardt and Antonio Negri, who insist that 'the people' is the moment of appropriation, the apparatus by which the constituted power adopts the power (*potentia*) and energy of the multitude.[4] In the coming chapters

I too want to focus on this crucial relation between the crowd and the people, but with a slight difference. I want to argue that we should focus on the crowds that are used to stage the people (or multitude). Thinking through the crowds is important because it draws our attention to the way in which the sense of the people is at least partially prefigured by the crowds that stage it.

The affective patterning that occurs within the crowd plays an important, if not determinative, role in the constituent moment. 'Patterning' is perhaps a strange term. I draw it from Margaret Wetherell's *Affect and Emotion.*[5]

> In affective practice, bits of the body (e.g. facial muscles, thalamic-amygdala pathways in the brain, heart rate, regions of prefrontal cortex, sweat glands, etc.) get patterned together with feelings and thoughts, interaction patterns and relationships, narratives and interpretative repertoires, social relations, personal histories, and ways of life. These components and modalities, each with their own logic and trajectories are assembled together in interacting and recursive, or back and forth, practical methods. Pattern layers on pattern, forming and reforming. Somatic, neural, phenomenological, discursive, relational, cultural, economic, developmental and historical patterns interrupt, cancel, contradict, modulate, build and interweave with each other.[6]

In Wetherell's hands, patterning becomes a way of tracing the forces that gather together in the flow of time. Thinking about patterning helps us see the way affect can 'thread across a scene, a site or an institution and is spatialised, too, in complex ways. Intriguingly, an affective practice can be "held" in a particular place [by patterning]. Further solidification comes into view when we consider the affective practices of entire social categories and historical periods'.[7] It is as important to see the affective ruts, grooves and forces that hold bodies in pattern, as it is to feel the dynamic patterns of change.

The Foucauldian sense of 'apparatus' has been a helpful way of thinking about the structuring of public order thus far. But I introduce 'patterning' in order to focus on a slightly different sort of connection.[8] Wetherell connects 'patterning' with Giles Deleuze and Felix Guatari's concept *agencement* or assemblage. She quotes Brown and Stenner:

> assemblage has the various meanings of 'arrangement', 'laying out' or 'putting together'. It also connotes the process activity of arranging things together. An assemblage of desire is then, like Foucault's apparatus, a heterogeneous arrangement of elements that are contingently laid out together.[9]

Alongside the sense of 'connection' that the English term 'assemblage' suggests, *agencement* also carries the sense of a temporary arrangement. John Philips explains that for Deleuze *agencement* connected to the state of becoming when two bodies (in the broadest sense) entangle. 'The unity, for instance, of a poison and the body poisoned can be regarded as a state of becoming and an event which is reducible to neither the body nor the poison. The body and the poison, rather, participate in the event (which is what they have in common)'.[10] In the broadest sense, then, this part begins to describe an 'assemblage of the people' as it emerges momentarily from below. I mean this in the sense that 'assemblages are productive, entering into polyvalent becomings to produce and give expression to previously nonexistent realities, thoughts, bodies, affects, spaces, actions, ideas and so on'.[11] Crowded protest generates new valences and resonances of the people but not as the static, fixed discursive function deployed by constitutions. The 'assemblage allows us to attune to movement, intensities, emotions, energies, affectivities, and textures as they inhabit events, spatialities and corporealities'.[12] This part will attune to what Wetherell calls the *patterning* element of assemblage analysis. It will not get into the nuances of contemporary assemblage theory, which would ultimately distract from the flow of the book.[13]

Notes

1 Martin Loughlin and Neil Walker, *The Paradox of Constitutionalism: Constituent Power and Constitutional Form* (Oxford: Oxford University Press, 2008).
2 Ernesto Laclau, *On Populist Reason* (London: Verso, 2007).
3 Jacques Derrida, 'Declarations of Independence', 7.1 *New Political Science* (1986), 7.
4 Antonio Negri, *Insurgencies: Constituent Power and the Modern State* (University of Minnesota Press, 1999). See also for instance the work of Andreas Kalyvas, 'Democracy and the Poor: Prolegomena to a Radical Theory of Democracy', 26 *Constellations* (2019), 538; Joel Colón-Ríos, *Constituent Power and the Law* (Oxford: Oxford University Press, 2020); or Emilios Christodoulidis, 'Against Substitution: The Constitutional Thinking of Dissensus', in Martin Loughlin and Neil Walker, *The Paradox of Constitutionalism: Constituent Power and Constitutional Form* (Oxford: Oxford University Press, 2008) for radically different approaches.
5 Wetherell, *Affect and Emotion*. See also Couze Venn, 'Individuation, Relationality, Affect: Rethinking the Human in Relation to the Living', 16.1 *Body & Society* (2010), 129. For a different sense of patterning as 'rhythmic materiality': Julian Henriques, 'The Vibrations of Affect and Their Propagation on a Night Out on Kingston's Dancehall Scene', 16.1 *Body & Society* (2010), 57.
6 Ibid., 13–14.
7 Ibid., 14.
8 For the contrast between assemblage and apparatus, see Stephen Legg, 'Assemblage/Apparatus: Using Deleuze and Foucault', in 43.2 *Area* (2011), 128.
9 Ibid., 15.
10 John Phillips, '*Agencement*/Assemblage', 23.2-3 *Theory, Culture Society* (2006), 109. See also Thomas Nail, 'What Is an Assemblage?' 46.1 *SubStance* (2017), 21. George Marcus and Erkan Saka, 'Assemblage', 23.2-3 *Theory, Culture Society* (2006), 101; Couze Venn, 'A Note on Assemblage', 23.2-3 *Theory, Culture and Society* (2006), 107.
11 Weheliye, *Habeas Viscus*, 47.
12 Jasbir Puar, *Terrorist Assemblages: Homonationalism in Queer Times* (Durham: Duke University Press, 2007), 215.
13 From Puar and Weheliye to Manuel De Landa *Assemblage Theory* (Edinburgh University Press, 2016).

12

AFFECTIVE PATTERNING

In which we try an experiment to evade sovereign thinking – we see the affective patterning of crowds – and explore the dangers of a decontextualised thinking of affect.

The promise of the book was always to identify the common sphere of affect between protest and the state. Thus far we have seen this field primarily from the perspective of the state. The book has developed both a sense of sovereignty as an affective–aesthetic form and a public order as the terrain of the government of affective sovereignty. The crowd has largely remained a projection of those who sought its repression. It is now time to turn our attention to it more systematically. To crystallise the sense of this shift I want to attempt a kind of visual experiment. The aim is to demonstrate in aesthetic terms the manner in which sovereignty dominates the political scene.

I want to treat John Baldessari's 1984 photomontage *Two Crowds* (*With Shape of Reason Missing*)[1] as a methodological invitation. Baldessari's photomontage consists of two photographs of crowds, with blank shapes (in white) obscuring 'the reason' that has gathered the crowd. The first image consists of two parallel crowds, with the pure white stripe diagonally obscuring the space between them. It has also been cropped so that we cannot see the events that the hushed crowds observe. The photograph conveys quiet obedience, perhaps of a church or occasion of state. The second crowd gathers around an oval blank, with bodies turned towards the absence at the centre of the image. Clearly, the crowd is in a street, and although the bodies are organised in concentric circles around the 'shape of reason', the crowd is less clearly ordered or distributed than in the first image. In both images – as their title suggests – the reason for the crowd is obscured. This 'masking of the focal point does not so much subtract meaning as repress its specificity while directing attention to formal configurations of space, and hence

FIGURE 12.1 John Baldessari, *Two Crowds with Shape of Reason Missing,* 1984. Courtesy of the Estate of John Baldessari. Two black-and-white photographs mounted on board; 48 × 30 in. overall dimensions.

power'.[2] The repression of the focal point directs us to the internal rhythms and patterns, the internal shape and distribution of the crowd become obvious. The circular (or oval) crowd seems almost to centrifugally revolve around the centre point; in the linear crowd there is a sense of a focal point that abstracts the crowd from itself. They seem to be turned towards a leader or a priest; the crowd becomes at once a distraction and intensification of the linear relation of the congregation to the priest/leader. Baldessari's images preserve 'the abstract "shapes" of power, characterised by clear geometry, reflexive symmetry and hierarchical relation to the leader or ritual'.[3] Baldessari draws our attention to the mimetic element of the crowd, to the manner in which it produces or patterns itself.

I introduce Baldessari's image as a methodological invitation. It invites us to repress the shape of its 'reason' and instead to begin to see the crowd. However, unlike Baldessari's images, the aim here is not to permanently destroy the 'shape of reason'. The effect of the repression of the shape of reason is to unmoor the crowd from its historical specificity. Without the 'shape of reason' the crowd becomes a sort of pure immediacy. But in this pure immediacy, the crowd closes in on itself, pointing only to its own mimetic dynamics. This sense of immediacy is important because it tells us about immanent affective relations, but its pure immediacy is also dangerous, as we will see. The aim here (and in the coming chapters) is to investigate the relation between immediacy and mediation. Therefore, instead of a permanent concealment, I want to momentarily repress the shape of reason. I want to suggest a flicker between obscuring and proclaiming. This will maintain a tension between the shape of reason (its history, specificity, context, situation) and the patterns that gather around it.

The first work is the painting *Mobilmachung 1914* (*Mobilisation 1914*) by the minor landscape artist Fritz Genutat. Genutat's painting portrays Kaisar Wilhelm's address to the people declaring German mobilisation in Berlin at the beginning of the First World War. The regality of the sovereign is conveyed by his clothing, his individuality, the sweeping gesture of unity and, most of all, the height from which he speaks. Genutat's perspective places the viewer on the balcony with the royal party, looking down and out across the assembled masses. Following Baldessari then, the Kaisar is precisely the focal point that should be repressed. Without him, the crowd below is seething and undifferentiated; it seems to overflow from the street into the nearby park. It is a foaming ocean of people, surging around trams, a fountain and the street architecture. It forms simply in relation to the newly obscured balcony above. Without the Kaiser's gesture which directs them down the distant boulevard, the masses are revealed in their passivity. *This is the crowd as a landscape*, rendered merely scenic by the aerial perspective. The image makes sense only in a linear relation between the crowd and the (now obscured) sovereign. Flickering between the sovereign presence and absence, we begin to see both the passivity of the crowd-as-landscape and the transcendence of the sovereign 'shape of reason'.

In contrast, Isaak Israelovitch Brodsky's more accomplished *Lenin at Putilov Factory in May 1917* (1929) gives us a very different perspective. Lenin stands above the crowd, but only at head height on a roughly hewn scaffold. Like Wilhelm, he gestures, but his gesture is not towards something visible. Instead, Lenin points away from the visible horizon of smoky factories, away from the world of work. Lenin addresses the crowds that have gathered around him, but Brodsky's perspective places the viewer in among the crowd, looking out just over the heads of the gathered workers. With Lenin repressed, the crowd seems to take up all of the possible space, defined at its edges only by the industrial buildings. These buildings define not only the space of the crowds but also their sense. These are industrial workers, their clothes and flat caps confirm their plebeian status. But unlike Genutat's crowd, these are real people, distinguished by

FIGURE 12.2 Isaak Brodsky, *Lenin at Putilov Factory in May 1917* (1929), Chronicle/Alamy.

character and activity. They stand in rapt attention to the speaker, but they are thoughtful and powerful. One man runs his hand through his hair in a gesture of perplexity, another draws his shoulders together, with his hands clasped behind his back. Genutat's crowd on the other hand is merely a projection and extension of the sovereign's power. They are there because the sovereign has called them; as we learn from the title, he has mobilised them. He gestures for them to march. They must move through the city's boulevards (just visible in the painting below the sunburst) that have been fashioned by the sovereign for precisely such a military adventure.

A key distinguishing feature of the paintings is the different heights from which they take-in the crowd: Brodsky hovers just above the ground, while Genutat's balcony defies the actual architecture of the Kaiser's palace to fly far above street level. From the degree of aeriality, the politics of the images unfolds: Brodsky's proletarian solidarity and Genutat's aristocratic distance. It is clear from both pieces that we need some height above the crowd from which to understand its patterns and shapes, but with great height we begin to lose the immanent sense of the crowd. We can introduce a third image to our visual experiment, at this point. On first glimpse, Umberto Boccioni's *Riot in the Galleria* (1910) seems to peer down from the ceiling of an early-twentieth-century *galleria* in Milan at a disordered crowd in movement below. In the *galleria* the crowd seem to pulse towards two women fighting outside a glass fronted café. While painted a year after Marinetti's publication of the first Futurist Manifesto,[4] it is quite unlike the angular, thrusting and abstract futurism with which we are now familiar. *Riot in the Galleria* is almost impressionist in its swirls and fug. Its colours are divisionist, and it is pointillistic in technique. But despite this, key futurist themes are

FIGURE 12.3 Umberto Boccioni, *Riot in the Galleria* (1909), Alamy.

present and these allow us to begin to understand the perspective that Boccioni invites us to take on the crowd.

The key lies in the electric light radiating from the café window and glowing like orbs at the ceiling of the *galleria*. The lights electrify the scene, and Boccioni draws a parallel between their harsh radiating light and the waves of the crowd. As he would later write: 'Oh divine electric light! … Electrify the crowds! Set them on fire! Dominate!'[5] The crowd is a pulsing and radiating movement, 'waves of individuals flow toward the women, as if compelled by a magnetic force that extends to the far reaches of the arcade'.[6] The figures seem to have thrown their arms out in front of them as they charge forward. As Christine Poggi comments, 'these individuals exemplify the propagation of sentiment, as if by contagion or electrical current'.[7] Indeed, the electrical current/waves of sentiment pervade the entire scene, conveyed by the pointillist flecks of colour. While there is a focal point in *Riot in the Galleria*, unlike both Genutat and Brodsky's works, obscuring it does not radically alter the image. The women at the centre of the image are not its 'shape of reason'; quite the contrary, the affects that flow through them also flow through the entire image. Poggi explains: 'Hysteria spreads like a form of contagion outwards to entrap all of those within its field, while it also precipitates a stampede inward toward the centre'.[8] We might think of it as a painting of atmosphere. Bocconi tries to capture the force that compels movement, rather than the figures themselves. As Poggi writes, the figures seem almost to vibrate with energy which reaches its climax before the incandescent dazzle of the café window. Many of the figures seem to 'dissipate into a charged, atmospheric flux'.[9] There is a fizzle, an effervescence and a resonance within the figures, that means that the atmosphere is more significant than the way in which it is manifested in any one figure.

This shift towards the atmosphere is crucial. Bocconi forces us to look again at Genutat and Brodsky, insisting that we think beyond the internal rhythms of the crowd, and instead to the atmosphere that is patterned. Genutat's atmosphere is marked by a transcendence of the sovereign and the imminent war as the cleansing force. The clouds of war gather in the top left of the painting, but even in this menace there is a sunburst. The sun breaks through over the boulevard to which the Kaisar directs the crowd in their mobilisation. The atmosphere primarily radiates from the balcony. The Kaiser's gesture sends the crowd to war. But it also purifies the people of their individuality; it makes them a crowd governed by his common purpose. He directs them as a nation into the fire and glory. In Brodsky's work, there is some fervour (bodies on the right, in particular, seem to lean towards the makeshift stage, capturing movement and commitment), but the primary affects are pensive and thoughtful. The atmosphere is made up of a series of tensions: between the crowd and the factories that surround it; between different workers, their focus and demeanour; and between the movement of Lenin and the hushed crowd. The crowd has been drawn out of their spaces of work, drawn by the magnetic presence of the shape of Lenin.

This experiment directs our attention both to the patterns and rhythms of the crowd. But with Bocconi's intervention, it also forces us beyond. We must begin to examine the atmosphere of crowded moment rather than simply its 'object of reason'. We must understand the affective conditions of the crowd, and the manner in which the crowd conditions the atmosphere. In the previous parts we have been too bound into sovereignty and government. We need to begin to explore what happens when the affects and atmospheres of the state of unrest begin to bubble up from beneath.

Notes

1 Reproduced in John Tagg, 'A Discourse (with Shape of Reason Missing)', 15.3 *Art History* (1992), 351.

2 Christine Poggi 'Mass, Pack and Mob: Art in the Age of the Crowd', in Jeffrey Schnapp and Matthew Tiews, *Crowds* (Stanford University Press, 2006), 193.

3 Ibid. 195. Tagg reveals that beneath the repression are two key performative utterances. The first image is a church, which he imagines to be a wedding ceremony ('I do')

and the second image is famously of the declaration of war in 1914 in Berlin ('I declare') (Tagg, 'A Discourse' 356). In this sense, the repression is even more compelling. Baldessoni seems to ask as to compare the function of the crowd in these performatives. What is a sovereign declaration of war without the crowd.

4 The painting can be read as a direct response to Marinetti's 'Founding and Manifesto of Futurism', which announces: 'We will sing of great crowds excited by work, by pleasure, and by riot; we will sing of the multicolored, polyphonic tides of revolution in the modern capitals; we will sing of the vibrant nightly fervor of the arsenals and shipyards blazing with violent electric moons … and the sleek flight of planes whose propellers chatter in the wind like banners and seem to cheer like an enthusiastic crowd'. Filippo Marinetti, 'The Founding and Manifesto of Futurism', in Umbro Apollonio (ed.) *Futurist Manifestos* (London, 1973), 22.

5 Boccioni, 'Genius in Culture' quoted in Christine Poggi, '*Folla/Follia:* Futurism and the Crowd', 28.3 *Critical Inquiry* (2002), 727.

6 Poggi, 'Mass, Pack and Mob', 159.

7 Ibid.

8 Poggi, '*Folla/Follia*', 721.

9 Ibid., 722–723.

13

A SOMNAMBULIST OR TURBULENT PEOPLE

In which we introduce imitation, contagion, resonance and other key affective dynamics – we explore the imitative dynamics of the crowd – the manner in which they might calm or excite the populace – we meet Gabriel Tarde.

The paintings discussed in the last chapter are suffused with the crowd theory of their time. They capture that sense of the atmosphere of the crowd precisely because the theoretical currents that were circulating brought the masses and the manifestation of their crowded politics to the foreground. Thus, before exploring two contemporary moments where the crowd stages the people, we will step back into French *fin-de-siècle* crowd theory. In particular, the work of Gabriel Tarde helps us think through this idea of the way a crowd might 'pattern' the people. At the heart of crowd theory was the idea that crowd behaviour was governed by the affective forces of that particular moment. The crowd releases these forces, which then govern the crowd's behaviour. There is an instantaneity about crowds. Gabriel Tarde wrote:

> A *mob* [the French term is *foule* and so is better translated as 'crowd'] is a strange phenomenon. It is a gathering of heterogeneous elements, unknown to one another; but as soon as a spark of passion, having flashed out from one of these elements, electrifies this confused mass, there takes place a sudden organization, a spontaneous generation. This incoherence becomes cohesion, this noise becomes a voice, and these thousands of men crowded together soon form but a single animal, a wild beast without a name, which marches to its goal with irresistible finality.[1]

In *The Crowd*, Gustave Le Bon, the great populariser of crowd theory and a notorious racist, 'presents the crowd as a distinct form of collectivity. The crowd is not a community. It doesn't rely on traditions. It doesn't have a history'.[2] There are no rituals of public performance, no social repertoire of protest.[3] There is nothing social that holds a crowd together. It 'is a temporary collective being. It holds itself together affectively via imitation, contagion, suggestion and a sense of its own invincibility'.[4] In other words, the crowd is an immediate thing. It creates immediate forces that are not mediated by language or reason. The forces are instantaneously affective, immediately altering the bodies present.

It is tempting to contrast Le Bon's image, with the version that appears in E. P. Thompson's seminal essay 'The Moral Economy of the English Crowd in the Eighteenth Century'.[5] Thompson focuses on the tradition of food riots in England in the eighteenth century. Carefully reading contemporary accounts, he gives voice to historically specific crowds that attempt to right the wrongs done against the social fabric (of tradition/moral economy). His crowds usually act with restraint and precision, directing their ire against specific opponents. Le Bon's writings, on the other hand, present an abstract, ahistorical agent. The crowd is a pure irrationality governed only by the immanent forces of suggestion and contagion. These crowds release a feverish savagery. In this sense, Le Bon's crowd operates precisely to exclude the type of sociality that Thompson identifies. While there are types of crowds in Le Bon, what connects them is never the social fabric (place, trade, employer, class) but some aspect of their temporality, rhythm, race or desire. Indeed, Le Bon's sense of 'de-individuation' precisely precludes the type of socio-historical mediation that Thompson describes. This leaves 'the crowd' as a free-floating, abstracted, trans-historical agent, with nothing but heredity to colour its temper. Le Bon's is the ultimate view from outside. The crowd is oceanic: it surges and churns; it is tempestuous, wild, angry, raging, boiling, seething, agitated. Le Bon compares its dynamics 'to the waves, which are the expression on the surface of the ocean of deep-lying disturbances of which we know nothing'.[6] This is a classic trope: after Le Bon, the American crowd psychologist Boris Sidis described the 'savage fury of a hurricane' which rises to the surface from crowds;[7] before him Hippolyte Taine referred to the crowd as growing from a stream to a torrent and then to a cataract which hurled itself against the dyke of the forces of law and order.[8] This tradition understands the crowd from outside; it asks us to imagine the tumult as it crashes against the walls and doors of 'our house', smashing windows and lighting fires against the state with which we are supposed to identify. The crowd's terrible power is supposed to immediately threaten the reader. But Susan Buck-Morss challenges this vision. Writing with precisely the same oceanic metaphor, she says: 'The ocean waves that in the child's eye rise menacingly before crashing on the seashore, harbour a secret calm. You have only to dive under the threatening curl of their crest to enter their sanctuary as the foam churns overhead'.[9] This is Thompson's point too. When viewed from within, the apparent anarchic fervour of the eighteenth-century bread riot becomes an attempt to resolve a customary injustice. It is not abstract and ahistorical but a moment full of history, full of social forces.

Le Bon does not come off well from this comparison. His ideas are narrow and tainted with an utter hatred for crowded forms. I adduce him here in order to underline that de-historicising tendency that sees affect without history or constitution, simply a biological connectivity. Gabriel Tarde provides a more compelling response to Thompson's challenge.[10] Tarde's theory insists that crowd dynamics 'crystalized the very essence of society at a micro-sociological scale'.[11] This was because the 'common characteristic of all social acts is that they are imitative'.[12] By focusing on imitation, Tarde insists that we think about sociality through its capillary relations. In *Penal Philosophy* Tarde 'outlined a 'social embryology', according to which there are 'two distinct germs of societies, the family and the crowd' ... every society can be traced back to one of these two forms, family or crowd'.[13] This duality allowed Tarde to distinguish between two different types of imitation: fashion-imitation and custom-imitation. The 'family produces an imitation of customs, a kind of conservative imitation which prevails in the countryside. The crowd, on the other hand, generates imitation of rapidly changing fashions and this type of imitation is primarily found in the metropolis'.[14] Tarde thus distinguishes the urban crowds from those enmeshed in the (largely) rural paternalistic social relations described by Thompson. But while Tarde could begin to respond to Thompson in this way, it would only underline the difference of approach. For Thompson, the crowd gathers because of a breach of the (perceived) moral economy. This 'moral economy' is a form of *sui generis* custom; it is 'ambience, *mentalitie*, and ... the whole vocabulary of discourse, of legitimation and of expectation'.[15] In this sense, custom evidences the (objective) social structure of the moral economy. In Tarde there is no social structure, *only* imitation and invention. Social imitation is a 'semiconscious' state. Initially, in his work it is a sort of somnambulism and later a mutual influence.[16] 'Tarde suggests that people are not split between rational choice and irrational desire, but act according to a semiconscious imitation that mingles the two'.[17] 'There is not a military or civil requirement that you obey', he writes, 'which you have not copied from some living model'.[18] The crowd does not evince societal structure, but being social is akin to a crowded-state of being transfixed; 'it is especially in the great tumultuous assemblages of our cities that this characteristic force of the social world ought to be studied'.[19] The crowded scene and the social are fused for Tarde.

This does not preclude custom, context and history. Quite the contrary, for Tarde the two forms of imitation are orientations towards temporal flows. Custom-imitations are old forms of repetition, often long established. They are conventional or customary. Fashion-imitations, on the other hand, are those new imitations that emerge swiftly, effecting changes 'in short periods of time'.[20] In this sense, Tarde sought to distinguish an imitation where changes come and go (fashion) and an imitation where social relations are established (custom). However, within each of these forms of imitation there is novelty, each repetition introduces tiny changes leading to a distinctly vibrant process. What is more, the types of imitation crucially articulate with one another:

> We might have added … [crime like other social facts] becomes changed or develops through intermittent insertion of new buds or new grafts of *imitation-fashions* which come to replenish and nourish, sometimes drive back, a stock of *imitation-customs*, but they themselves have a tendency to take root, to swell the legacy of custom and tradition. … Every science, every art, every language, every religion, obeys this law of the passing from custom to fashion and the return from fashion to custom, but custom which has expanded.[21]

In Tarde's social theory, society (as a series of transcendent forces) drops away, being replaced instead by the immanent forces of imitation, invention and opposition. The best way for a social scientist to understand this is through statistics and observation. With this he claims that you could see the 'beliefs and desires' as they went rippling through society.[22] As Clark explains, novel inventions are introduced into the social system and then spread like ripples across a pond, until they meet an obstacle. 'The obstacle, however, is likely to be the imitation of some earlier invention, and when they collide, from their opposition is likely to emerge a new product – that is, a new invention – which in turn is imitated until it meets further obstacles, and so on, ad infinitum'.[23] Tarde was the head of statistics for the Ministry of Justice from 1894 to 1900, and he thought that we could statistically trace these ripples of belief and desire, by seeming their material correlates.[24] At the same time, through observation, we could understand them from below. Ultimately, Tarde's is a system of 'modification or communication'.[25] Each imitation both solidifies and alters social practice.

Tarde faded into obscurity after his death in 1904, remembered only as Émile Durkheim's minor rival, debunked for the twin evils of psychologism and individualism. It was the like of Giles Deleuze and Guattari (among others) who began a return to Tarde, portraying him as this radical other at the heart of conventional sociology. In *A Thousand Plateaus*, it was Tarde's 'micro-sociology' rather than the established macro analyses of objective social conditions that could provide an understanding of the potentiality of May 1968. Reading Tarde, Gilles Deleuze and Felix Guattari posit that 'a flow is always of belief and of desire'.[26] In May 1968, a 'flow was escaping, miniscule at first, then swelling'.[27] This was perceptible only to those who paid attention to the affective patterns of daily life. With this everyday affectivity in focus, it was possible to trace the gradual development of atmospheres of unrest which began to spread and intensify. In this way, Tarde's sociology was increasingly read by those who sought to understand the affective flows of revolt and protest. For our purposes, Tarde would *first* seem to be a theorist of this emergent unrest. Irrespective of the grand socio-historical state of society or the economy, Tarde points us instead to those 'molecular flows' of desire and belief, wherein people become politically or socially restive. He provides a way into thinking about what we earlier identified as the 'temper of the people', and what we will see in the next two chapters as the articulation of the people and the crowd. Unlike Burke, temper here is not a unitary thing but a form of affective life in which eddies and ripples of affect circulate and shift. On this reading, 'temper' is not a broad, abstract sociological field; instead it is a patterning or communication of beliefs and desires that should be understood epidemiologically.[28]

However, despite this radical afterlife, Tarde's actual politics were much more conservative. Alberto Toscano's reading of *Les Transformations de Pouvoir* makes this patently clear.[29] Toscano points out that Tarde's theory of somnambulism and imitation lent itself readily to a sort of *empowering pacification*. Tarde imagined that 'the political aspect of the movement of amplifying repetition seems to be schematized as a top-down process, where equality attained within a "social elite" ... is seen to spread to inferior strata'.[30] Invention was generally speaking the remit of the individual who stands out from the heaving surges and eddies of social imitation. The social then was a sort of somnambulistic state, a not quite conscious state of suggestive imitation. This state of sociality then lends itself to a certain idea of power. Tarde links political power to

> an affective anthropology of obedience, a vision of the passive subjects of power as inhabited by a need for security in submission. Voluntary servitude is not just a rational calculation for security, however, but a 'passionate kneeling', based on the presence of men of a 'general need for subordination and obedience' which gives submission to authority a kind of libidinal content, to the extent that political power is supposedly perceived as a salve against the anxious malady of doubt and uncertainty.[31]

As Andrew Barry points out, Tarde 'was more concerned with the problem of how to monitor and govern the desires of the populace than with how to foster them'.[32] His politics is made up of a patrician great-man theory alongside a trickle-down propagation. Even despite the association with the crowded assemblies that Tarde thought had ripped the nineteenth century apart, he argued that 'it is the deep logic of imitation that can turn men into obedient creatures, into a "nation of copyists"'.[33] This is both an observation and a political programme. Ultimately, the most readily applicable of ideas for those in political power would be to generate imitative pacifying dynamics. He wrote: 'Political life consists in directing these [affective] currents, either by containing them or activating them, in the direction of their greater convergence or lesser divergence'.[34] The state (and sovereignty) is ultimately a government of the temper of the people, what Toscano calls a 'network management'.[35] It might begin to calm the undercurrents of communism, syndicalism and anarchism that he saw as tormenting *fin-de-siècle* society. With this in mind, we might also point to Tarde as a key thinker of the sovereign peace, described in the second part of the book.

Rather than try to settle this apparent bifurcation in Tarde's legacy, I want to suggest that there is nothing contradictory in the adoption of Tarde either as a theorist of the radical upsurge of unrest or as a theorist of habitual pacification and the sovereign peace.[36] In fact, it is precisely this double sense that I find so useful. This is because, as we will see in the next two chapters, 'the people' holds this same double sense. It is called to presence in those crowded assemblies that surge forth and it is the name of that habitual pacification beneath an established constitutional order. But this double sense is not simply a bifurcation, because neither the state nor a revolt is unitary. Tarde himself made this clear: 'the state is almost never unified, it is almost always multiple, like the self [*moi*], almost always prey to internal rebellions, to dissidences that tend to fracture the nation into two or more factions'.[37] The state is multiple – it is nothing, Taussig would say[38] – internally fractured and inconsistent, made of competing rationalities and behaviours. When it calls on 'the people', it seeks to give itself a unity, appropriating energy and authority, while at the same time trying to calm the temper of the crowds.

Notes

1 Gabriel Tarde, *Penal Philosophy* (Little, Brown and Company: Boston, 1912), 323.
2 Jodi Dean, *Crowds and Party* (Verso, London, 2018), 9.
3 Charles Tilly, *From Mobilization to Revolution* (New York: McGraw-Hill, 1978); Charles Tilly, 'Repertoires of Contention in America and Britain 1750-1830' in Mayer Zald and John McCarthy (eds) *The Dynamics of Social Movements* (Cambridge: Winthrope, 1979), 126. For an excellent contemporary example of this type of analysis see Patrick McCurdy, Anna Geigenbaum and Fabian Frenzel, 'Protest Camps and Repertoires of Contention', 15.1 *Social Movement Studies* (2016), 97.
4 Dean, *Crowds and Party*, 9.
5 Edward P Thompson, 'The Moral Economy of the English Crowd in the Eighteenth Century', 50 *Past &Present* (1971), 76–136.
6 Le Bon, *The Crowd*, 9.
7 Boris Sidis, *The Psychology of Suggestion: A Research into the Subconscious Nature of Man and Society* (New York: D Appleton and Company, 1898), chapter 2, available at https://www.sidis.net/pscontents.htm
8 Hippolyte Taine, *The Ancient Régime* (1876) (Gloucester, Massachusetts: Peter Smith, 1962), 379.
9 Susan Buck Morss, 'Compatings and Loosenings' in Jeffrey Schnapp and Matthew Tiews, *Crowds* (Stanford University Press, 2006), 91.
10 For Tarde the contemporary antagonism lay with Emile Durkheim. Borch underlines that 'late nineteenth century French sociology was, by and large, animated by conservative concerns about how to restore social order after a century of recurrent insurrections' (Christian Borch, *The Politics of Crowds: An Alternative History of Sociology* (Cambridge University Press, 2013), 64). Tarde's was a non-rationalist response, coming like Bergson and Sorel from the 'Spontaneous tradition'. (For a discussion of the Spontaneous and Cartesian traditions, see Terry Clark, 'Introduction' in Gabriel Tarde, *On Communication & Social Influence: Selected Papers* (Chicago: University of Chicago Press, 1969), 7–12.) It attempted to explain that social relations were based in irrational dynamics, of which for Tarde the crowd provided a ready example. Durkheim responded with a rationalism, one that increasingly found favour with the new republican French political establishment of the early twentieth century. For him, people were individual desiring entities held back by object social forces. These social forces therefore demanded an objective science rather than a sort of inter-psychology. In 1894, Tarde himself explained the burgeoning argument with Durkheim. We begin the quote while Tarde is in the middle of explaining Durkheim's well known idea of sociology as the objective study of social facts: '"Each

social fact consists either of a belief or a tendency or a practice which is that of the *group taken collectively and which is something quite different from the forms under which it is refracted in individuals*'" (italics in the original). But how could it be refracted before it exists, and, to speak intelligibly, how could it exist *outside* of *all* individuals? The truth is that any social thing, a word in a language, a religious rite, a trade secret, an artistic process, a legal provision, a moral maxim, is transmitted and passed not from *the social group taken collectively* to the individual, but from one individual – parent, teacher, friend, neighbour, comrade – to another individual, and in this passage from one mind to another it is refracted. The totality of these refractions, starting from an initial impulsion due to some anonymous or illustrious inventor, discoverer, innovator or modifier, is all the reality of a social thing at any given moment' (Gabriel Tarde, 'Sociology, Social Psychology, Sociologism' (1894), in *On Communication & Social Influence: Selected Papers* (Chicago: University of Chicago Press, 1969), 115). Lisa Blackman renders this as 'association' rather than 'inscription' (Lisa Blackman, 'Reinventing Psychological Matters: The Importance of the Suggestive Realm of Tarde's Ontology', 36.4 *Economy and Society* (2007), 574–596, 576). Durkheim mischaracterised Tarde's theory of imitation as reducing social facts to individual psychology. For Durkheim, 'there are ways of acting, thinking and feeling which possess the remarkable property of existing outside the consciousness of the individual'. He complained that Tarde's theory misunderstood what happened in crowds (transformation not imitation), and confused this with the force of social norms. Indeed, it entirely missed the coercive power of social facts, and worst of all, it represented a threat to the objectivity of sociology and its scientific character.

11 Borch, *The Politics of Crowds* 58; see also Andrea Mubi Brighenti 'Tarde, Canetti and Deleuze on Crowds and Packs', 10.4 *Journal of Classical Sociology* (2010): 291.
12 Tarde, 'Sociology, Social Psychology, Sociologism', 114. See also Gabriel Tarde, *Social Laws: An Outline of Sociology* (1897) (Massachusetts: Macmillan, 1899).
13 Borch, *The Politics of Crowds*, 55–56.
14 Ibid., 56.
15 Edward P Thompson, *Customs in Common* (Penguin, London 1993), 2.
16 See Borch's discussion (*The Politics of Crowds* 59-63) of Jac van Ginneken, *Crowds, Psychology and Politics 1871-1899* (Cambridge: Cambridge University Press, 1992).
17 Rosalind Williams, *Dream Worlds: Mass Consumption in Late Nineteenth-Century France* (Berkeley: University of California Press, 1982), 349-50, quoted in Borch, *The Politics of Crowds*, 58.
18 Tarde, *Social Laws*, 41.
19 Tarde, *Penal Philosophy*, 322–323.
20 Ibid., 326.
21 Ibid., 363.
22 Andrew Barry, 'Tarde's Method: Between Statistics and Experimentation', in Matei Candea *The Sovial After Gabriel Tarde: Debates and Assessments* (Routledge, 2010), 177–189.
23 Clark, 'Introduction', 21.
24 In *Social Laws* Tarde defines desire as a 'subjective tendency or mental eagerness' and belief as 'intellectual grasp or mental cohesion and constraint' (33). These form 'one homogenous and continuous stream. Though variously tinged with the different shades of affectivity pertaining to each separate mind, it nevertheless flows identically in each, now spreading and dividing, now uniting and contracting, and passing freely from one person to another, and from one perception to another in each person, without change' (Tarde, *Social Laws*, 33–34).
25 Andrew Barry, and Nigel Thrift, N. 'Gabriel Tarde: Imitation, Invention and Economy', 36.4 *Economy and Society* (2007), 509–25, 514.
26 Gilles Deleuze and Felix Guattari, *A Thousand Plateaus: Capitalism and Schizophrenia* (Minneapolis: University of Minnesota Press, 1987), 219.
27 Ibid., 216.

28 Nigel Thrift, *Non-Representational Theory: Space, Politics, Affect* (Routledge, 2007), 229.
29 Alberto Toscano, 'Powers of Pacification: State and Empire in Gabriel Tarde', 36.4 *Economy and Society* (2007), 597–613.
30 Ibid., 605.
31 Ibid.
32 Barry, 'Tarde's Method', 177, citing Toscano, 'Powers and Pacification'.
33 Tarde, *Les Transformations de Pouvoir*, quoted in Toscano, 'Powers and Pacification', 605.
34 Tarde, *Les Transformations de Pouvoir*, quoted in Toscano, 'Powers and Pacification', 608.
35 Toscano, 'Powers and Pacification', 608.
36 Certainly Tarde would have favoured one reading over the other, but written work always escapes its author.
37 Tarde, *Les Transformations de Pouvoir*, quoted in Toscano, 'Powers and Pacification', 609.
38 Michael Taussig, *The Nervous System* (Routledge, 2001).

14

THE CROWD AS POLITICAL TECHNOLOGY

In which we begin to examine the relation between the crowd and the people – Jodi Dean explores the energetic element of crowded behaviour – Elias Canetti is read as a theorist of atmospheres – the crowd is understood as a political technology for staging the people.

Jodi Dean begins *Crowds and Party* with a story of a particular moment during Occupy Wall Street in 2011. The general assembly were discussing whether to add an occupation in Washington Square, as well as Zuccotti Park. Under intense time constraints sentiments began to grow in favour of the new occupation. Dean writes:

> Speaker after speaker, amplified by the People's Mic … , urged us to take the park. *We are many. We outnumber them. We can do it. We must do it.* Upraised hands twinkled approval in waves of support round and round the circle. Then, a tall, thin, young man with curly dark hair and a revolutionary look began to speak.
>
> We can take this park!
> *We can take this park!*
> We can take this park tonight!
> *We can take this park tonight!*
> We can also take this park another night.
> *We can also take this park another night.*
> Not everyone may be ready tonight.
> *Not everyone may be ready tonight.*
> Each person has to make their own autonomous decision.
> *Each person has to make their own autonomous decision.*
> No one can decide for you. You have to decide for yourself.

> *No one can decide for you. You have to decide for yourself.*
> Everyone is an autonomous individual.
> *Everyone is an autonomous individual.*
>
> The mood was broken .... We were no longer a 'we', a collective. Asserting ourselves as individuals, we became individuated, concerned first with our own particular preoccupations.[1]

There is a key momentum within the movement. This mood or energy is crucial for Dean. She insists that the affects at play in crowded events like Occupy opened the possibility of staging the people. The key to the power of Occupy was not the anarchist inspired individualism,[2] but its ruptural collective energy.

The suggestion that 'the people' might be staged by Occupy, or by any particular crowd, will raise certain heckles. So at the outset let me clear away some of the misunderstandings. Firstly, 'the people' does not simply mean all of the people in a state. If that was the case then it would be impossible for the people to act. There is no political position, no institution or representative which could infallibly claim the entire and unchanging allegiance or support of every single part of the populace. Yet, we commonly say 'the people have spoken' when a proportion of people cast their votes in an election or when a ruler has been overthrown by popular unrest.[3] To make sense of this we must either reject the idea of the people could act (as some do) or more convincingly accept that there is something more complex going on when we speak about 'the people'. Hans Lindahl argues that the people should not be conceived as a full unity-in-action. Instead, we should think about it as a discursive production that emerges retroactively.[4] After the fact, the crowded disorder may be constructed as the event of political creation *or* as a seditious riot.[5] In this sense, there is a sort of fundamental undecidability in the moment: a crowd may have been the people or it may have been a mob. This is the fundamental instability of the constituent moment for Lindahl. He argues that this instability extends through the new order. When people exercise the constitutional rights established in the constituent moment, 'they retroactively take up the first-person plural perspective of a "We" that has (already) enacted a constitution'.[6] They attribute themselves, as citizens, to their moment of constituent power. But this attribution is to a 'past that has never been present'[7] because the vitality of 'the people' is maintained in these acts of attribution.

Jodi Dean explains that the crowd is never certainly the people. Drawing on Alain Badiou, she argues that the sense of the event is made after the fact. The crowd opens the possibility of the people. It 'forces the possibility of the intrusion of the people into politics. Whether the people is the subject of a crowd event is up for grabs. The crowd opens up a site of struggle over its subject'.[8] The crowd opens the possibility of the people, by way of its energy. For Dean, the crowd itself is not a political subject. The people is the political subject. Politics happens 'when meaning is announced and the struggle over this meaning begins'.[9] 'The crowd is not the people. ... Rather, the people appear as the subject of politics when the rupture of the crowd event can be attributed to them retroactively'.[10] The crowd produces a surge of energy that transforms those present.[11] We might gloss both Lindahl and Dean by identifying the crowd as a political technology for staging the people. It opens the possibility of the political subject emerging retroactively (Dean) or of the constitution retroactively being attributed (Lindahl). The crowd is not the people as such, some other operation is necessary to approach this completion. Identifying the crowd as a 'political technology' is important because it helps us to grasp both the end for which it is instrumentalised and also the specificity of the technological apparatus itself. A palette knife and paint brush are instruments of painting, but to understand them simply through the painting produced with them is to miss the specificity of their instrumentality. The crowd is a political technology which can be deployed to stage the people. But the patterning of the people that happens in the crowds of revolt or protest is crucial to the sense of the people that might emerge.

Dean draws on Elias Canetti's concept of the 'discharge' to explain what is essential to crowded staging of the possibility of the people. This is the specificity of the crowd as a political technology. The 'discharge' is the moment when those grouped together individually suddenly lose a sense of themselves. It is a sudden release from everyday alienation, and it moves through the crowd like an electric charge. After the discharge, each person takes part in the crowd in an ecstatic manner. Differences of rank, status and possessions are set aside. 'In the crowd the individual feels that he is transcending the limits if his own person'.[12] Discharge is the moment when a group of individuals become a crowd by way of a sharing equality – a 'blessed moment, when no-one is greater or better than another'.[13] For Dean then, 'Canetti gives us the crowd as a strange attractor or *jouissance*, a figure of collective enjoyment'.[14] Once the crowd has discharged Dean reads Canetti's crowd as a manifestation of desire:

> Canetti's crowd desires. It wants to grow, to increase and spread. It will persist as long as it is moving toward a goal … . Canetti attributes to crowds traits suggestive of what psychoanalysis treats as desire: growth and direction. The urge to increase is a push to be more, to eliminate barriers, to universalize and extend the crowd feeling such that nothing is outside it. Direction intensifies equality by providing a common goal. If the crowd is to continue to exist, the goal must remain unattained. Expressed in Lacanian terms: desire is a desire to desire.[15]

She later glosses this: 'Crowds exert force or, better, they are a force of desire exerted by collectivity'.[16]

Crucially, this force of desire is not the fully political expression of an alternative world. At best it is a 'positive expression of negation' – the crowd 'breach the given, installing a gap of possibility'.[17]

> The crowd by itself, unnamed, doesn't represent an alternative; it cuts out an opening by breaking through the limits bounding permitted experience.

> It mis-assembles what is present and threatens what is not yet there (I say 'mis-assemble' because 'assemble' would imply order and 'dis-assemble' would imply destruction without subjectivization). People are there, but, thorough the active desire of the crowd, differently from how they were before … . Together, previously separate people impress the possibility of the people as the collective subject of a politics.[18]

The crowd surges forth with a momentum of its own, mis-assembling the space of politics. And in this it opens the possibility that the people might appear. 'The energy of the crowd opens to political subjectivity, but it is not the same as political subjectivity … . For the crowd to become the people, representation is necessary, representation faithful to equality, to the "blessed moment" of the discharge'.[19]

Dean's account tears through contemporary critical theory with great momentum. But without wishing to challenge the overall drive of the book, I want to pause for a moment on the question of the discharge. Dean's reading of Canetti is partial, though in a way that is completely understandable. His *Crowds and Power* is a really odd book. In an interview with Canetti, Adorno said its method was 'something of a scandal … the reader cannot quite shake off the feeling that in the development of your book the imagination … is in fact of a greater significance than' the experience of the real.[20] Rather than a systematic reading of Canetti, Dean abstracts the discharge and uses it as a fulcrum around which desire is shifted from the individual to the collective. However, if we put discharge back into context with the other crowd dynamics that Canetti identifies, we find a slightly more complex framing.

Canetti begins his account of the crowd with the fear of being touched. This affective structure is ever present in contemporary society Canetti claims:

> There is nothing that man fears more than the touch of the unknown. He wants to *see* what is reaching towards him, and to be able to recognize or at least classify it. Man always tends to avoid physical contact with anything strange … . The repugnance to being touched remains with us when we go about among people; the way we move in a busy street, in restaurants, trains or buses is governed by it.[21]

The fear of being touched structures life, he argues. But the crowd releases 'Man' from this fear. As bodies press together and lose a sense of themselves, that fear of touch also dissipates. Canetti's use of 'Man' (in the sense of 'mankind') unintentionally reveals the gendered nature of this moment, which is essential. But let us come back to this in the next chapter where we will explore the role that the gender violence of a 'touch' can play in patterning the constituent moment.

Canetti moves rapidly, initially identifying two types of crowd: open and closed. The open crowd is 'open' in the sense that it is un-boundaried. Its simple rule is growth, as we have seen. The crowd arrives suddenly, mysteriously. Most people do not know why they have been drawn to it, but within it they move with an intense determination. 'It seems as though the movement of some transmits itself to others. But that is not all; they have a goal which is there before they can find words for it. This goal is the blackest [densest] spot where most people are gathered'.[22] The crowd has a mass, a density and a gravity, and this gravity draws people in and re-orients their behaviour. 'The open crowd exists so long as it grows; it disintegrates as soon as it stops growing'.[23] It is to be distinguished, Canetti tells us, from the closed crowd which is determined by its boundary.

> The closed crowd renounces growth and puts its stress on permanence. The first thing to be noticed about it is that it has a boundary. It establishes itself by accepting its limitation. It creates a space for itself which it will fill. This space can be compared to a vessel into which liquid is being poured and whose capacity is known. The entrances to this space are limited in number, and only these entrances can be used; the boundary is respected whether it consists of stone, of solid wall, or of some special act of acceptance, or entrance fee. Once the space is completely filled, no one else is allowed in.[24]

The boundary – usually a building – remains even when the crowd disperses. The open crowd operates by sharing out the equality of its happening. With the closed crowd, however, the 'building is waiting for them; it exists for their sake and, so long as it is there, they will be able to meet in the same manner. The space is theirs, even during the ebb, and in its emptiness it reminds them of the flood'.[25] It is only then that Canetti turns to the discharge, even though he claims that it is 'the most important occurrence within the crowd'.[26]

Although it is not a term used by Canetti in any technical sense, I want to suggest that we can read Canetti's analysis as setting up a thinking of atmospheres, or at least what he calls the crowd's 'feeling space'.[27] Putting the analyses into atmospheric terms, we find the feeling of alienation and separation that dissolves in the crowd; the festive buzzing of an open crowd that draws people to its mass; the inward intensity of the closed crowd in a theatre; the echoes of that empty space that seems imprinted with the absence of a crowd; or the promise of a new crowd (an empty theatre perhaps or a stadium). By focusing on the morphology of crowds, Canetti underlines the manner in which the space of the crowd and its affective patterning relate together. This only intensifies after he introduces the 'discharge'. His concepts are modulated through the atmospheres/feeling-spaces that they involve. So for instance, he writes:

> *Destructiveness* ...
> the noise of destruction adds to [the crowd's] satisfaction; the banging of windows and the crashing glass are the robust sounds of fresh life, the cries of something new-born. It is easy to evoke them and that increases their popularity. Everything shouts together; the din is the applause of objects.[28]

Or again: '*The Eruption*' is the crowd as it overflows 'some well-guarded space into the squares and streets of a town where it can move freely, exposed to everything and attracting everyone'.[29] It is the 'passionate determination to reach *all* men'.[30] '*Persecution*' is a shared sentiment: 'One of the striking traits of the inner life of a crowd is the feeling of being persecuted, a peculiar angry sensitiveness and irritability directed against those it has once and forever nominated as enemies'.[31] There is also domestication, panic and rhythm. And all of this is before Canetti even begins his sections on the 'Classification of Crowds According to Their Prevailing Emotion'.[32] The point here is not to enter into an extended exegesis of Canetti but simply to suggest that much of his apparently scattered account is connected by an unspoken sense of atmospheric or affective intensity. Canetti gives us a morphology of crowds that is largely structured by an understanding of their feeling-space.

If we re-orient *Crowds and Power* to this sense of atmosphere, a slightly different question emerges. The discharge remains important; it might even be the most important moment in these mis-assembling crowds. But it loses its definitional quality. For Canetti, 'discharge' is what makes a collection of individuals into a crowd. Without the discharge, it is simply a collection of people gathering in the same space. But put into atmospheric terms, the discharge is simply one way in which an atmosphere might be affected by a crowd and, in turn, might affect the crowd. There are other atmospheres that can increase or decrease the energy or capacity to act of the crowd. The moment of forgetting yourself is not the culminating moment of a crowd's being. It is one among many moments of a crowded atmosphere. There are some important reasons why Dean might prefer Canetti's singular account of discharge over this plural thinking of atmospheres. The aim of *Crowds and Party* is to draw a bright line connecting crowded protest and the role of a party as the affective orientation necessary to ensure that the crowd's rupture is sustained. The discharge gives Dean a simple way to deal with the crowd's energy, but it only works by focusing on one type of crowded moment, one type of affective intensity, one sort of collective energy. As the climax of a crowded assembly, the discharge orients the crowd in one direction. This helps Dean's account, where energy moves from those collected in the moment of discharge, to a party as the site of struggle for the people.

> Charge, atmosphere, pressure, expectation, excitement: the affective sensibility of the collective becomes desirable in itself, the shared sense of the power of numbers. This sense lets us construe the crowd as the positivity of negation, a positive expression of the negation of individuality, separateness, boundaries and limit.[33]

The crowd is the positivity of negation, the site in which 'we' are more than 'each of us'. Atmosphere then is the orientation of this 'we' towards a feeling of mutual power. Discharge creates a crowd that is capable of becoming the people.

If we shift away from the discharge as the essential moment, then other sorts of crowded activity come into focus: those quiet moments of occupation where small groups gather, a strange intimacy fashioning new bonds of friendship; the shared sentiment of exhaustion, that low flatness in minor defeats. We could go back to Dean's account of the moment in Occupy Wall Street when the crowd decided whether or not to occupy Washington Square Gardens. Dean says that 'mood was broken' when the 'revolutionary looking' man reminded everyone about their own personal concerns. We can imagine the fervid atmosphere as the crowd builds towards that new occupation and then the slow tempo of regret and disappointment as it dissipates. But this collective deflation is also an atmosphere, and like the discharge it also orients or conducts people. These 'negative', energy-sapping atmospheres are not the type that Dean is interested in. That flatness and exhaustion are not the sentiments of a vibrant political party. But I want to argue that if we are to understand the state of unrest (the affective tone that the crowd can produce), it is not enough to simply look for the ecstatic discharge; we must also see these negative affects as they circulate.

Pluralising Dean's account of crowded atmospheres opens up a more complex relation between the crowd and the people. The patterning of the crowd affects the people that might be staged. We can think about the wide variety of atmospheres that provide different affective situations for staging the people. These different affective tones help stage the people differently, in the same way that different stagings of sovereignty generated different affective resonances. This difference within the (immediate) affective resonance then colours the mediation that emerges from the resonance. In the next chapter we turn to one of these situations: an attempt to pattern the people in Tahrir Square.

Notes

1 Dean, *Crowds and Party*, 3–4.
2 For Dean it instantiates everything that is wrong with an anarchist inspired left; 'Each [of us] is told, repeatedly, that she is unique and encouraged to cultivate this uniqueness. We learn to insist on and enjoy our difference, intensifying processes of self-individualization. No one else is like us (like me)' (Ibid. 31).
3 Aside from the young who are excluded by their age from voting, foreign citizens who are excluded by their nationality, and the great body of people who do not vote for a wide variety of personal and political reasons, there is often less than 50% of the population who actually cast a vote. There are significantly fewer who cast their vote for the winning party or politician. But yet we attribute the will of the people to these elections. In more informal processes like revolutions, a majority do not make their will be known on the streets. But yet, like elections, we still say that the 'people speaks' in these moments.
4 Hans Lindahl, 'Constituent Power and Reflexive Identity', in Martin Loughlin and Neil Walker, *The Paradox of Constitutionalism: Constituent Power and Constitutional Form* (Oxford University Press, 2008), 19.
5 For further discussion see Douzinas, *Philosophy and Resistance in the Crisis.*
6 Hans Lindahl, 'Constituent Power and Reflexive Identity', 20. See also Illan rua Wall, *Human Rights and Constituent Power: Without Model or Warranty* (Routledge, 2012).

7 Ibid., 19, quoting Merleau-Ponty.
8 Dean, *Crowds and Party*, 8.
9 Ibid., 125.
10 Ibid., 115–116.
11 For Dean's use of prefiguration see *Crowds and Party*, 124.
12 Canetti, *Crowds and Power*, 20.
13 Ibid., 18.
14 Dean, *Crowds and Party*, 121.
15 Ibid., 122–123.
16 Ibid., 124.
17 Ibid.
18 Ibid.
19 Dean, *Crowds and Party*, 125.
20 Theodore Adorno and Elias Canetti, 'Elias Canetti: Discussion with Theodore Adorno', 45 *Thesis Eleven* (1996), 2.
21 Canetti, *Crowds and Power*, 15.
22 Ibid., 16.
23 Ibid., 16–17.
24 Ibid., 17.
25 Ibid.
26 Ibid.
27 Ibid., 49.
28 Ibid., 19.
29 Ibid., 22.
30 Ibid.
31 Ibid.
32 Ibid., 48.
33 Dean, *Crowds and Party*, 120.

15

SECURING THE PEOPLE

We explore the manner in which gender violence might 'pattern' the emergence of the people – we see the festive atmosphere and the affective frenzy of the group sexual assault in Tahrir Square – sexual violence as a 'purification' of the populace.

Towards the end of *Notes toward a Performative Theory of Assembly* Judith Butler clarifies a point that had quietly simmered throughout the book. She distinguishes between the performative element wherein the crowd performatively stages its common precarity before the forces of the state (a performative alliance) and the affective dynamics of the 'surging multitude'. 'I am less concerned', she writes:

> with the ostensible vitality of surging multitudes or any nascent and promising life force that seems to struggle to belong to their collective action than I am with joining a struggle to establish more sustaining conditions of liveability in the face of systematically induced precarity and forms of racial destitution.[1]

The affective dynamics of the crowd are important, it seems: they constitute 'a new "lived" sense of the people'.[2] But Butler worries about endorsing a surging life force as such: 'There are, after all, all sorts of surging multitudes I would not want to endorse (even if I do not dispute their right to assemble), and they would include lynch mobs, anti-Semite or racist or fascist congregations'.[3] She does not deny the energy that is released within crowds, instead she worries that crowded action does not necessarily manifest any particular politics. There is nothing determinative about the affective energy of the crowd. For Dean this indeterminacy allows her to focus on certain crowds and their potential articulation with a putative party. For Butler, the impossibility of vouching for the surging energy of the crowd brings caution about crowds in general. In this chapter I want to take this question of the dangerous energies of crowds further. Rather than flashing them up as an indeterminate threat, we will explore the brutal energy of the crowd, focusing on the contestation of the meaning of the people that went on in Tahrir Square in 2011. This is a contestation that occurred at the very level of patterning of the crowd, as those involved struggled for the place of women at the symbolic site of the revolution. The question is simply, 'Can the crowd be trusted?'

We must start six years before the events of Tahrir Square, at 2 pm on the 25th of May 2005. That day, a relatively small demonstration had gathered outside the Press Syndicat in Cairo to object to the Article 76 referendum that would allow President Mubarak to extend his term in office. Two hours before, the crowd had been broken up by riot police and the organised supporters of Mubarak's National Democratic Party (NDP). As the protest formed again the journalist Nawal 'Ali Mohamed Ahmed was passing on her way to her office. Following an order from a riot police officer she was surrounded by a small crowd of NDP supporters who pushed her to the ground. They tore her clothes 'fondled' her 'private parts', and seized her bag and documents.[4] She finally escaped, but the NDP crowd struck again and again that day. Twelve women in total were sexually assaulted on what would become known as Black Wednesday. Crucially, it is also the first recorded use of 'group sexual assault' as a security tactic against protesters.[5] The NDP crowd acted with frenzied desire, encircling and isolating Ahmed from anyone who might have come to her aid. She was groped, her clothes were torn, she was bruised and battered by frenzied hands that tussled with one another to get close to her. The desire of the NDP crowd appears to have been a noxious mix of sexual frenzy *and* security strategy. What better way to express support for the regime, to shore it up, than to humiliate and violate those who would contest its legitimacy. It is a violence associated with the domestic scene, where the *oikonomic* power is exercised over women's bodies.

To the shock of many, Tunisia was set alight in December 2010, after Mohammed Bouazizi self-immolated in Sidi Bouzid. The crowds began gathering in public space, reaching Tunis on the 27th of December. And then, in the *Place du 14 Novembre* the intensity grew. Ben Ali was deposed by mid-January. But the conditions and relations crystallised by the Tunisian Revolution resonated with Egyptians and by 25th of January there were 50,000 people in Tahrir Square.[6] The space of Tahrir Square was differentiated from the rest of the city by the occupation. Ahmad Shokr comments that: 'In the days that followed [its beginning], the excitement of entering the plaza never subsided. Crossing the popular checkpoints, one was greeted, like a hero, by a chorale of young men chanting, "Welcome revolutionaries!"'[7] The affective intensity of the square was already heightened. Shokr describes stalls of free food, live music and a 'spirit of mutual aid'. 'The atmosphere evoked an endless carnival, whose visitors were enticed by every stall'.[8]

> By moving into the square en masse, the people of Tahrir defied the exclusionary logic that had governed their urban space for years. What they created was an anti-city of sorts. The pervasive sense of impatience and never having enough time that characterizes everyday life in a metropolis suddenly vanished. Social codes that customarily define appropriate interactions between people collapsed. In Tahrir, there were no strangers; everywhere people talked to each other with a newfound ease.[9]

Until January, Tahrir Square was dominated by the massive roundabout at its centre, but suddenly the space was redrawn. It manifested an affective intensity, opening the potentiality of the people.

At the same time as this crowded vital energy, this 'surging multitude' or performative assembly, there was another set of crowded intensities being performed. Nazra for Feminist Studies, the El-Nadeem Centre for Rehabilitation of Victims of Violence and Torture and the New Woman Foundation *have* collected harrowing testimonies of survivors of the group sexual assaults. From their text we may begin to discern the patterns of the frenzied crowds: The women often reported initially feeling crushed or mobbed as they moved from one part of the square to another. The intensity of the crowd seemed to grow around them in a way that many struggled to put their finger on. Then suddenly they were isolated; friends were torn from one another, isolated by brute presence in numbers. The survivors often remembered the first individual touch of a hand.[10] But the first hand was followed by others. An individual touch seemed to cascade as the crowd began to 'take possession' of their prey.[11] Once alone a woman became the centre of a new focused pack, circles of people formed around her. Many of the victims reported not hearing any cursing or swearing: 'to the contrary, [the attackers] say "we are protecting you" or "stay away from her she is like your sister"'.[12] But these words were cover for brutality. The men often said these things while they groped and digitally penetrated their victims. In fact, some of the survivors seemed to suggest that these phrases, and their cries of distress, seemed to drive the crowds onwards into ever deeper frenzies. Most of the testimonies collected by Nazra et al., describe the terror where every hand became indistinguishable, where the victim could not tell which was seeking flesh and which was seeking to protect.[13] The frenzied circle around the women became a bubble, a micro-atmosphere of sexual violence. These ordeals would go on for anything between a few minutes and up to an hour! And in most cases they only stopped after concerted effort to get the victims out of the crowd. Even the exit was full of danger as men sought to lure women into private places with a view to raping them.

Tahrir Square held both the carnivalesque intensity *and* this sexually violent intensity. The danger of this doubling of the affective accounts of Tahrir Square is twofold. Firstly, there is the danger of creating a clear line of idealisation between the crowd (qua people) and the crowd (qua mob). With this type of absolute distinction we can simply dismiss the sexual assaults because they are of a different order to those of the appearance of the people. Equally problematic is the idea that we treat the two crowds as directly related – a linear causality, as though the crowded intensities of Tahrir lead inexorably to the group sexual assaults. These are two sides of the same coin, and both stem from moralising commitments on crowded protest and revolt. As Khalil argues, it is an essential shift away from 'a moral-laden evaluation of crowds as either progressive or reactionary', and instead begin to think about 'how they perform articulations or positions within a crowded discursive [and affective] field'.[14] It is easy to dismiss revolt by pointing to violence as a simple outcome, but it is equally problematic to suggest that the only way to support crowded action is to defend *all* crowded politics. If neither of these positions is particularly useful, then how are we to understand the relation between the joyful sense of Tahrir and the crowded sexual assaults?

We might begin by remembering that the crowd sexual assaults were from the outset a security technique. In the square they continued to fulfil this function. They were an attempt to secure the square first for the state, and then for particular forms of public appearance. The group sexual assault was an attempt to 'purify' the space of appearance and render women 'improper' to that public space. This becomes particularly clear when we periodise the assaults. In the first phase of the revolution, before Mubarak was ousted, the security forces and thugs organised by the regime were deployed to brutalise, charge, beat and otherwise maim protesters. While there were some group sexual assaults in this phase, they had not yet reached the intensity that they would after the 11th of February when Mubarak resigned. In this second phase the number of group sexual assaults increased exponentially. It appears that in this second phase, the sexual assault crowds were not simply instigated or controlled by the security forces, nor were they necessarily associated with a particular party. At the same time, however, they were not reducible to opportunistic sexual violence.

Activist and survivor Sally Zahoney explains that the sexual assaults aimed 'to scare people and shame the girls that demonstrate, and ostracize the largest number of people possible from the political sphere'.[15] The assaults and rapes were punishment for presence and sought to prohibit the women's presence in future demonstrations. The sexual assaults represent a patriarchal disciplining of unruly women, an abject cleansing of the public sphere. They would do this by making crowds the primary site of women's insecurity. The violence sought to preclude and punish women's presence in the crowd. It did so by confirming the very worst suspicions that the crowd is a violent and irrational entity, with sexual frenzy being aroused and rapidly escalated. The group sexual assaults operated to insert an instability into the sense of the crowd: the violence was done in Tahrir Square among the crowd (of protesters) and by the crowd (of rapists). It remains impossible to know to what extent the crowd of protesters and the crowd of rapists overlap, and because people cannot know, the entire crowd becomes suspect. This is equally the significance of the women never knowing who was there to rescue them or to intensify the assault. Even in the moment of the assault, the instability is maintained. The public space produced by the crowd was secured by producing the crowd as an object of insecurity for women.

This is security as a horizontal relation, rather than along the vertical axis of state/subject. The violence seeks to establish the terms under which one could enter public space. And therefore to police the subjects who perform the public in this constituent moment. Let us not forget, as one of the survivors notes, during and after the revolution,

> [w]omen and men from all walks of life stood in a spirit of national solidarity calling for social justice and for an end to political oppression. Many women said they felt reborn, that it was the first time that they felt free and equal in public life. They hoped and believed in a new Egypt in which women and men would be able to pursue their lives in an atmosphere of mutual respect.[16]

Tahrir Square was the radiating centre point of a constituent moment. First Tunisia and then Egypt were centres of hope before the militarisation of the so-called 'Arab Spring' in Bahrain, Libya and Syria. The presence of women in Tahrir Square was an essential dynamic of the revolution, it marked an important break. Taylor, Tan, Sloane, Tiernan and Mahmood explain that on a societal level the Egyptian revolution was a liminal moment where actors were 'betwixt and between successive lodgements in jural political systems'.[17] They say that the revolution was a 'rupture [that] allowed women to make choices outside of the "normative social behaviour" dictated by the old order'.[18]

By rendering the crowds insecure for women, the sexual assault crowds gender the constituent moment.[19] Through a constitutive exclusion, these sexual assault crowds sought to secure the gendered nature of the order that might emerge. The raw sexual violence effected an extreme symbolic exclusion of women from the moment of great national significance. The women were rendered utterly alone and isolated precisely at a point of political togetherness, and by the same mechanisms as that of the constituent moment. That is, they gathered as a part of a crowd that stood for the people, but it was a crowd that rendered them utterly alone, right there among the people. One unnamed survivor described this as a deep uprooting:

> we were raped in the middle of Tahrir [liberation] Square among throngs of Godless people, human wolves that are ravaging us, violate all that is private stripping us from our bodies. Violence, lust, and instincts and no one can save us; to face death and rape merely because I am female. In this situation, I am solely a female. The mother, sister, daughter, neighbour, and friend are just females, on the corner of Mohammed Mahmoud street,

> the martyrs street and the Eyes of Freedom street. They stripped me off my nationality and my sense of belonging to that scene.[20]

The woman came to Tahrir Square to be part of the national moment, as she saw it. But the group sexual assault stripped her of that 'belonging'. She felt reduced to a bare gendered body, no longer part of the crowds of the revolution (the people), no longer bound to the nation through its martyrs. She was detached from the scene of collective freedom and rendered utterly alone, uprooted from every sense of nationhood and the polity.

We have seen that there is a major uptick in the sexual assaults after Mubarak was removed from office. The government of the square as a form of public space of appearance is unhitched from the state. But Alessandro Petti, Sandi Hilal and Eyal Weizman draw our attention to a different government of the space, in exactly the same period as the sexual assaults:

> In Arab cities, the term 'public' is associated with the state and its repressive mechanisms; that is to say, the 'public' was never owned by the people … . It was only when protestors in Tahrir began cleaning up the square [the day after Mubarak was toppled] that they finally took real communal use of it – and of the future of Egypt – as uncertain, contradictory and full of dangers as that may be … . In Tahrir, the cleaning of the square (as many commentators have suggested) is what has turned it from being a 'public' space – the space of the regime – into an effective political common.[21]

Tahrir Square became public, in the sense of a political common, only after the ouster. Cleaning the space therefore was not simply an act of government but rather a horizontal relation enacted among the occupiers. The spatial relations in Tahrir Square were reconstituted; it was no longer the property of the regime, policed and managed by and for them. But we can say the same about the group sexual assaults, for certain men the square needed to be cleansed of the presence of women. It needed to be governed. Once the space was no longer the property of the regime, the responsibility for the conditions of appearance shifted.

The crowd is crucial to both the 'festival' of Tahrir and the group sexual assaults. In both instances it is used to affect the conditions under which the people (that will be constituted by the political struggle to come) can appear. In this sense, the group sexual assaults intervene in the affective patterning of the square. They try to shift the potential of the crowd's affective intensity. At each point of passing through a crowd, a woman must ask whether this is a political excitement of which she is part (the carnival, the 'spirit of Tahrir') or a sexual excitement of which she is the object. The effects of this patterning can be readily seen in discursive and symbolic stakes. The gendered 'cleansing' of public space has an effect on the types of demands that can be made; it changes the way that the political contestation is constituted. On a symbolic level, Tahrir Square stands for an attempt to shift the social and political constitution. The gender violence that marks this moment of intense symbolic significance will play out in any institution that claims lineage from that moment of rupture.[22] In short, the affective intensities that are staged in the constituent moment fold into the mediation of the people, just as the mediated people has multiple affective intensities of its own.

Notes

1 Judith Butler, *Notes Toward a Performative Theory of Assembly* (Harvard University Press, 2016), 183. 'Getting out of hand' is an anxiety that returns for Butler in her more recent book *The Force of Non-Violence* (London: Verso, 2020), 14. There it was violence, rather than crowds that might escape the ends to which it was directed. We will return to this in the next part.

2 Ibid.

3 Ibid.

4 Four of those subject to this sexual violence successfully took a case to the African Commission for Human Rights in EIRP and *Interrights v Egypt* [2011] ACHPR 85.

5 The state was there, certainly, from the official instigating the events to the security forces who held back the crowd of protesters who tried to intervene. Nicole Grove, 'The Cartographic Ambiguities of HarassMap: Crowdmapping Security and Sexual Violence in Egypt', 46.4 *Security Dialogue* (2015), 358.

6 Gaston Gordillo, 'The Speed of Revolutionary Resonance', *Critical Legal Thinking* (14/03/2011) http://criticallegalthinking.com/2011/03/14/the-speed-of-revolutionary-resonance/

7 Ahmad Shokr, 'The 18 Days of Tahrir,' 258, *Middle East Report* (Spring, 2011) http://www.merip.org/mer/mer258/18-days-tahrir

8 Ibid.

9 Ibid.

10 'R' reports: 'Suddenly I felt a hand grab my butt, I turned around and saw the young guy and stared him down, a few men saw and tried to push me forward away from him, the young man backed away once he saw I looked directly at him. He cowered away' ('R', in Nazra, El-Nadeem, and New Woman Foundation 'Sexual Assault and Rape in Tahrir Square and its Vicinity: A Compendium of Sources, 2011-2013') https://nazra.org/sites/nazra/files/attachments/compilation-_of_sexual-violence_-testimonies_between_20111_2013_en.pdf (viewed on 06/04/2020).

11 'N' describes how she was separated from her friend who was brutally assaulted: 'my heart aches for her and I keep playing the whole thing in my head ... she was right there in front of me then someone grabbed my ass so I looked behind then looked back and she was gone, I kept looking for her I couldn't see her anymore, it was as if I was in high sea and all the waves are just tossing me all over the place' (N, Ibid., 11). The similarity of these descriptions to Canetti's description of the 'baiting crowds' is uncanny. 'Everyone wants to participate; everyone strikes a blow and, in order to do this, pushes as near as he can to the victim. If he cannot hit him [the victim] himself, he wants to see others hit him. Every arm is thrust out as if they all belonged to one and the same creature' (Canetti, *Crowds and Power*, 49).

12 H's husband, Nazra, 'Testimonies on the Recent Sexual Assaults in Tahrir Square', 28.

13 'I didn't know who was trying to help and who wasn't. The only person I trusted was my friend. Others said they were helping but really just trying to get in the first row, getting a piece of the cake. Others were actually helping but it was impossible to know who' ('C' Ibid. 13). 'One of the men was trying to undo my belt and pull my pants down. He was grabbing me really tightly, putting his arms around me and screaming 'Leave her alone you sons of ...' pretending to protect me. While he was

yelling at the crowd, he was sticking his fingers inside my pants. I was very dizzy and felt like throwing up', Sally Zahoneny, Ibid., 44.

14 Andrea Khalil, *Crowd and Politics in North Africa: Tunisia, Algerian and Libya* (Routledge, 2014), 2.

15 'This has been the tactic of the regime for a while, even since 2005, then the virginity tests, beating of female protesters and dragging them across the streets'. Sally Zohney, Nazra et al., 'Sexual Assault and Rape in Tahrir Square and Its Vicinity', 17.

16 Nancy Gallagher, 'Sexual Harassment in Tahrir Square,' *E-International Relations* (27/06/2013) http://www.e-ir.info/2013/06/27/sexual-harassment-in-tahrir-square/

17 Serena Taylor, Amy Tan, Phoebe Sloane, Maggie Tiernan, Faiqa Mahmood, '"When She Stands among Men': Sexual Harassment of Women at Political Protests in Cairo, January 2011–August 2013', *Al Nakhlah; Online Journal of Southwest Asia and Islamic Civilisation* (2014) quoting Victor Turner, *Dramas, Fields and Metaphors: Symbolic Action in Human Society*. Ithaca, NY: Cornell University Press, 1975.

18 Ibid.

19 It may also be, perhaps that the rapist crowds sought to prevent the revolution – as the regime's use of crowd sexual assault before the revolution.

20 Nazra et al., 'Sexual Assault and Rape in Tahrir Square and its Vicinity', 24.

21 Alessandro Petti, Sandi Hilal and Eyal Weizman *Architecture after Revolution* (Sternberg Press, 2013), 171.

22 Honig, *Democracy and the Foreigner.*

16

EXCURSUS 3

Crowds and populace

In the introduction I suggested that 'the populace' was distinct from 'the population' (as the object-subject of governmentality) and 'the people' (as the subject of constituent power). The populace correlates to the population in the sense that it is the object-target of the governmental machine. But the populace is never quite as neutral as 'the population' because it always carries that sense of a rabble. The populace is governable, but unlike the population, it is never a perfect subject-object of government.[1] If the population is all the people in a territory with all their issues aggregated so that they can be analysed and managed and the people is the crowning glory of the crowded revolt, then the populace is the aggregate of affective life. As such, it must be carefully managed by the security apparatus to ensure that a state of unrest is not precipitated. The question for the security apparatus when crowds do begin to gather over a particular issue is whether this particular crowd bears the affects of the populace. Is there a strength of feeling behind the force of numbers, or will that strength of feeling build once the state tries to suppress these crowds? This is essential because the populace is the affective background from which crowds spin out.

Seeing the relation between populace and crowd helps us to escape the empty representational framing of the people in revolt. When crowds grow in the city squares, when they return again and again, liberals begin to ask whether this movement *represents* 'the people'. Their problem is that this sort of manifestation of the people comes with no warranty. Unlike elections which are regulated mechanisms for establishing the will of the people, crowded revolt is ungoverned by law. The representative idea, where the crowds would stand for the majority, is a trap. It confuses the matter, because as we have seen 'the people' is the *result* of crowded revolt. Its presence cannot be established in a particular crowd except retrospectively.[2] We have already seen in the last part how the energy and intensity of the crowd can begin to open a rupture in everyday relations from which 'the people' might emerge. Before the people is said to emerge, what exists is the energy and enthusiasm of the crowds *but also* the possibility of a populace that is behind the action. The crowds help us think about the affects and atmospheres of unrest, but the populace opens this up beyond the confines of the public square. It draws attention to the affective life of revolt that does not take place in Tahrir Square in Cairo, Zuccotti Park in New York or Tamar Park in Hong Kong. The minor or ordinary affects of revolt are found in those little groups of friends, in the family relations, the quite streetscape or workplaces.[3] This is as important to the affective life of the populace as the spectacular sites of unrest.

When the security apparatus releases its public order exceptionality, the object-target is the disorderly crowd. As we have seen, contemporary public order deploys affective interventions in order to exhaust particular crowds. But it is important to see that the police aim at the specific crowded protest precisely because of the relation it might have to the populace. Even with very minor disturbances, the risk for the police is that the crowds will be fed from the populace. This particular crowd might give rise to more crowds; it might draw others to the cause. If this process spirals further, then the risk is that the police begin to lose control as the state of unrest unfolds and intensifies. In this sense, we might say that the state of unrest does not belong to the crowd. Certainly, crowds are essential in mis-assembling the public sphere so that new atmospheres begin to seep out. These atmospheres of unrest change the capacity of the populace to act. They render the habitual relations of public order in question. But if crowded protests are successful in generating a state of unrest, the crowds become merely a sign of the perturbation in the affective life of the populace. In this way protest operates at a level which is essential to sovereignty. Protest excites the temper of the populace. It pulls more and more people out onto the streets so that increasingly the sovereign order begins to doubt whether it can continue to rely upon habitual calm. Without a calm, orderly populace, all that is left to the state is blind force.

Notes

1 In *Security, Territory Population,* Foucault discusses the problem of scarcity in the eighteenth century. He poses the right working of the grain market. This account features everyday fluctuations in price leading to rational decisions among suppliers and importers about releasing grain to market and forbearance among the consumers of dearness at certain points. This is 'behaviour such that every individual functions well as a member, as an element of the thing we want to manage in the best way possible, namely the population. They really act as members of the population' (Foucault, *Security, Territory, Population*, 43).

2 For an extensive discussion of this see Wall *Human Rights and Constituent Power.*

3 Sabrina Lilleby, 'Extraordinary Happenings, Ordinary Affects', 1.1 *Capacious* (2017), 20–21.

PART IV
The enmity of unrest

The new patterns of the state of unrest disrupt the habitual relations upon which sovereignty relies. Unrest is a wrenching experience: it breaks up the patterns of social and economic life; it disrupts people's projections of their life course; it throws them into dangerous situations, into contact with different people. Familiar relations are now rendered difficult or dangerous as friends and relations turn on one another. At the heart of this moment of popular unrest is the emergence of an enmity. Major protests and revolts resonate broadly with people, one way or another. Some are called to the unrest. It makes them into para- and proto-revolutionaries or it makes them into unsuspecting supporters of the regime. The unrest sucks them in and pushes them to express themselves collectively on this matter of great importance. Others try to live on in spite of the disorder that surrounds them. But the unrest weaves its way through their lives as well.

We have seen throughout the book that the affective life of the populace rests in a state of indeterminacy. It is impossible to know what affects are circulating at any given time and to predict whether particular actions, images or other interventions will resonate. As we saw in the first part of the book, sometimes these interventions land where they were supposed to and sometimes they don't. The opacity of the affective life of the populace means that the state is often surprised by outbreaks of protest or revolt. However, in this final part I want to underline the manner in which this begins to change. In the state of unrest, a fundamental enmity emerges between the state and that part of the populace that seeks its change or overthrow. It is a mutual enmity. The protestors object in great numbers. They gather in squares and on roads to show their disgust and anger at the sovereign order. What's more, the state increasingly sees its populace as an enemy that must be suppressed. The initial confidence in the face of minor protests becomes increasingly shrill as they grow in number and sentiment. The violence of the state of exception is deployed, and it further sours relations. Everything is now tinged with the feeling of betrayal, mistrust and discontent. And so the return to a state of habitual relations of the sovereign's peace is increasingly difficult. For our purposes, however, it is important to note that these new relations of antipathy are actually a momentary and partial resolution in the affective life of the populace. No longer is it indeterminate and unknowable. Instead, the state looks on in horror as the affective life of the populace clarifies itself in an apparently unrelenting hatred of the sovereign order.

The spectre of 'violence' is crucial in the emergence of this enmity. But as Butler cautions, it is important to recognise 'the ways that violence is figured and attributed within a field of discursive, social and state power'.[1] Thus for instance the state's monopoly of the use of force 'depends upon a naming practice, one that often dissimulates violence as legal coercion or externalises its own violence onto its target, rediscovering it as the violence of the other'.[2] So, when the police crush a protest that obstructs some major road, they claim not to be violent, because their actions were 'necessary'. In this logic, the crowd was violent because it disrupted the flow of the city and the situation itself required the police to break it up. The hard physical violence done by the police officers therefore is attributed to the protestors. As Butler comments: 'When states or institutions do this, they seek to rename non-violent practices as violent, conducting a political war, as it were, at the level of public semantics'.[3] What can be named as violence and non-violent is therefore dependent upon the 'episteme' in which 'it gather[s] credibility'.[4]

Butler's *The Force of Non-Violence* is a fascinating attempt to defend an ethical practice of non-violence that goes beyond liberal shibboleths of dignity and humanity. There is much to commend it, but in this part I want to develop a very different analysis. Where Butler seeks to develop a normative account based in a 'thoroughly egalitarian approach' to non-violence,[5] this book settles on a description of the affective dynamics of the state of unrest. In its multiple senses, violence is a central part in the production of the state of unrest. By this, I mean the baton strikes, property damage, disruption, arrests and detention, fights, menaces, charges, gassing and rubber bullet fire. Violence generates instabilities, 'it is the type of phenomenon that is constantly getting "out of hand"'.[6] As a part of this production of unrest, violence also generates very different types of bonds. What Butler might call new collective selves.[7] Throughout this book, we have seen various forms of these affective and emotional bonds that are born in violence. For instance, we saw how the colonial police sought to produce an *esprit de corps* among their men. Besides the repetitive drilling, this was built in everyday banal acts of brutality and in the manifestation of extreme violence against the colonised. This violence was supposed to generate a type of hyper-masculine bond between the police. In a different way, we have seen the precarious and temporary bonds that emerge in crowded protest. These bonds are not what Butler figures as 'bodies in alliance' but something much more intense and spontaneous.[8] Jodi Dean emphasised the energetic element, a momentum or movement that connects the crowds in a sense of purpose. This bond is also born from violence, but here it is from the attacks of the police (or their thugs) as they try to clear the squares or parks of occupation. Violence is not just 'an attack on "bonds"', as Butler says;[9] it also generates new bonds for the crowds in protest. This part is not a celebration of violence. It is an attempt to grapple with the affects and ambiences that shimmer throughout the scene of violence.

We have just three chapters in this part, drawn from three very different theorists writing in very different situations: from the mid-1990s Jacques Rancière explains to us the manner in which the sudden transparency of the affective life of the populace is marked by surprise. From the turn of the twentieth century George Sorel draws our attention to the affective patterning of enmity, and from the early 1960s Frantz Fanon focuses us on an atmosphere of violence. What binds the three is a close attention to this patterning of antagonism in the state of unrest.

Notes

1 Judith Butler, *The Force of Non-Violence* (London: Verso, 2020), 6.
2 Ibid.
3 Ibid., 2–3.
4 Ibid., 6.
5 Ibid., 56.
6 Ibid., 14.
7 Ibid., 52–55.
8 Butler, *Notes Toward a Performative Theory of Assembly.*
9 Butler, *The Force of Non-Violence*, 16.

17

THE SURPRISE OF UNREST

We begin to explore the ruptural quality of disorder – we see the surprise which marks disorder and the way that dissipates – with Jacques Rancière we see a new force which the event of disorder crystallises.

Since 2011, the story has been told over and again to the point where it seems to be exhausted: the fruit seller set himself alight, and his act of self-immolation sparked a series of protests from December 2010 and into January 2011. These increasingly insistent crowds began to spread, sweeping across the interior of the country. Resonating from town to town, they finally reached the capital. And with that the demands shifted.[1] The ever-growing numbers exerted a pressure of refusal; they violently wrenched the situation, and Europe's favourite North African dictator fell. And then other populaces felt emboldened, others states in the region began to look shaky. This is all so familiar that it is hardly necessary to insert the names of people and places (Bouazizi, Sidi Bouzid, Tunis, Ben Ali and the apparent catch-all event, the 'Arab Spring'). Looking back from early 2020, the events of 2011 seem so obvious. All that was needed was a spark and the populaces of North Africa would rise up. It also seems predictable how it would turn out. This apparent obviousness is interesting precisely because of its intimate relation to the surprise that had preceded it. It is important to see that the jaded and weary obviousness obscures precisely the feelings of surprise which marked the event.

Jodi Dean writes that 'there is something about [an] insurrection that was unimaginable prior to its enactment'.[2] It takes the casual viewer, the professional observer and indeed the participants themselves by surprise. It never quite comes when, or from whom it is expected. But afterwards … well, afterwards as I've said it seems so obvious. There is a sort of affective arc. We might call it a script, as we saw in Chapter 2, but we would have to be careful to note that mass insurrections do not have puppet-masters pulling the strings. It is a script only in the sense that events produce mass expectations, affective projections of what will happen. These expectations give an affective pattern the movement. They give it a temporal extension. When a script has played out, it is usually very difficult to understand what it felt like at the outset. In other words, we must not let this familiarity blind us to the erstwhile surprise. In this chapter I want to draw attention to this *affective patterning* by focusing in on the surprise. I want to suggest that in the context of unrest, surprise has an affective structure which we might understand by thinking about it temporally and in its energetic dimensions.

Although seldom remarked upon, Rancière's political writings of the nineties are riven through with a subterranean thinking of surprise. From its broadest aims (nothing less than redefining what should be understood as politics) to its specific political analyses (the shock of the *sans part*), he recovers a sense of surprise. Rancière identifies an aesthetic order wherein constituencies are rendered perceptible and through their identification it becomes possible to manage their interests. He calls this a 'police' order, deploying an old sense of 'police' as the management of interest, need and desire. 'Police' names any order that 'determines hierarchical relationships between human beings'.[3] It is 'an order of bodies that defines the allocation of ways of doing, ways of being, and ways of saying, and sees that those bodies are assigned by name to a particular place and task; it is an order of the visible and the sayable'.[4] Or as Chambers explains: 'The term *policing* can therefore be used to designate a broad set of phenomena concerned with structuring and ordering a social formation. The police *arranges reality*, in the sense that it distributes people and things into locations and roles'.[5] It is an aesthetic-material constellation which conditions perception. The affective patterning of the police order is a deadening, anaestheticising normalisation. For a critical theory audience, this designation of the social order as a police order would seem to imply a critique, but Rancière maintains that 'police' is a neutral term. It is not a 'levelling mechanism' which suggests that all governments are fundamentally and equally oppressive. As Rancière himself makes clear, 'there is a worse and a better police'.[6] Chambers explains that modes of the police order 'may make more of less space for the emergence of democratic politics'.[7] So 'police' in Rancière does not come covered in ACAB graffiti.[8] Rather, the term is used to crystallise a difference from 'politics'.

The police order, for Rancière, is fixated on identifying who and what counts. Although it is not an association that Rancière makes himself, the police order is essentially a form of public order; it is a manner of maintaining the sovereign's peace or governing the temper of the people. In this, it must first identify the economic, political and social interests of parts of society, in the process creating a sense of society as made up of various parts. These sectional interests are then to be balanced against one another in one way or another. Rancière claims that 'politics' occurs when this ordering is disrupted. The dissensus makes visible and audible what was previously invisible and inaudible: the crowds which emerge to surprise the police order because they are a part of society but are not counted as a part in the police order. Rancière calls this the 'part of no part' (*sans part*). It is a part of society that finds no part within it. The 'part of no part' lacks the possibility of prior identification by the police order. The 'part of no part' shocks because 'it is the part that only comes to be through politics [understood as rupture of the police order]. Thus, the unintelligible [*sans part*] is not *hidden* … [before its makes its demand] rather, [it] … is not there at all'.[9] Neither the police order nor critical theory can reveal the 'sans part', nor can they unmask it. 'Only politics can do that' because it is only in the political moment that it comes to presence.[10] The crowd 'defines the common of the community as a political community, in other words, as divided, as based on a wrong that escapes the arithmetic of exchange and reparation'.[11] It comes to be through its 'contentious commonality'.[12]

It is helpful here to step back to Chapter 8 for a moment. The apparatus of public order seeks to govern the affective life of the populace. It identifies domestic security risks and tries to neutralise them. We can think about this for a moment through Donald Rumsfeld's much derided security epistemology:

> there are known knowns; there are things we know we know. We also know there are known unknowns; that is to say we know there are some things we do not know. But there are also unknown unknowns – the ones we don't know we don't know. And if one looks throughout the history of our country and other free countries, it is the latter category that tend to be the difficult ones.[13]

In the context of public order management, the known knowns would be those heavily infiltrated groups, which would have little chance of ever surprising the police. Known unknowns would then equate to those groups that are known about, but which are not yet infiltrated or subject to the requisite levels of surveillance. Finally, Rumsfeld worries about the unknown unknowns. These would be those groups which are so clandestine, or so isolated in their organisation, that they are not yet known to the security apparatus. The security forces act as though these unknown unknowns exist, seeking out signs of their activity that might lead to their discovery.

This security epistemology is a microcosm of what Rancière calls the 'distribution of the sensible' or the 'police order'. The problem is that politics (on Rancière's understanding) is insensible to this security epistemology. The problem of 'unrest' for the security forces is not the agitation of particular groups (known or unknown unknowns). Instead, the real danger comes from the imperceptible social forces that might emerge rapidly. In other words, unrest emerges not because of the activities of particular groups (identified or un-identified) but because the affective life of the populace begins to share a growing sense of unease, crystallising around a particular issue or protest.[14] With that something new enters the field of social mediation. Public-order technicians have come close to understanding this at various stages, perhaps none more so than Raymond M. Momboisse who called for police and other security officials to take 'the pulse of social circulation', to attune themselves to the social 'signs of tension'.[15] The problem that Momboisse saw in 1967 was that unrest was the moment where a previously un-constituted force emerges into being. Security forces always seek out conspiracies and organisation, and in this they are not wrong. But what they often miss is that unrest takes hold because of shifts in affective life. Momboisse cautioned that the police should watch radicals, but not because they were organising a tightly knit secret mass movements. Instead, it was because the radicals responded to the affective life of the populace and were capable of striking when affects were building behind them. Rancière naively suggests that the state does little about the 'part of no part' because it cannot recognise something that does not yet exist. The security apparatus is well aware of this problem, but nonetheless Rancière is entirely correct to identify it as the site of surprise.[16]

Everyone that arrived in the *Place du 7 Novembre* in Tunis on the 27th of December 2010 was a part of society; each one was identifiable individually and in their friendship and kinship groups. But the crowd itself was unthinkable to Ben Ali's order. This was a crowd that refused to conform to the timid challenges of the 'loyal opposition',[17] and instead simply refused Ben Ali's rule in its entirety. To the police order, this crowd did not exist. Before these people came to the streets, they were many different things to the regime. Some were docile (if unhappy) subjects; others were subtly resistant; and still others were 'disloyal', covertly organising against the regime. But the point is that for the regime *and for these people themselves*, there was nothing common between them. They would only discover what was common in the act of resistance. Their political move then was to declare themselves together. In this act of staging a refusal, the protestors surprised both themselves and the regime. We could say the same about those who gathered for Occupy Wall Street. As the conservative media regularly reminded everyone, these were people who lived within a capitalist system. They bought their coffees at Starbucks, they rented or owned apartments, they worked for capitalist companies, some even had pensions that bought and sold bonds on Wall Street. These were people who had many diverse parts in the system. But when they came together against the structure by which their position was maintained, they constituted something new that could not be accommodated within the structure.

It is 'surprise' which marks the affective structure of Rancière's political analysis.[18] I do not mean that it is surprising that people are unhappy, that states weigh particularly heavily on particular parts, or that it is surprising that people will protest. Instead, I suggest there are two parts to this surprise: the first surprise of the *sans part* is a temporal jolt – it is happening now, in response to *this* particular event. *This* is the moment of unrest! As we have seen people often profess amazement amidst the events, but afterwards as they gain distance (and as the contest over their meaning begins to settle) the causes become obvious. The benefit of Rancière's account is that he attaches no preconditions to the *sans part*.[19] He allows their surprise to unfold in its immediacy. Later, when placed within a narrative of causes and effects, everyone can see that Ben Ali's regime had become unbearable, that *of course* 'stop and search' in London was affecting that populace unduly, that *obviously* the austerity and unemployment of the post-2008 crash was going to bring the indignant young of Spain and Greece onto the streets. In other words, the meaning of the event is struggled over and then settles. In the struggle for meaning, the raw surprise of unrest is anesthetised. It joins with all the known parts in the police order.

The second surprise of the *sans part* is for those involved. The crowds that gather in ever-growing numbers surprise themselves. The police order convinces everyone that they are alone in their discontent. The shock of seeing such numbers gathered together is immensely powerful. One of the key features of the idea of the 'strength of numbers' is that the co-presence of many people valorise each other. This is not just some sort of mutual recognition, nor is it simply the fact that numerically large crowds might stand for a majority. People also find themselves within an atmosphere which gives texture and depth to that feeling that lead them to the streets. The 'part of no part' comes with its own energetic/affective economy. This is precisely the object of the police tactics that we described in Chapter 9. Public order policing seeks to diffuse this energetic economy, to puncture the atmosphere, to confront the crowd with another force of numbers. In so doing, the police aim to reach beyond the particular crowd, to their dissensual/political challenge against the police order.

Surprise marks a temporal and energetic dimension of unrest. It is that excitement and energy that can come with newness. It is precisely the energetic element identified by Dean in *Crowds and Power*, but Rancière's analysis draws us to the question of surprise first and foremost. The problem, however, is that even though 'surprise' contains important insights for thinking the emergence of unrest and the affective structures that swirl around this, we might begin to get stuck. Rancière's theory in particular sees only the jolt of history and its gradual normalisation. It tells us very little about what else might be going on. Another way of thinking about this jolt of history is by framing it as a matter of violence. Understanding the identification of protest and disorder as 'violence' is essential to understanding the affective structures which are deployed around unrest. But it also opens up a different question about what violence (qua social upheaval) might begin to produce. To think about this we turn to two theorists who are often described as bloodthirsty: Sorel and Fanon.

Notes

1 See Alain Badiou, *The Rebirth of History* (Verso, 2012) for a discussion of this significance of this snowballing.
2 Dean, *Crowds and Party*, 146.
3 Samuel Chambers, *The Lessons of Rancière* (Oxford University Press, 2014), 42.
4 Jacques Rancière, *Disagreement: Politics and Philosophy* (University of Minnesota Press, 2004), 29.
5 Chambers, *The Lesson of Rancière*, 70.

6 Rancière, *Disagreement*, 30–31.
7 Chambers, *The Lesson of Rancière*, 72.
8 'All Cops Are Bastards'.
9 Chambers, *The Lesson of Rancière*, 153.
10 Ibid.
11 Rancière, *Disagreement*, 12.
12 Ibid., 9.
13 Donald Rumsfeld, 'US Department of Defence Briefing' (12/02/2002) https://archive.defense.gov/Transcripts/Transcript.aspx?TranscriptID=2636 (viewed on 19/03/2020).
14 This sounds like I am dismissing leadership and organisation, in the name of an anarchic spontaneous force. I am not. Leadership and organisation will take place before, during and after the moment of crowded protest. But the two are not (necessarily) related, and certainly not in a linear fashion. Anyone who has tried to organise a protest to which few turned out will attest to the fact that it must strike at the right moment, and it must resonate in the right way. These are the affective patterns to which this book has been oriented. Particular forms of leadership and organisation may intensify and attenuate, disgorge or abate the energies of unrest, but they are only one part of affective life.
15 Raymond Momboisse, *Riots, Revolts and Insurrections* (Charles Thomas Publisher: Springfield Illinois, 1967), 50.
16 In Berlant's terms, there are 'genres of the unprecedented' (Berlant and Greenwald, 'Affect in the End Times', 72). States deploy many different strategies in futural management that intervene in the present to ensure the possible disordered future never comes, from Momboisse's tension indicators to the algorithmic 'listening' to online chatter. But this is always an uncertain task, if the disorder that is mitigated against never comes, then the uncertainty about whether it was ever a possibility is only exacerbated. Or if the disorder does arrive, then by definition the futural analysis upon which the intervention was based was misguided in some sense. The success or failure of such modes of security is thus always difficult and uncertain (Ibid.).
17 See Beatrice Hibou, *The Force of Obedience: The Political Economy of Repression* (Polity Press, 2011).
18 It is essential to add here that Rancière and his commentators are clear that this applies just as much to liberal democratic states as autocratic modes of governance. We might say with Chambers that 'liberalism is unprepared for the surprise that is the emergence of a new political subject. In other words, the liberal counting system can never predict this novel political authority in advance; it can only count that which should be properly counted within the order of the police' (Chambers, *The Lesson of Rancière*, 103). Here Rancière raises heckles because so long as his work is thought of in 'authoritarian' systems it remains foreign and unthreatening. But to think it in the 'democratic' context is more challenging. Rancière insists that what passes for democracy today is precisely a police order. 'Policing is not so much the "disciplining" of bodies as a rule governing their appearing, a configuration of *occupations* and the properties of the spaces where these occupations are distributed' (Rancière, *Disagreement*, 29).
19 Here we could contrast Rancière with Badiou's theorisation of the inexistent – a structuring which shares a great deal. Politics happens for Badiou as something that 'breaks through a status quo that is based on a fiction of hierarchical order and is founded on the internal exclusion of invisible or inexistent elements' (Nina Power and Alberto Toscano, 'Politics' in A.J. Bartlett and Justin Clemens, *Alain Badiou, Key Concepts* (Routledge, 2014)). He insists that a historical riot succeeds in bringing 'the *inexistent* of the world' to a more intense existence. This is a long-standing part of Badiou's *oeuvre*. The controversial terminology of the 'inexistent' was developed in the context of the *sans-papiers* in France. But, as Feltham says, this 'is clearly a transposition of his earlier thesis on change beginning through naming the impossible'

(Oliver Feltham, *Alain Badiou: Live Theory* (Continuum, 2008), 67). The idea is simply that there are masses of people who are present in the world but who do 'not count'; they 'decide absolutely nothing' (Badiou, *The Rebirth of History*, 55–56). That they are 'inexistent' is true only for 'the state of the situation', which counts them as nothing. The event is a void that deviates from the state of the situation (Alexander Galloway, *French Theory Today: An Introduction to Possible Futures* (The Public School: New York, 2011), 17). Thus, '*a change of world* is real when an inexistent of the world starts to exist in the same world with maximum intensity' (Badiou, *The Rebirth of History*, 56, emphasis in original). Badiou continues that this sentiment is present in Tahrir Square, where people were saying, 'we used not to exist, but now we exist, and we can determine the history of the country' (Badiou, *The Rebirth of History*, 56). This means that the '*inexistent has arisen*' (Ibid.). Thus, in many senses Rancière and Badiou share much. However, Badiou has been clear that it is not enough for a riot to smash things up;; they must shift from an 'immediate riot' to a 'historical riot'. In particular, the riot only becomes historic when the 'negative growling of pure rebellion is succeeded by the assertion of a shared demand, whose satisfaction confers an internal meaning on the word "victory"' (Ibid. 35). The immediate riot rages on itself, burning itself out as it destroys the 'meagre symbols of the "wealthy" existence it is in contact with everyday' (Ibid. 23). The historic riot moves beyond the immediate riot to become the grounds of an event.

18

WHAT VIOLENCE MIGHT ASSEMBLE

In which we send Georges Sorel to contemporary Hong Kong – in his work we find a complex and compelling account of the enmity produced in the state of unrest – 'diremption' and enmity are connected to a violence that tears normal relations – the 2019 and 2014 unrest in Hong Kong are understood in these affective terms.

Walter Benjamin's 'Critique of Violence' makes the point more famously: at the heart of law is a violence that authorises itself. There is a difference between force and violence, with the former attributed to the state and the latter attributed to protesters and revolutionaries (as well as every variety of private individual). To be force, what is needed is proof of the 'historical origin' of violence, 'which under certain conditions is declared legal, sanctioned'.[1] But this 'force' is actually made of a law-preserving and a law-making *violence*. As Butler says, the state's naming practice furthers and dissimulates its own violence.[2] Benjamin's mysterious prose riffs off Georges Sorel's altogether more flabby *Reflections on Violence*.[3] He takes the ideas and makes them more dynamic, more incisive.[4] Reading Sorel after Benjamin is therefore a disappointing experience. There is a lingering sense that Sorel has taken exactly the same ingredients as Benjamin, and instead of something delicate and beautiful, he has served the most stodgy of meals. Because the 'Critique of Violence' is a germinal text for critical legal studies, it is difficult to read the *Reflections on Violence* without looking for the ideas that Benjamin would borrow. This often means that Sorel is *only* understood through Benjamin. But Sorel provides a compelling analysis of the affective structure of violence and the sharpening of a state of enmity in his own right. In this chapter I want to take two key concepts and underline how they might be used to think unrest differently.

Rather than becoming a dry exegesis of Sorel's work, the chapter will cross his insights with an analysis of contemporary unrest in Hong Kong.[5] It will introduce Sorel's affective reading of violence and unrest, using it to think about the 2019 unrest in Hong Kong. Obviously, we should be cautious about abstracting some trans-historical truth from Sorel's very particular account. He was writing in 1905, a generation after the Paris commune, and in the context of an ever-growing socialist and syndicalist movement in France. And more than anything, Sorel is a local thinker with the pages of *Reflections* full of score settling and admonishments aimed at contemporary politicians and leaders. As George Ciccariello-Maher points out, 'the *Reflections* was a book *for* a movement, it was meant to be *useful*' in France during the early years of the twentieth century.[6] But despite all of this caution, I think resituating some of his ideas in a radically different context can be useful both as a contrast to understand Sorel, and to push our understanding of the Hong Kong unrest much further. So let us flick backwards and forwards.

Towards the beginning of the *Reflections* Sorel makes a remarkable claim about the purpose of the book. It seeks to 'find out how the feelings by which the masses are moved form themselves into groups'.[7] This awkward little declaration points us towards collective feelings. It points towards a protean and dynamic assemblage of affective life. These collective feelings form themselves into clusters (what I will call 'feeling clusters'), as they move the masses. Sorel's idea then is to investigate the emergence of these feeling-clusters. What he called 'myth' was the way to diagnose affective relations and intervene in them.[8] For Sorel, myths were an assemblage of images, narratives and ideas that resonate with people in particular situations.[9] They

> enclose with them all the strongest inclinations of a people, a party or of a class. Inclinations which recur to the mind with the insistence of instincts in all the circumstances of life; and which give an aspect of complete reality to the hopes of immediate action by which, more easily than by any other method, men can reform their desires, passions and mental activity.[10]

Myths enclose investments, give them form and name their transmission. They give common inclinations an 'aspect' – an appearance, manner, quality. Myths operate by way of fully formed images, which resonate in ways that generate enthusiasm. These images (for instance, of the general strike) can also sustain energy in parts of the populace with whom they resonate. They sustain energy by crystallising the feeling-cluster into something perceptible, an image for the mind's eye. But the myth should not be reduced to those images, because what underlie its resonance are those shared inclinations, feelings and sentiments. In short, myth is an irruption of the affective life of (a part of) the populace. It is a way of thinking about the sudden perceptibility of the affective life of (a part of) the populace. The indeterminacy of affective life suddenly resolves, and the mists clear to reveal something into something that the syndicalist and revolutionary can work with. In this way it should recall the discussion throughout this book of the affective life of the populace, the examination of sovereign affects, the discussion of morale, the question of an affective public order and the manner in which the crowd might stage the people.

Let us use this to explore Hong Kong's recent unrest. It was the introduction of a new law that would allow extradition to China for certain crimes that began the spiral of unrest. Purbrick summarises:

> In the summer of 2019 Hong Kong has been shaken by prolonged protests, ostensibly regarding the issue of amendments to the extradition law but with deeper roots in the discontent of large parts of the population. The initially peaceful protests, on several occasions numbering according to the organisers at least a million people, frequently deteriorated into violent clashes between protesters and the Police, creating a cycle of violence that proved beyond the capability of the government to break. The protesters grew more radical and more willing to engage in violence to achieve their aims, or indeed as a nihilistic expression of discontent. The Police used traditional riot control tactics originating from the 1967 communist-related disturbances, applied colonial era laws, and on several occasions failed to distinguish between the majority of protesters who were peaceful and the minority who turned to violence.[11]

On the 12th of June the extradition bill was tabled for a second reading at the Legislative Council (LegCo). That morning, large numbers of protesters gathered outside the LegCo complex. This would be the turning point, where protest turned to genuine unrest. Drawing on Sorel, we might identify a small number of images and think about what these events do to the shifting feeling-clusters: the police overreaction on the 12th of June 2019; the tear gas and rubber bullets; the white shirts (triad members) who terrified train passengers on the 21st of July and the resulting action to 'take back' Yuen Long against the triad members; or the October face-mask ban and the emergency ordinance that we will return to in the next chapter. The problem, however, with all of these is that they emphasise the big events, at the expense of the everyday continuum. The great power of Sorel's *Reflections* is that he helps us grasp the long flow of affective life and the way that it is interspersed by moments of intensification and release. Thus, we need to take these scenes of violent eruption, and as E. P. Thompson encourages us, see them as part of the gradual shifting in the feeling-clusters. These eruptions force momentary resolutions in the affective life of the populace, its 'ambience, *mentalitie,* and … expectation'.[12]

Sorel's *Reflections* is a syndicalist text. It is focused on the emergence of radical union action which might use strikes to improve local conditions of labour, which might draw workers together against their class enemy and ultimately encourage the strikes that would form part of a greater struggle for socialism. For Sorel, a strike is an education in the force that the established order will bring to bear upon the workers. As Goldhammer comments: 'When strike violence does occur, Sorel anticipates the death of workers, not of bourgeois'.[13] In this sense, the *Reflections* is vaguely enthusiastic about force (legitimated state violence), because of its affective productivity. Workers would discover how bosses treated their apparently reasonable requests for fair pay, safer conditions or modest decreases in working time. In the strike a vast diremption takes place. As Sorel would say, the workers find out that they were always already at war. The strike shows the worker their place in a society of enmity. The striking workers *were* the enemy of their bosses and politicians. What is more, in the blood of their fellow workers, the myth of the general strike spreads epidemically.[14] Strikes produce 'feeling clusters' in which workers would understand their place in a class war. This is a form of 'diremption', a separation of a unity (society, social peace) in two (classes, class war). Sorel insisted that the strike liberated workers from the feeling that their interests might be accommodated within the established order by local bosses or even by socialist politicians. It drove them to develop a distinct proletarian morality. That is, a different affective order wherein violence has a different ethics.

The strike operates on an everyday level. It breaks apart the habitual relations of social reproduction, the drudgery of labour in the pattern of life. In the factory or the workshop, labour disciplined the populace. By way of necessity and specific techniques of disciplinary power, it generated docile bodies. This docility extended far beyond the factory floor. But in the strike these modes of discipline became increasingly visible. In 2014, the Umbrella Movement in Hong Kong sought to intervene in social reproduction but not at the workplace. Instead the protesters focused on the city as a site of social reproduction. The urban space is also a site of discipline. It generates docile bodies by managing the flow of bodies, determining the manner in which desires congeal in spaces of consumption and the movement through this space.[15] The occupations of the Umbrella Movement of 2014 re-made urban space in a different way. They generated new atmospheres where different forms of affective sociality took place.[16] However, for all of the non-violent organisation, the new forms of sociality-in-common, even the basic hope for a different city, the 2014 Occupy movement failed to break through and change the material conditions in Hong Kong. The new forms of life that emerged in the villages of Umbrellaville seemed to melt away. Soon after the occupations ended, I interviewed a number of people involved, and most of them described the deep exhaustion of the sentiments behind the occupation.

In 2019 the true significance of the Umbrella Movement was revealed. On the 1st of July protesters broke into the LegCo buildings, graffitiing the walls with slogans. One of these slogans that has re-appeared throughout the movement read: 'It was you who taught us that nonviolent marches don't work'.[17] The exhaustion of the 2014 umbrellas was productive of something new. What was exhausted was an unwavering commitment to *peaceful occupation*. The protests of 2019 would start from a fundamental antagonism. The lesson of 2014 was of the necessity of a diversity of tactics, with a large body of peaceful (and dynamic) protesters, and a smaller (but not insignificant) number willing to use violence (the 'fighters' or 'front line'). One of these protesters spoke to Reuters, explaining that: 'We learned a lot from our mistakes in the Umbrella revolution … . Definitely more people accept there will be some violence now. They may not like it, they may not want to be a part of it, but they don't condemn us. We are joined together as a force'.[18] Instead of aiming to produce the unity of the entire city (peacefully having a political discussion in the streets), the protesters in 2019 sought diremption (keeping the majority of people with them while alienating the supporters of the police and the government). They sought to clarify that there were two camps and that they could not be allowed to get along together. Often this political distinction came very close to an ethnocentric construction of the population. This would pit 'Hong Kongers' (usually born in Hong Kong, speaking Cantonese, capitalist, individualist) against the ethnic 'Chinese' (usually more recent immigrants to the region, speaking Mandarin, 'patriotic' towards China).

The protesters have gradually developed new repertoires of protest, new tactics to combat the strengths of the police.[19] The frontline protests have adapted the Bruce Lee instruction to be 'formless, shapeless, like water'. In particular, they have developed swarm tactics that allow crowds to appear suddenly, face off against inferior police forces ('be ice') and melt away ('be water') before the full strength of the police can be deployed. This prevents mass arrests.[20] They can then either disperse around the city via the Mass Transit Railway (MTR) ('be mist') or reappear around the same neighbourhoods. The journalist Erin Hale explained:

> 'Be water' can feel chaotic, with people running from one train station to the next, but it is backed by a highly disciplined strategy. Protesters are often following alerts on Telegram and a website documenting police locations or protest groups needing backup. [One explained:] 'If we find stopping in one place is not workable, we will go around to different place to block the gate of a police station or a government department'.[21]

Another protester told *Reuters*:

> I have thrown rocks, I have acted as a shield with umbrellas for others, I have been helping to build barricades, to bring supplies, to take injured people to a safe zone. I have also been hit by police with batons. We're all slowly getting used to this. We have to.[22]

In all of this, the crowds learn enmity. They show with each protest that the police are part of a different order. The 'feeling clusters' of diremption gather force.

The acclimatisation of crowds to police force and their own violence is a significant problem for the police. The entire affective power of the public order model is premised on a latent exceptionality, deployed with surprise against sporadic protest. To understand this we need to go back to the tactics that we saw in

Chapters 9 and 10. The protesters' diremption effects strangely mirror the tactics deployed by the police, which focus on exciting terror among the crowd. They seek to render the crowds as a 'savage' other. Against this faceless violence, the good police set in to exceptionally defend the rule of law. As Purbrick explains,

> The 1967 communist riots had a deep effect on the structure and culture of the Police. The structure has remained largely similar from the 1970s to 2019 with the same ranks, districts, and the ability of the Police to change from the routine daily policing mode to an internal security structure, known as 'Force Mobilisation' (or FORMOB). These Police formations have substantial firepower and equipment to suppress riots or internal security challenges. However, this change of district police structure to a paramilitary internal security mode raises problems for the Police. District policing is put aside and replaced by a structure that visibly projects force to the community. This projection of force is ideally kept temporary to ensure that the majority of the community remains supportive of the Police, but if maintained for too prolonged a period or if the paramilitary force negatively impacts on ordinary people there is a danger of the loss of support from the community for the Police.[23]

In the 2014 unrest around the Umbrella occupations, the police could move between latent exceptionality and low-level community-style policing. The decision to shift from one form to the other was entirely responsive to the strategic decisions of the police. As a static and defensive block, the occupiers could only respond.

In 2019 the protesters reversed this relation. Because the crowds are capable of deploying massive numbers *and* significant force, the police were forced to maintain their exceptional paramilitary force throughout the protests. Instead of *latent* exceptionality, there is an extended period where exceptional paramilitary policing is deployed. In this way the exceptional becomes everyday and therefore loses its alien quality. The crowd and the populace become acclimatised to the exceptional order, and with this the feeling-cluster around the police changes. They are associated with intense violence against school children and university students; they are closely associated with their deeply unpopular political leaders in Hong Kong and later in Beijing. The populace in general no longer perceive them as an independent, fair and well-trained force. Instead, discourses of illegitimacy begin to circulate. The 2019 protests thus demonstrate how it is possible to finally exhaust the latent exceptionality of the Hong Kong police public-order structure.

Diremption is one of Sorel's key insights, but myth is perhaps his most important addition to the field. The methodological problem that we have seen throughout the book is that it is remarkably difficult to sense the shifting patterns within the affective life of the populace. One has to wait for the populace to show itself. This is particularly the case while a moment of unrest is still unfolding and the affective resonance of particular moments is being felt. So let me merely identify Sorel's approach to this, before sketching some potential ways this might be used to understand the events in Hong Kong. For Sorel, myths were a way of understanding the affective dynamics of a situation, but they must also 'be judged as a means of acting on the present'.[24] Importantly, myths were a means and not an end. They were not predictive 'astrological almanacs' that would give a scientific path to victory.[25] Nor did they generate a utopian image of the end point of the struggle. Instead they would help the syndicalist attune to the affective life of the proletariat, the feeling-clusters which form them as a proletariat. Myth helped the syndicalist understand the affective flow in which they stood. From this, it would be possible to act to further shape desires and beliefs. For Sorel, it was the myth of the general strike that was of particular importance; it was 'admirably adapted to the working-class mind'.[26] It crowded out the desires instilled by the parliamentary socialism, who sought a quietist proletariat that they could represent to the country. The general strike 'is so effective as a motive force that once it has entered the minds of the people they can no longer be controlled by their [parliamentary socialist] leaders'.[27] The myth operated like a germ, infecting people, disrupting extant patterns of thought.

> *It is the myth in its entirety which is alone important*: its parts are only of interest in so far as they bring out the main idea. No useful purpose is served, therefore, in arguing about the incidents which may occur in the course of a social war, and about the decisive conflicts which may give victory to the proletariat; even supposing the revolutionaries to have been wholly and entirely deluded in setting up this imaginary picture of the general strike, this picture may yet have been, in the course of the preparation for the Revolution, a great element of strength, if it has embraced all the aspirations of Socialism, and if it has given to the whole body of Revolutionary thought a precision and rigidity which no other method of thought could have given.[28]

The general strike is not a fully worked out rational strategy that the syndicalists might use to plan out their class war. Sorel argues that it is not a rational plan *at all*. It is an affective strategy; once grasped the feeling of the general strike gives the proletariat a new set of inclinations and ideas.[29]

The 2019 Hong Kong protests made five demands, but it is clear that these are not the final political objects of the protest.[30] While ideas of genuine universal suffrage, democracy and even independence have simmered in the background of the protests, they have not been formally adopted. The protests have not been immediately structured by utopian ideas of the 'end' of the struggle, because putting them at the core of the protests risked precipitating direct Chinese military intervention. Instead, the intermediate demands have been given force by the creation of an *atmosphere of unrest*. This atmosphere is produced in material terms through a gradual escalation of the violence, fluctuating numbers of protesters and the variety of disruptive and turbulent tactics. Without occupying particular spaces, the protesters have changed the feel of the city at particular times of protest intensity – the smoke of small fires; the graffiti and rubble left strewn around the city; the presence of riot police in full armour. They leave a mark on the urban space itself, which stands for the unrest. The generalised state of unrest is then felt as a condition for political change.

We might think therefore about 'unrest' in Sorelean terms. Images are crucial for him. They give the populace a mental picture which crystallises the feeling-clusters through which they move.[31] The image of masked protesters, of massive numbers on the streets, or even of riot police emerging from their own tear gas, crystallises that sense of unrest.[32] In those images, it is possible to grasp the possibilities that might be opened if government is frustrated at a fundamental level, without having to identify what those possibilities actually might be. Possibility is figured as such. In this sense, the unrest does not operate as an object/end of struggle, but rather a sort of means without end.[33] The potentialities of the protests shift as the protests themselves unfold. The triads fighting on behalf of the state,[34] the November local election results[35] or the 'Christmas Shopping' protests would all have been unthinkable in June when this began.[36] Unrest is the means by which the social movement builds itself in the moment. Unrest is produced as the condition of possibility of shifts in the political order. Its motive force (as a feeling-cluster) lies in its projection of a future that cannot be measured by realist analysis or in technical detail. And its motive force stems from the fact that it is not some distant utopian possibility but an already vibrant feeling of the city.

Finally, Sorel also helps to mark a significant danger of the events in Hong Kong. The problem would be that as a movement it simply deploys violence at its energetic core. In European thought this is associated with fascism's celebration of war as a rebirthing of the spirit of a nation.[37] The sacrificial logic of Sorel's violence whereby a new proletarian morality emerges from the death and injury of striking workers proved remarkably powerful when deployed in German and Italian fascism. European fascism sought to generate cycles of sacrifice that would purify the nation. But the nation can never be sufficiently pure, and so there would always need to be scapegoat populations that had to be cleansed (Jews, socialists, Roma). These logics spiralled into incessant and infinite sacrificial cycles.[38] Once set loose, this violent *energia* of sacrifice proved deeply contagious. There were already hints of this release in Hong Kong, with a number of instances of violence against people of 'Chinese' ethnicity (as opposed to those from Hong Kong). We must be cautious about these, not to deny their occurrence but because the significance of this feeling-cluster is not clear. Equally, we should be careful about the easy association of Sorel with fascism. His ideas were certainly intensely useful for Mussolini. But fascism also radically reshaped Sorelean ideas: it amplified the role of sacrifice, repositioned violence as *the* dynamic *energia* beneath the movement, re-articulated the quasi-anarchic patterning of strike through the prism of strong leadership and military organisation, and ultimately shifted the boundaries of othering from an economic to a national/ethnic relation. The fascism that would emerge in Italy in the 1920s was certainly an appropriation of Sorelean ideas. But it was not the only reading of Sorel. The anti-liberal *Reflections* is an ambivalent, polyphonic text.

The lessons of fascism in the early twentieth century would suggest that social violence and mythic sacrifice provide a potent cocktail, which overcomes weak democratic institutionality. Hong Kong's institutions may not be particularly well equipped to deal with the violent release, but they are certainly not Weimarian. Behind them lies an immensely powerful Chinese state, which had imprisoned over 1.5 million Uighur Muslims in 're-education centres' in Xinjiang at the same time as the events in Hong Kong.[39] A director of one of these 'vocational education and training centres' described them as a security apparatus aimed at preventing political unrest: 'If we leave the terrorism thoughts to be developed, it is very easy to have riots or other issues. We prevent this from happening … . Our center is to prevent terrorism thoughts from happening'.[40] At the same time, the protests do not resemble the early storm troopers of European fascism. The lack of a central leader is essential here. Without this centralisation of power, there is no authoritarian core that crystallises the violent *energia*. Without the channelling of violence onto particular minorities, it remains frayed, anarchic. The mythic structures are interrupted, constantly in a state of rearticulation. They have not finally congealed around an ethnic/national othering, as they would have to for fascism. In short, by the time their expression was cut short by the outbreak of the Coronavirus, they were still in that state of flux.

As I wrote at the outset, Sorel is thought of as bloodthirsty. He is seen as a proponent of violence. Yet his work is based upon the revaluation of 'violence'. It is something done to the proletariat, something which is formative. They must put themselves in a position to be subjected to the 'force' of the police system. They must strike. But every strike is 'violent' in the sense that it ruptures the capitalist system, making the class antagonisms palpable, generating feeling-clusters around the myth of a general strike. Violence names the act of protest and revolt. In all of this Sorel gives us a different way to approach the affective life of the populace. He gives us a set of tools that might help us think differently about the affective resonance of a movement, and perhaps more importantly he points us to the scene of unrest. In this setting, the affective life of the populace begins to resolve into strong attachments and antagonisms. Because when the strategy of diremption is successful, what emerges is a society of enmity. In this the proletariat become increasingly unified against the quietism of the bourgeoise. This is what violence might assemble for Sorel.

Notes

1 Walter Benjamin, 'Critique of Violence' in *Reflections: Essays, Aphorism, Autobiographical Writings* (Schocken Books, New York, 1986), 280.
2 Butler, *The Force of Non-Violence*, 104.
3 Georges Sorel, *Reflections on Violence* (London: George Allen & Unwin, 1916).
4 There is too much in Benjamin's short essay to really begin to underline here in a footnote, but by distinguishing the force of the state into law-preserving (*rechtserhaltende*)

and law-making (*rechtsetzende*) violence, underlining the generative power of violence in the generation and maintenance of social and political order, Benjamin gives birth to a lively strand of critical legal thinking.

5 This reading across traditions has a number of very significant dangers. Sorel's *Reflections* is rooted in the possibility of socialism, even if it is a heterodox version. It is a labour struggle for a new world. But not only are the Hong Kong protests not oriented towards labour strikes, but they are struggling against a (sort of) communist state. In this sense, the basic orientation is radically different. While we might begin to differentiate the modern Chinese state from the idea of socialism that Sorel proposed, it is not difficult to find protests elements that would be deeply inimical to a struggle for socialism. In particular, the appearance of what appears to be an ethno-nationalist strand, or the role of the former or neo-imperialist powers of Britain or the US, should trouble this account. Thus, it should be clear that deploying Sorel to understand Hong Kong in 2019 is not without its difficulties. If the argument was simply that Sorel could be applied to Hong Kong, that their contexts and normativity were the same, then the ideas should be dismissed. But that is not the argument here. Instead I want to suggest that it is possible to abstract key elements of Sorel's account of syndicalism, in order to understand very different setting. This wrenching of certain concepts from their own normativity leads to a shallower sense of Sorel, but one which is nonetheless incisive for contemporary unrest.

6 George Ciccariello-Maher, 'Identity Against Totality: The Counterdiscourse of Separation beyond the Decolonial Turn', PhD Thesis, UC Berkeley (https://escholarship.org/uc/item/3c66g2x0), 54 (emphasis in the original).

7 Sorel, *Reflection on Violence*, 44.

8 We need to be very clear here that for Sorel myth did not simply take a textual form – he was certainly not describing that genre of classical 'myths and legends'. As Jesse Goldhammer explains, Sorel was describing 'modern myths' which 'are forms of affective communication'. These 'modern myths are dynamic and creative. Their images, narrative structure and affectivity inspire collective action on the part of individuals captivated by this thinking' (Jesse Goldhammer, *The Headless Republic* (Cornell University Press, Ithaca (NY), 2005), 140).

9 He does not give many examples, but when he does they come from very different contexts: For instance the 'dreams of Christian renovation' (from the first generation of Christians for the 'return of Christ and the total ruin of the pagan world' to the 'hopes which Luther and Calvin had formed of the religious exhalation of Europe') are rendered as 'pictures which created the enthusiasm of [the] first adepts'. Sorel, *Reflection on Violence*, 134.

10 Ibid., 133.

11 Martin Purbrick, 'A Report of the 2019 Hong Kong Protests', *Asian Affairs* (2019), 1.

12 Thompson, *Customs in Common,* 2.

13 Goldhammer, *The Headless Republic,* 113.

14 See Goldhammer's reading of Sorel (Ibid., 140).

15 Illan rua Wall, 'Atmospheres of Protest' in Shirin Rai and Silvija Jestrovic, *Oxford Handbook of Politics and Performance* (Oxford University Press, forthcoming). More broadly, for an affective and atmospheric account of urban space, see Cameron Duff, 'On the Role of Affect and Practice in the Production of Place', 28 *Environment and Planning D: Society and Space* (2010), 881.

16 Daniel Matthews, 'Narrative Space and Atmosphere: A Nomospheric Inquiry into Hong Kong's Pro-Democracy "Umbrella Movement"', 26.1 *Social and Legal Studies* (2017), 25.

17 Trey, 'A History of Hong Kong's Contentious Politics: "It was you who taught us …"' *Comparativist* (28/08/2019) https://www.comparativist.org/2019/08/28/a-history-of-hong-kongs-contentious-politics-it-was-you-who-taught-us/ (viewed on 30/03/2020).

18 Marius Zaharia, Felix Tam and Claire Jim, 'Frontline Protesters Make Case for Violence in Hong Kong Protests', *Reuters* (22/08/2019) https://www.reuters.com/article/us-hongkong-protests-violence-analysis/frontline-view-making-the-case-for-violence-in-hong-kong-protests-idUSKCN1VB2LV (viewed on 30/03/2020).
19 Tilly, *From Mobilization to Revolution*. See also Baz Kershaw, *The Radical in Performance: Between Brecht amd Baudrillard* (Abingdon: Routledge, 1999), 89–125.
20 The MTR public transport system had been essential to help the protesters disappear. But during the protests it became a key site of unrest. At the same time, when the police, or triad thugs entered the MTR system some of the most controversial violence occurred. Erin Hale, 'Hong Kong Protesters Use Flashmob Strategy to Avoid Arrest', *The Guardian* (13/10/2019) https://www.theguardian.com/world/2019/oct/13/hong-kong-protesters-flashmobs-blossom-everywhere (viewed on 30/03/2020).
21 Erin Hale, '"Be water": Hong Kong Protestoers Adopt Bruce Lee Tactic To Evade Police Crackdown', *The Independent* (07/08/2019) https://www.independent.co.uk/news/world/asia/hong-kong-protest-latest-bruce-lee-riot-police-water-a9045311.html (viewed on 30/03/2020).
22 Incidents where tear gas was fired within the system or where thugs attacked train carriages have underlined the sense of a form of state violence out of control (Zaharia, Tam and Jim, 'Frontline Protesters Make Case for Violence in Hong Kong Protests').
23 Purbrick, 'A Report of the 2019 Hong Kong Protests', 13–14.
24 Sorel, *Reflection on Violence*, 135.
25 Ibid.
26 Ibid., 139.
27 Ibid.
28 Ibid., 136 (emphasis in the original).
29 Joshua Clover summarises this well: 'The general strike unifies the experience of quotidian miseries and the fragmentary glimpses of something beyond them, allowing the individual worker an intuition of the world toward which the revolution strives, obtained "as a whole, perceived instantaneously"' (Joshua Clover, *Riot, Strike, Riot: The New Era of Uprisings* (London: Verso, 2016), 96).
30 The five demands were the withdrawal of extradition bill, the retraction of characterisation of the protests as riots, the release of arrested protesters, an independent commission on police violence and the resignation of Carrie Lam.
31 It is worth noting that this too is the point of the analysis in Chapters 3 and 4, where we saw the Tunisian and US government releasing images which sought to resonate with the populace. These images were specifically deployed to play on the affective life of the populace.
32 In a slightly different vein, Andrew Pilsch's paper 'Lachrymator: Persuasion's Tear Gas', delivered to the 17th Biennial RSA Conference in 2016, is particularly useful in thinking through the sort of Latourian agency of the billowing clouds of tear gas.
33 Benjamin, 'Critique of Violence'; see also James Martel, *Divine Violence: Walter Benjamin and the Eschatology of Sovereignty* (Routledge, 2011); Giorgio Agamben, *Means without End: Notes on Politics* (University of Minnesota Press, 2000).
34 Lily Kuo and Verna Yu, 'Where Were the Police? Hong Kong Outcry after Masked Thugs Launch Attack', *The Guardian* (22/07/2019) available https://www.theguardian.com/world/2019/jul/22/where-were-the-police-hong-kong-outcry-after-masked-thugs-launch-attack (viewed on 30/03/2020).
35 Protester-friendly candidates swept the board, taking all but one of the local councils: Emma Graham-Harrison and Verna Yu, 'Hong Kong Voters Deliver Landslide Victory for Pro-democracy Campaigners', *The Guardian* (25/11//2019) https://www.theguardian.com/world/2019/nov/24/hong-kong-residents-turn-up-for-local-elections-in-record-numbers (viewed 30/03/2020).

36 Mat Booth, Dayu Zhang, Wallis Wang, 'Hong Kong "Christmas Shopping" Protests', *South China Morning Post* (15/12/2019) https://www.scmp.com/video/hong-kong/3042200/hong-kong-christmas-shopping-protests (viewed on 30/03/2020).
37 Ernst Jünger is perhaps the apogee of this sort of logic, whereby the violence and blood of war are necessary evils in the emergence of a new civilisation. His war diaries insist that 'war is confirmed as a sacrifice that forms the foundation of a new order'. Elisabeth Krimmer, *The Representation of War in German Literature* (CUP, 2010), 83.
38 Jean-Luc Nancy, *The Inoperative Community* (University of Minnesota Press, 1991).
39 Stephanie Nebehay, '1.5 million Muslims Could Be Detained in China's Xinjiang: Academic', *Reuters* (13/03/2019) https://www.reuters.com/article/us-china-xinjiang-rights/15-million-muslims-could-be-detained-in-chinas-xinjiang-academic-idUSKCN1QU2MQ (viewed on 30/03/2020).
40 Kier Simmons, 'Inside Chinese Camps Thought to Be Detaining a Million Muslim Uighurs', *NBC News* (04/10/2019) https://www.nbcnews.com/news/world/inside-chinese-camps-thought-detain-million-muslim-uighurs-n1062321 (viewed on 30/03/2020).

19

ENMITY AND THE ATMOSPHERE OF VIOLENCE

We begin to think about the affective situation in which protest and revolt emerge – we closely read Fanon's atmospheric account of the 'atmosphere of violence' of anti-colonial struggle – enmity is produced in the state of unrest.

On the 20th of October 2019, the Chilean president Sebastián Piñera addressed the nation: 'We are at war against a powerful, implacable enemy that has no respect for anything or anybody'.[1] An other was amongst the Chilean people, an alien force that Piñera called *los encapuchados* (the '*hooded ones*'). This alien force had 'a degree of organization, logistics, typical of a criminal organization', and worse still, this 'powerful enemy' *was willing to use* '*violence without any limits*'.[2] He created a vacant faceless figure of absolute enmity in response to the school kids who were organising a fare evasion campaign to protest increases public transport fares. For Piñera and his supporters, this faceless enemy who deployed a limitless violence required nothing less than a state of emergency.[3] Tanks rolled down the avenues, tear gas and rubber bullets fired into the growing crowds. But as Piñera was about to find out, sometimes those faceless *encapuchados* are only the tip of the ice berg. Sometimes a great swathe of the populace will turn on its government. In this moment the affective life of the populace began to resolve into a state of enmity. Between the action of the fare dodgers and the response of the army, a new social force began to resonate. Achille Mbembe's description of the society of enmity in *Necropolitics* is readily transposed to this situation:

> A disconcerting figure of ubiquity, the enemy is henceforth more dangerous by being everywhere: without face, name or place. If the enemy has a face, it is only a *veiled face, the simulacrum of a face*. And if the enemy has a name, this might be only a borrowed name, a false name whose primary

> function is dissimulation. Such an enemy advances, at times masked, at other times openly; among us, around us, and even within us, ready to emerge in the middle of the day or in the heart of the night, each time his apparition threatening the annihilation of our way of life, our very existence.[4]

Piñera deployed the army on the streets and Chile erupted.

A simple parallel exists here between Piñera's characterisation of the *encapuchados* and the unrest in Hong Kong. The masks used by protesters became a key point of intervention for the government. As we saw in the last chapter, protests broke out in June over proposed legislation on extradition. Hong Kong's chief executive, Carrie Lam, characterised the protesters as 'violent radicals who have used the extradition bill drama as a pretext to foment "revolution"'.[5] As the protests escalated, so too did the policing reaction. Creeping towards an all-out emergency declaration, Lam deployed a 1922 emergency regulation to ban face masks in association with any form of public assembly. On the day of the emergency announcement Lam was cautious in her language – the use of colonial emergency provisions was deeply unpopular and seemed to confirm the protesters' arguments about creeping authoritarianism. But after the face mask regulation was declared unconstitutional, Lam reverted to the language of enmity: the faceless protesters were 'enemies of the people'.[6]

The enmity that emerges between the protesters and the state seems such an obvious place to finish this book. Of course they hate each other, you might say. But I want to suggest that there is much more to this enmity than it might initially appear. As we saw at the beginning of this part, the 'surprise' that the state and protesters feel, at the unfolding of unrest, sensitises us to the new social force that emerges in the moment of unrest. This social force was not just a secret before it emerged; it didn't exist as such. In the moment of unrest the affective life of the populace begins to resolve into a new patterning. In the state of unrest, the opacity of the affective life of the populace begins to dissipate (even momentarily) and there is suddenly a more transparent relation of aggression between parts of society and the state. Perhaps the greatest account of this process that I have come across in writing this book over the last decade has been Fanon's psycho-affective account of 'the atmosphere of violence'. Fanon is well known as a theorist of enmity. This enmity is usually understood through the racial division of the colonial space. In the map of the colonial and native cities, Fanon finds the perfect instantiation of the racial ordering of the colony. This racial ordering gives clarity to the politics of enmity that emerge in the struggle. But what is less rarely emphasised is the importance of the affective state of unrest in *producing* the enmity that already exists. The racial order of the colony is already given, but as Fanon shows over and again, the insults and anxieties that it produces are turned inwards. The native suffers psychotically for her place in the colonial order. At the beginning of *The Wretched of the Earth*, Fanon explains how this might be reversed. He explains how the division of native and colonial can be made into an operative structure that might spur people on to the difficult task of anti-colonial liberation. In other words, it is by the creation of a state of unrest that the enmity between the colonial and the native is operationalised.

Fanon's account begins with a protest. 'When the political leader summons the people to a meeting, there could be said to be blood in the air'.[7] The political leaders of the anti-colonial movement seek to strengthen their hand by calling for a popular show of force. The colonised come to the streets, showing their force of numbers. These leaders, however, are 'mainly preoccupied with a "show" of force'; they do not want to *use* the force of the crowd.[8] Yet, there is an important excess at play here. The crowd's energies are not limited to fulfilling the leader's desires: 'The excitement that is fostered – the comings and goings, the speech making, the crowds, the police presence, the military might, the arrests and the deportation of leaders – all this agitation gives the people the impression the time has come for them to do something'.[9] By gathering as a crowd the excesses of desire and belief are suddenly made present. Their vitality seems to bubble over, beyond the power of the leaders. There are forces of resistance and revolution that are not containable. The leaders are worried about this excess. They do not call for more protest. Instead they seek to instil calm. They block the popular energy. Sorel would sympathise here with Fanon. These leaders' positions are, to some extent at least, based on what they perceive to be their duty to maintain social peace. If they can harness the popular anger, while holding it in check, they will increase their standing. The colonial power will have to deal with them because of the threat of unleashing the flow of brutal energy from below.

Fanon suggests that when this flow of passions on the street is obstructed by its leaders, a second sort of affective flow emerges. 'In order to maintain their stamina and their revolutionary capabilities, the people also resort to retelling certain episodes in the life of the community'.[10] Myths and popular histories of the heroic outlaw emerge, the stories of national resistance against foreign invasion are revived once more. Fanon implicitly contrasts the struggle myths with those that emerge because of the (repressed) rage at the colonial system. These rage myths and ritualised dances stand in for 'the No that [the colonised] dare not voice, the murders they dare not commit'.[11] The struggle myths, on the other hand, deepen and mature the movement. The emergence of these stories indexes the people's preparations 'to march again, to break the lull introduced by colonialism and make History'.[12] The myths mediate the affective intensity that the crowds had manifested, continuing it beyond the space and atmospheres of the moment.

It is an external event that unblocks the affective flow in Fanon's account: the colonised are primed and ready when a new hope (a potentiality, an opening of the situation) lends a new possibility to their aestheticised resistance, re-intensifying the potentiality of the situation. The news of the successes of other anti-colonial movements leaks out. These events resonate with the populace, shifting their energies. The Vietnamese victory against the French at Dien Bien

Phu becomes a victory for every colonised people: 'A Dien Bien Phu was now within reach of every colonized subject'.[13]

> Colonized peoples are not alone. Despite the efforts of colonialism, their frontiers remain permeable to news and rumours. They discover that violence is atmospheric, it breaks out sporadically, and here and there sweeps away the colonial regime. The success of this violence plays not only an informative role but also an operative one.[14]

The possibility of success is there, a possibility floating in the air above each colony: 'This pervading atmosphere of violence affects not just the colonized but also the colonizers who realize the number of latent Dien Bien Phu's. The colonial governments are therefore gripped in a genuine wholesale panic'.[15] The external events *crystallise* the state of unrest.[16] The 'atmosphere of violence' then intensifies; 'the colonized subject identifies his enemy, puts a name to all of his misfortunes, and casts all his exacerbated hatred and rage in this new direction'.[17] In this, the atmosphere of violence takes on an immanent corporeality. Fanon describes this with an irresistible poetry as 'rippling under the skin'.[18] Atmospheres are not simply out there in that square or room; they get under your skin, agitating the body and driving it to attune.[19] They infect the body.

'But how', Fanon asks, 'do we get from the atmosphere of violence to setting violence in motion? What blows the lid?'[20] Here we reach the sticking point for many, as they read Fanon. The conservative response (shared by many liberals)[21] is that his work – particularly *The Wretched of the Earth* – legitimates anti-colonial violence. Like Sorel's *Reflections on Violence*, Fanon's later work is damned as a bloodthirsty manifesto for anti-colonial mass murder. But in fact, violence in Fanon is part of an economy of force which pervades the colonised world.[22] As Cornell and Seely put it: 'every day-to-day activity *is* violence and cannot be otherwise in the colonized world'.[23] In an extended description they explain:

> Fanon over and again tells us that colonialism is violence: every aspect of daily life is disruptive and this disruption is robbed of any symbolic meaning. You can be grabbed off the street and thrown into prison for no reason at all other than that you are black and white people felt threatened by you walking with your hands in your pockets. Your partner can be raped because someone in a nearby township dared to organize a demonstration and the colonizers wanted to issue a warning. You can be raped because your husband joined the armed struggle and you did not even know it – you can be raped simply because the colonizers felt like having 'sex' and you were there. Your children can be shot simply because they were on the beach in your occupied territory playing soccer, and their bodies stored in ice cream freezers because the morgues have reached capacity. And you can make no sense of this violence because it is not attributable to anything you can do, imagine, or symbolize. The violence of the colonial situation

> therefore breaks up any 'imaginary domain' in which a person is allowed to configure her own bodily integrity.[24]

Violence invades and perverts the social order, stripping the colonised 'of their language, their intellectual heritage and their symbolic forms'.[25] The 'colonized are ... stripped of their own world'.[26] There is violence everywhere in the realignment of desires and beliefs necessary to sustain the colonial order, and it leads to a sort of 'enforced psychosis' among the colonised.[27] Fanon uses the term 'atmosphere of violence' to signify the complex nature of this violence. There is a violent manipulation of desires and beliefs; there is a symbolic violence that tears the colonised from their language and cultural forms; and of course, there is the material violence that is a regular phenomenon for some and an ever-present threat for all.

We might think of this as the space through which the boomerang (of Arendt and Césaire) flies, before returning to the metropole from which it was originally cast. The reader will recall Césaire's observation that 'colonization ... dehumanizes even the most civilized man ... that the colonizer, who in order to ease his conscience gets into the habit of seeing the other man as an animal accustoms himself to treating him like an animal, and tends objectively to transform himself into an animal'.[28] There is a colonial economy of force, and it is from this that the anti-colonial economy of force is born.[29] It is in this context that Fanon sees the importance of anti-colonial violence. For 'the West', anti-colonial resistance is violent *both* in the sense that it is rendered illegitimate by not emanating from a state authority *but also* because it must be brutal in the face of escalating colonial brutality. When Fanon describes it as an *atmosphere* of violence he points to the way in which violence seems to hang in the air. He identifies the latency, potentiality or virtuality of violence. It is 'operative' in the sense that it shapes the capacity of those within the atmosphere to act. The 'atmosphere of violence' increases the potentiality of the colonisers over the colonised, but at the same time it increases the potentiality of the colonised to overthrow the colonisers. Each new brutality adds to the belief and desire of the colonised to destroy the colonial order. Fanon identifies an 'atmosphere of violence' as the affective life of *both* colonial relations *and* anti-colonial struggle. It is a shared atmosphere, despite the asymmetry of its violence.

> First of all there is the fact that such a development [the increasing atmosphere of tension] has a certain impact on the colonist's state of bliss. The colonist who 'knows' the colonial subject realizes from several pointers that something is in the process of changing. The good 'natives' become scarce, silence falls when the oppressor approaches. Sometimes looks harden and attitudes and remarks are downright hostile. The nationalist parties become restless, call for more meetings, and, at the same time, security is increased and troop reinforcements are dispatched. The colonists,

> especially those isolated on their farms, are the first to become alarmed. They demand drastic measures.[30]

These are the capillary changes that Tarde identified in his microsociology. The mood hardens in those small encounters with the coloniser. The suppleness of the basic order of racial superiority is suddenly frozen. The colonisers feel their precarity. Their order feels brittle, and so they demand an intense police response. The great wager of the colonial project is that for long periods the atmosphere of subjection will hold the colonised in place. When the atmosphere shifts to embolden the colonised to explicitly refuse, only an extreme violence can contain them and return them to an atmosphere of subjection. So, the colonial authorities deploy the tactics and techniques that they have developed for precisely such occasions. They begin with a show of force: 'they arrest one or two leaders, organize military parades, manoeuvres and fly-overs. These demonstrations of military power, these sabre-rattling exercises, this smell of gunpowder which now fills the atmosphere does not intimidate the people. These bayonets and heavy gunfire strengthen their aggressiveness'.[31] Atmosphere for Fanon is a material sense. Here it is filled with the smell of cordite and the clatter of weapons. The colonised do not respond as the colonisers had intended. The colonial force has mis-understood the affective dynamics of the situation. The show of force which was designed to frighten the populace into submission instead intensifies the mood of violence.

At this point in Fanon's account, the atmosphere has become hyper-intense. The tension is quite palpable; it is in the fibres of the flesh in a way that is immediately perceptible. Fanon describes a spiral of action and reaction which intensifies (and changes) the atmospheric dynamics that were latent at the outset.

> A dramatic atmosphere sets in where everyone wants to prove he is ready for anything. It is under these circumstances that the gun goes off on its own for nerves are on edge, fear has set in, and everyone is trigger-happy. A trivial incident and the machine-gunning begins: you have a Setif in Algeria, the Central Quarries in Morocco, and Moramanga in Madagascar.[32]

A flashpoint! A moment of release! The competing flows of belief and desire (from the colonisers and the colonised) culminate in the actualisation of the atmosphere of violence. The latency snaps into a manifest state. The colonists turn their machine guns on the colonised, and the colonial tensions of the atmosphere of violence have turned to the anti-colonial war and colonial suppression, or they dissipate, only to return more intensely in weeks or months or years.

Fanon's 'atmosphere of violence' is very different to many of the atmospheres that we have seen before – the one litigated in the Jefferson Memorial, the crowd atmospheres understood by the public order police manuals, in the theories of Gustave Le Bon. Like Sorel, Fanon's account suggests that we could think about atmosphere as the patterning that is replicated in innumerable encounters. It is not just in a particular place, but like the analytics of morale, it extends on a national or regional scale. Renisa Mawani explains that Fanon 'conceptualizes the atmosphere to be a material product of the colonial encounter'.[33] The atmosphere emerges precisely from the types of subjection and violence practised upon the colonised. It emerges over time and across different colonial settings. It is the violence of these encounters that is common. It ripples beneath the skin of the colonised. Crucially, atmosphere also takes us beyond this corporeal idea of subjectification. The 'atmosphere of violence' is in-common. It both transcends particular bodies and encounters *and* it immanently suffuses each particular encounter of every body in the colonial space. The atmosphere of violence entwines all within the colony.

Through the course of *The Wretched of the Earth*, the valence of atmosphere gradually shifts: from the crowd who sense that 'blood is in the air' but are calmed; to the ripples of excitement and panic that reverberate through the colony with the news of Diem Bien Phu; to attempts to intimidate the colonised by the show of military force; to the dramatic and edgy atmosphere where the precipitating violence finally occurs. Quite clearly the feeling of the atmosphere, its emotional force, will shift in each of these moments. The crowded fervour of the initial protests is different to the atmosphere which reverberates with echoes of the colonists machine guns. But Fanon does not differentiate these moments. Quite the contrary, they are each captured under the 'atmosphere of violence'. In this way he suggests a relation between the general (affective milieu) and the particular. Atmosphere does the theoretical work of connecting different events spatially and temporally. This gives rise to a dynamic tension where the 'atmosphere of violence' can retain an apparently stable sense, while still causing and being effected by the changing situation.

In his preface to *The Wretched of the Earth*, Jean-Paul Sartre argued that violence names the 'process of history'. Sartre identified a direct line between Engels and Fanon, identifying only three theorists capable of drawing out the violent ruptures whereby history progresses. He wrote: 'if you set aside Sorel's fascist utterances, you will find that Fanon is the first since Engels to bring the processes of history into the clear light of day'. Ciccariello-Maher points out, however, that 'Sartre's dismissal of Sorel takes the paradoxical form of an affirmation, since he tacitly admits that Sorel falls within that exceptionally perceptive group of thinkers who recognized the role of violence in history'.[34] Thus, despite Sartre's dismissal, it is important to see something common between Fanon's *Wretched of the Earth* and Sorel's *Reflections on Violence*. As Ciccariello-Maher shows, enmity is the key to this articulation. In Fanon, this enmity is there in the colonial relation in black and white. It is a racialised line that divides the coloniser from the colonised. But colonial public order operates to supress any violence that might emerge because of it. The colonial order functions to turn aggression inwards. The atmosphere of violence is the affective condition in which the native externalises the hatred of this brutal order. In this sense, it produces that which was already there.

As with Sorel in Hong Kong, we have to be careful about simply transposing Fanon into contemporary scenes of unrest. Fanon's colonial atmosphere is a racialised affective structure which is not (or not simply) what is in question in Hong Kong or Chile. Without underplaying this difference, however, we can transpose Fanon's sense of unrest as a means of producing an affective state that was already there. Looking back now we see the contours of 2019's unrest in the 2014 Umbrella Movement, in the 2008 Chilean student movement, in the 'one country, two systems' model, in the post-Pinochet system which baked neoliberalism into the constitutional order, the 'atmosphere of violence' which emerged and intensified as Hong Kong and Chile saw protest and repression, etc. These are the spurs of enmity. This is the 'atmosphere of the storm' that Bataille saw in the first sentence of this book.[35] It is the way in which disorder and unrest generate new forms of resonance and intensity.

Notes

1 Terri Gordon-Zolov and Eric Zolov 'The Walls of Chile Speak of a Suppressed Rage', *The Nation* (07/11/2019) https://www.thenation.com/article/chile-protest-art/ (viewed on 19/03/2020).
2 Aislinn Laing, Natalia Ramos Miranda, 'Chile's Piñera Extends State of Emergency, Says "We Are at War"', *Reuters* (20/10/2019) https://uk.reuters.com/article/uk-chile-protests/chiles-pinera-extends-state-of-emergency-says-we-are-at-war-idUKKBN1WZ0F0 (viewed on 19/03/2020) (my emphasis).
3 The rhetoric seems to suggest a most extraordinary series of attacks on state infrastructure, but in reality this was a fare evasion campaign to protest a small increase in public transport fares. Initially, students would jam the fare-gates of stations open. After police escalated the force being deployed, there were a number of arson attacks on public transport infrastructure, exploding into a massive movement as Piñera declared his emergency. Setting aside the rights and wrongs of the Chilean unrest, we can very clearly see the discursive importance of the force/violence distinction.
4 Mbembe, *Necropolitics*, 49 (my emphasis).
5 Erin Hale, 'Be Water'.
6 Sarah Clarke, 'Hong Kong's Carrie Lam: Protestors Now People's Enemy', *Al Jazeera* (11/11/2019) https://www.aljazeera.com/news/2019/11/hong-kongs-carrie-lam-protesters-peoples-enemy-191111184126199.html (viewed on 19/03/2020). For an excellent examination of some of the politics of masking laws, see Jennifer Spiegel, 'Masked Protest in the Age of Austerity: State Violence, Anonymous Bodies, and Resistance "In the Red"', 41.4 *Critical Inquiry* (2015), 786.
7 Fanon, *The Wretched of the Earth* (Grove Press, New York: 2004), 29.
8 Ibid.
9 Ibid.
10 Ibid., 30.
11 Ibid., preface, liii.
12 Ibid., 31.
13 Ibid.
14 Ibid., 30.
15 Ibid., 31.
16 Fanon explains that in their panic, the colonists begin to decolonise: 'In answer to the strategy of a Dien Bien Phu defined by the colonized, the colonizer replies with the strategy of containment-respecting sovereignty of nations' (Ibid.).
17 Ibid.

18 Ibid.
19 Kathleen Stewart, 'Atmospheric Attunements', 29 *Environmental and Planning D: Society and Space* (2011), 445.
20 Ibid., 32.
21 There are too many different shades of this thought to begin to describe in this brief footnote, but for instance: Kenneth Taylor, 'Fanon, Violence and the Struggle Against Colonialism', *Philosophy Talk* (29/01/2018), https://www.philosophytalk.org/blog/fanon-violence-and-struggle-against-colonialism (viewed on 31/08/2019).
22 The reference here is loosely to the work of Patricia Owens *Economy of Force: Counter-Insurgency and the Historical Rise of the Social* (Cambridge: Cambridge University Press, 2015).
23 Drucilla Cornell and Stephen Seely, *The Spirit of Revolution: Beyond the Dead Ends of Man* (Polity Press, 2016), 96.
24 Ibid., 110.
25 Ibid., 103.
26 Ibid.
27 Ibid., 101.
28 Césaire, *Discourse on colonialism*, 41.
29 Owens, *Economy of Force.*
30 Fanon, *Wretched of the Earth*, 32.
31 Ibid.
32 Ibid. In Constance Farrington's original 1963 translation, these sentences read slightly differently: 'The atmosphere becomes dramatic, and everyone wishes to show that they are ready for anything. And it is in these circumstances that the guns go off by themselves, for nerves are jangled, fear reigns and everyone is trigger happy. A single commonplace incident is enough to start the machine-gunning: Setif in Algeria, the Central Quarries in Morocco, Moramanga in Madagascar' (Frantz Fanon, *The Damned* (Presence Africaine, Paris, 1963), 53).
33 Renisa Mawani, 'Atmospheric Pressures: On Race and Affect', York University Department of Sociology Annual Lecture (26/02/2019), unpublished draft.
34 George Ciccariello-Maher, 'To Lose Oneself in the Absolute: Revolutionary Subjectivity in Sorel and Fanon', 5.3 *Human Architecture* (2007), 102.
35 George Bataille, *Visions of Excess*, 162.

20

EXCURSUS 4

The state of unrest

The state of unrest is a disturbance in the affective life of the populace. It operates at many levels at once; it is there in the atmospheres of the 'public order situation'; it is in the ambiences and rhythms of the city as the streets clear and the faint smell of tear gas and smoke waft; it burrows into the anatomy of national feeling, pulling the strings of attachment with fear and hope of the new; and it resonates nationally and sometimes internationally as countries with similar situations begin to reverberate together. The state of unrest is not a static form but made up of multiple flows of affect. It is experienced differently by people, depending on mood, situation, status, etc. But actually, the state of unrest is most important for the sovereign order. As we saw in Chapter 11, an atmosphere of calm normality is central to the affective sense of public order. Public order has to disappear into the background to be effective in shaping the beliefs and desires of the populace. The state of unrest undermines this calm normalisation; it makes public order *the* question. It is a *major* challenge to the sovereign order because the field of affective flows that had gathered around the sovereign order begin to realign. The methods of governing public order shift gear from background shaping and surveillance, to emergency provisions. In this state of flux, new atmospheres, ambiences and affective flows that exceed the sovereign order begin to coalesce. Now that public order has to be enforced, the populace is increasingly drawn into a state of enmity. In the ordinary course of things, the affective life of the populace is opaque; it is indeterminate. What is most remarkable about the state of unrest, however, is that in this moment of disorder the affective life of the populace becomes *less* opaque. The tacit approval or habitual obedience that the sovereign order normally relies upon is disrupted. Crowds gather demanding change, refusing to be moved, returning again and again to disrupt and undermine. Some or many of the populace refuse. They begin to say, 'No'.

Carl Schmitt's *Constitutional Theory* underlines precisely this dynamic. For Schmitt, the people are not a 'stable, organised organ'. However, they must be able to express their constituent power. He writes: 'Even if they have a determinative will only in less definitive moments and express themselves recognizably, they are nevertheless capable of and in a position for such willing and are able to say yes or no to the fundamental questions of their political existence'.[1] The people must make its will known, but it cannot be by way of 'a normatively regulated process', because this would place the normative order above the people.[2] Instead, in a slightly perplexing way Schmitt comments: 'the will of the people to provide themselves a constitution can only be made evident through the act itself',[3] through the act of willing, that is. As Costas Douzinas puts it, this 'is a will that wills what does not exist or what is prohibited, a will that finds its force in itself and its effect in a world not yet determined'.[4] Schmitt then introduces the concept of 'acclamation':

> The natural form of the direct expression of the people's will is the assembled multitude's declaration of their consent or their disapproval, the *acclamation*. In modern, large states, the acclamation, which is a natural and necessary life expression of every people, has changed its external form. In these states, it expresses itself as 'public opinion'. However, the people can always say yes or no, consent or reject, and their yes or no becomes all the more simple and elementary, the more it is a matter of a fundamental decision on their own existence in its entirety. In times of peaceful order, these types of expression are rare and unnecessary. That no special will is perceived expressed simply signifies the enduring consent to the existing constitution. In critical times, the no that directs itself *against* an existing constitution can be clear and decisive only as negation, there is a direct, independent affirmation of a form of existence, which is contradictory and evident to others.[5]

Schmitt's reference to 'public opinion' is interesting because he later explains that it should not be understood as the sum of all individual votes. He imagines an apparatus which would allow every person to 'continuously express his opinions on political questions' 'without ever leaving his apartment'.[6] This, he explains would not capture 'public opinion'. It would merely be an aggregation of all of the many private opinions. For Schmitt, 'public opinion' exists in 'an "unorganised" form. Precisely like [the] acclamation [of the multitude]'.[7] At this point, Schmitt gestures in the direction of the affective life of the populace. It does not arise

> in secret out of nothing. It is influenced and even made by parties or groups. Nevertheless, that can never be recognized legally and made official, and, in some sense, it remains uncontrolled. In every democracy, there are parties, speakers, and demagogues, from the [*prostatai*] of the Athenians up to

> the *bosses* in American democracy. Moreover there are the press, film, and other methods of psycho-technical handling of great masses of people. All that escapes a comprehensive set of norms.[8]

In other words, there are apparatuses for managing the affective life of the populace, but nonetheless, it remains 'unorganised' and opaque.

'Acclamation' is essential to sovereignty. As Agamben shows, it is constitutive of the affective sphere of 'glory', 'a veritable sphere that is constitutive of sovereignty'.[9] We have seen this in a very different way in the first part of the book, which we might think of now as a series of glorious scenes. But as Schmitt says these moments of positive acclamation where a populace reaffirms their affective commitment to the state order are rare. They are unnecessary precisely because in the ordinary course of things, habitual relations leave the sovereign order unchallenged. But Schmitt's reflection on acclamation also shows that the glorification of the sovereign order operates on *the same level* as the multitude which refuses it. This is the crucial point of my analysis of the state of unrest. As we have seen in the third and fourth parts of this book, the affective conditions of this refusal operate on the same level as the affective conditions of habitual obedience to, and positive affirmation of, the sovereign order.

Schmitt's account emphasises an 'elementary' idea of 'the will'. This is a key fulcrum around which his fundamental commitment to decisionism revolves. Because it is a basic building block of his political theology Schmitt can skip over both the question of crowds and the question of atmosphere. He avoids what he would see as the rudimentary practical question about which actually existing acclamation expresses the will of the people. And he avoids what motive force drives the acclamation of a collective will. Thus, both with and against Schmitt, I want to insist upon the importance of the state of unrest where the affective life of the populace momentarily and partially resolves itself against the sovereign order. That affective life that was unknowable in its plurality and fluidity for so long begins to gather into a more determinate form. *This is not a 'will'.* It is an affective force that is manifested by the crowds. And it is an affective environment in which the sovereign order begins to fail. As Joshua Clover puts it: 'Riot and crisis arrive together, each the herald of the other'.[10] Both the affective environment and the affective interventions of the crowds are signs of unrest. After the protests or the revolution, the jurists will gather and talk about 'will', but that is only a handle to grasp something that is much too slippery for lawyers.

In the state of popular unrest, the state of enmity that emerges is very clear for all to see. A key part of the affective life of the populace hardens into a refusal – an enmity between the state and a portion of its populace. The question for the state becomes whether it can be isolated or whether it will resonate with large swathes of the populace. They find themselves asking how contagious this state of enmity might be. They are not worried that everyone will renounce the sovereign order. But that with enough public manifestation of refusal, the feeling begins to grow that the government lacks control. In this moment, the populace begins to look for other structures and groupings that might carry their ardour. As this sentiment grows, the populace increasingly becomes ungovernable because the simple unquestioning habits of being governed are interrupted. The government think about the pandemic of ungovernability. They fear the moment when they will have completely lost control. If that occurs, they must either step aside or declare war on the populace.

Notes

1 Carl Schmitt, *Constitutional Theory* (Duke University Press: Durham, 2008), 131.
2 Ibid.
3 Ibid.
4 Douzinas, *Philosophy and Resistance in the Crisis*, 86.
5 Schmitt, Constitutional Theory, 131.
6 Ibid., 274.
7 Ibid., 275.
8 Ibid.
9 Agamben, *The Kingdom and the Glory*, 177.
10 Clover, *Riot, Strike, Riot*, 129.

CONCLUSION

Notes from the tumult

The book was finished. A few footnotes needed to be checked. That was all. And then Covid-19 entered its early pandemic stage. Suddenly, the affective life of the world's populaces was cast into disorder. This was a tumult but not the disorder that I have spent the last twenty chapters analysing. Covid-19 threatened to overwhelm the health system of every state. The crisis in the Chinese province of Wuhan, in Iran and in Northern Italy showed what might happen. Increasingly, it appeared that this virus had a relatively low mortality rate (around 1%, perhaps even lower). But it was highly infectious. Initial numbers from China and Italy suggested that as many as 20% of those infected might need hospitalisation, and perhaps 10% would need intensive care and ventilation. The problem with Covid-19, then, was not essentially its complete novelty. This was not a virus like AIDS. The problem was that the volume of patients would quickly fill the available intensive care beds. Health care systems that had suffered decades of underfunding and privatisation were not in any position to care for the sheer number of the sick. In these circumstances, initial mortality rates in Northern Italy were in excess of 8%. With various European governments talking about 60% of the population being infected, the death toll would be in the millions. To try to slow the spread of the disease, governments around the world declared various sorts of emergency and shut down social and economic relations.

In late March, Agamben briefly reflected on the affective reactions to the pandemic in Italy. While his initial writings in early March had seemed to resort to cheap conspiracy theories,[1] by the end of the month he had begun to make more sense. In 'Reflection on the Plague', he wondered about 'the ease with which the whole of society [in Italy] has united in feeling itself afflicted by a plague'.[2] It was certainly remarkable how the usual reaction to exceptional governmental interventions (like protests) had not occurred in Italy or indeed in most countries. Instead, the populace seemed to actively desire the extreme isolation measures.

Agamben suggested that this demonstrates that the '[c]onditions of life had evidently become such that a sudden sign [like a plague] was all that it took for the situation to appear for what it was – intolerable'.[3] From this he drew a number of more tenuous arguments about religion and bare life, but I suggest that he is absolutely right both about the intense resolution of affective life and about the way that Covid-19 crystallises this change. Like a moment of popular unrest, the surprise comes from the fact that the disorder has crystallised a new social force. The affective life of the populace has shifted suddenly, and in ways that were unimaginable before the event. Whether this is because the populace has internalised the state of exception, as Agamben claims, or because there is something particularly resonant about a pandemic that seems to target the old and vulnerable is unclear.

In the UK, the response seems to rely upon many of the elements examined throughout the book. At 8 pm on Sunday, the 5th of April, Queen Elisabeth II addressed the nation. She sought to stage a sovereign encounter, a moment where the sovereign could deploy her *auctoritas* to settle the populace, to lift their horizon beyond the situation.[4] The address sutured together three different affective temporalities: the spirit of the Second World War, the contemporary actions of essential workers (especially the national health service) and a future where the virus would have passed. The Queen asked each viewer to imagine a time in their future when they would look back at their actions.[5] This temporality of the future selves looking back mirrored her own contemporary reflection on the spirit of the Second World War. She suggested that those future selves would look back with pride at the 'self-discipline', 'quiet good-humoured resolve' and 'fellow-feeling' of the Coronavirus generation.[6] The address was an attempt to steady the national mood, to deploy the Queen's aura of unchanging stability to affect the populace. It finished with a final flourish: 'We should take comfort', she said, 'that while we may have more still to endure, better days will return: we will be with our friends again; we will be with our families again; we will meet again'.[7] She seemed to say: 'This will have been the time when we defeated the virus!' Soon after, the news broke that Boris Johnson had been taken into hospital, where he was later transferred to an intensive care unit. This clarified further the purpose of the Queen's address. She was deployed by the government to intervene at the moment of their greatest anxiety, when the risk of panic was at its greatest. She insisted that this time 'will be remembered as an expression of our national spirit'.[8]

Alongside the appearance of the sovereign, the British response to the pandemic has been marked by growing anxieties about the 'new' public order. The governmental apparatus aims at the object-target of 'morale' and its opposite, 'panic'.[9] Morale is articulated as a unified and cooperative populace struggling in a national effort. In an everyday sense, this means hand-washing, only shopping for essentials, clapping for essential workers every Thursday, exercising once a day and generally staying at home. Panic is coded as a disorderly individualism which will require more strict governmental intervention. It is to be found in empty supermarket shelves and in figures of social irresponsibility – kids coughing at health workers,[10] inadequately spaced shopping queues or parks, people lying in the sun.[11] The police are key to the socially distant public order. They intensify surveillance and institute check-points. In the UK there has anger as they over-reach themselves: people were stopped by the police as they shop for Easter eggs;[12] stop and search is applied to shopping trolleys. In all of this, there is a redrawing of the object-target of public order. The affective management of public space begins to descend on those (formerly deemed to be) 'honest citizens', and no longer just the 'suspect populations'. But this broadening of the 'suspect population' also involves the intensification of its racialised and class-based dimensions.

Public order is a key terrain of the sovereign order's reaction to the pandemic. As I finish this book in early April 2020, there are already signs that this massive upheaval in social reproduction might lead to new ruptures in the management of affective life. As governments mutter about the need for draconian austerity after the crisis, an ambience seems to grow. Captured by the slogan projected on buildings during its unrest in Chile, and later scrawled in graffiti on walls of Hong Kong during the pandemic, it feels like: after this 'we can't return to normal, because the normal that we had was precisely the problem'.[13]

In the end, this book makes a very simple point. Sovereignty is a structure which must remain meaningful to the populace. It operates within and upon the affective life of the populace. The sovereign order involves both as a distant sovereign figure who must be occasionally glorified and an intense form of management of the affective life of the populace. In tumultuous times, sometimes the populace begins to claw at the sovereign order. The temper of the people begins to rise. The state responds with ever more complex modes of force. They deploy exceptional violence, learned from the suppression of colonised bodies. As this intensifies, the negotiation and denouncements give way to gas, water cannon, horse charges and baton rounds. If these fail, the state resorts to live fire, torture and an abstract brutality. But this violence often leads to an intensification of the enmity that had been emerging. As more and more are touched by the tumult, the populace is drawn into the public order situation. And everywhere people begin to think about a public order that is not determined by the state; they begin to think of different orders that belong to and are determined by the public. In other words the state of unrest opens up an imagination of different orders. It unblocks the desires and beliefs, for so long tangled up in the sovereign order. No longer do these desires and beliefs relate to the extant sovereign order. But now they begin to focus on different ways of being together. And on the streets, crowds begin to perform these other orders. This book has developed a theory of sovereignty, an analysis of atmospheres of sovereignty and the affective public order that the sovereign order rests upon. It has also developed a theory of protest, one that does not simply valorise social movement or rights to public speech or assembly. This book has been about the crowds that are at the heart of popular protest, and the way in which they intervene within the everyday structures of sovereignty.

Notes

1 Giorgio Agamben, 'The Invention of an Epidemic' (26/02/2020), *European Journal of Psychoanalysis* http://www.journal-psychoanalysis.eu/coronavirus-and-philosophers / (viewed on the 27/03/2020). He wrote that Covid-19 was just like flu but that the media and authorities were doing everything that they could to spread panic. Quickly, there were a series of critiques and comments, Jean Luc-Nancy wrote 'Viral Exception', Roberto Esposito 'Cured to the Bitter End', and Sergio Benvenuto's 'Forget about Agamben' is particularly pointed. All available *European Journal of Psychoanalysis* http://www.journal-psychoanalysis.eu/coronavirus-and-philosophers / (viewed on the 27/03/2020). There were also a number of important critical legal responses, particularly Tim Christaens 'Must Society Be Defended from Agamben?' (https://criticallegalthinking.com/2020/03/26/must-society-be-defended-from -agamben/ (viewed on the 27/03/2020) and Panagiotis Sotiris 'Against Agamben: Is a Democratic Biopolitics Possible?' https://criticallegalthinking.com/2020/03/14/ against-agamben-is-a-democratic-biopolitics-possible/ (viewed on 27/02/2020).

2 Giorgio Agamben, 'Reflection on the Plague' https://medium.com/@ddean3000/ reflections-on-the-plague-giorgio-agamben-b616763b6259 (viewed on 27/03/2020).

3 Ibid.

4 In the media much was made of the exceptionality of this encounter with the sovereign. She had only ever made four previous televised addresses: the first Gulf War, on the death of Princess Diana, the death of the Queen Mother and her own Diamond Jubilee.

5 She said: 'I hope in the years to come everyone will be able to take pride in how they responded to this challenge. And those who come after us will say the Britons of this generation were as strong as any'. 'The Queen's Coronavirus Speech Transcript: "We Will Succeed and Better Days Will Come"' (*The Telegraph*, 05/04/2020) https://ww w.telegraph.co.uk/news/2020/04/05/queens-coronavirus-speech-full-will-succeed -better-days-will/ (viewed on 06/04/2020).

6 Ibid.

7 Ibid.

8 Ibid.

9 Here we can obviously think of Ben Anderson's analysis of morale and panic, discussed in Chapter 4, but also Anna Gibbs, 'Panic! Affect Contagion, Mimesis and Suggestion: In the Social Field', 14.2 *Cultural Studies Review* (2008), 130; and Jackie Orr, *Panic Diaries: A Genealogy of Panic Disorder* (Durham: Duke University Press, 2006).

10 'Police Stop Group of Youths for Coughing at NHS Workers', *The Warrington Guardian* (28/03/2020) https://www.warringtonguardian.co.uk/news/18341961 .police-stop-group-youths-coughing-nhs-workers/ (viewed on 30/03/2020); Tom Duffy, 'Kids Joke "We've Got Coronavirus" while Coughing in NHS Workers' Faces', *The Liverpool Echo* (28/03/2020) https://www.liverpoolecho.co.uk/news/kid s-saying-coronavirus-cough-nhs-17999054 (viewed 30/03/2020).

11 Jason Burke, 'South African Police Fire Rubber Bullets at Shoppers amid Lockdown', *The Guardian* (28/03/2020) https://www.theguardian.com/world/2020/mar/28 /south-africa-police-rubber-bullets-shoppers-covid-19-lockdown (viewed on 30/03/2020).

12 BBC News. 'Coronavirus: Easter egg Crackdown over Essential Status "Wrong"' (30/03/2020) https://www.bbc.co.uk/news/business-52090441

13 Stefan Kalmár, *The ICA Daily* (27/03/2020) https://www.ica.art/ica-daily/satur day-28-march-2020 (viewed on 30/03/2020); Vijay Prashad, 'We Won't Go Back to Normal, because Normal Was Part of the Problem', *Monthly Review Online* (27/03/2020) https://mronline.org/2020/03/27/we-wont-go-back-to-normal-be cause-normal-was-the-problem/ (viewed on 11/04/2020).

BIBLIOGRAPHY

Adey, Peter, 'Security atmospheres or the crystallisation of worlds', 32 *Environment and Planning. part D, Society and Space* (2014), 834.

Adorno, Theodore, and Elias Canetti, 'Elias Canetti: Discussion with Theodore Adorno' 45 *Thesis Eleven* (1996), 2.

Agamben, Giorgio, *Homo Sacer: Sovereign Power and Bare Life* (Stanford: Stanford University Press, 1998).

Agamben, Giorgio, 'K', in Justin Clemens, Nicholas Heron, and Alex Murray (eds), *The Work of Giorgio Agamben: Law, Literature Life* (Edinburgh: Edinburgh University Press, 2008), 25.

Agamben, Giorgio, *Means without End: Notes on Politics* (Minneapolis: University of Minnesota Press, 2000).

Agamben, Giorgio, 'Reflection on the plague', https://medium.com/@ddean3000/reflections-on-the-plague-giorgio-agamben-b616763b6259 (viewed on 27/03/2020).

Agamben, Giorgio, *State of Exception* (Chicago: University of Chicago Press, 2005).

Agamben, Giorgio, 'The Invention of an Epidemic', *European Journal of Psychoanalysis* (26/02/2020) http://www.journal-psychoanalysis.eu/coronavirus-and-philosophers / (viewed on the 27/03/2020).

Agamben, Giorgio, *The Kingdom and the Glory* (Stanford: Stanford University Press, 2011).

Agamben, Giorgio, *The Signature of All Things* (New York: Zone Books, 2009).

Agamben, Giorgio, *What Is an Apparatus? And Other Essays* (Stanford: Stanford University Press, 2009), 3.

Ahmed, Sara, 'Happy objects', in Melissa Gregg and Gregory Seigworth (eds), *The Affect Theory Reader* (Durham: Duke University Press, 2010).

Ahmed, Sara, *The Cultural Politics of Emotion* (Edinburgh: Edinburgh University Press, 2014).

Allen, Carelton Kemp, *The Queen's Peace* (London: Stevens and Sons, 1953).

Anand, Dibesh, 'The violent vocabulary of policing, *Critical Legal Thinking* (13/12/2010) http://criticallegalthinking.com/2010/12/13/the-violent-vocabulary-of-policing/

(Viewed on 04/04/2020), See also Neal, Opitz, and Zebrowski, 'Capturing protest in urban environments', 1055.

Anker, Elisabeth, *Orgies of Feeling: Melodrama and the Politics of Feeling* (Durham: Duke University Press, 2014).

Applegate, Rex, *Riot Control: Materiel and Techniques* (PA: Stackpole Books, 1969).

Aradau, Claudia, and Rens van Munster, 'Exceptionalism and the 'War on Terror': Criminology meets international relations', 49.5 *British Journal of Criminology* (2009), 686.

Arendt, Hannah, *The Origins of Totalitarianism* (New York: Meridian Books, 1958).

Ascoll, David, *The Queen's Peace: Origins and Development of the Metropolitan Police 1829–1979* (London: Hamish Hamilton, 1979).

Austin, John, *Lectures on Jurisprudence or The Philosophy of Positive Law* (London: John Murray, 1869).

Ben Anderson, *Encountering Affect: Capacities, Apparatuses, Conditions* (Farnham: Ashgate, 2014), 39.

Ben Anderson, and James Ash 'Atmospheric Methods', In Phillip Vanni (ed), *Non-Representational Methodologies* (Abingdon: Routledge, 2015).

Badiou, Alain, *The Rebirth of History* (London: Verso, 2012).

Bailey, Richard, 'Up against the wall: Bare life and resistance in Australian immigration detention', 20 *Law and Critique* (2009), 113.

Barry, Andrew, 'Tarde's method: Between statistics and experimentation', in Matei Candea (ed), *The Social After Gabriel Tarde: Debates and Assessments* (London: Routledge, 2010), 177–189.

Barry, Andrew, and Nigel Thrift, 'Gabriel Tarde: Imitation, invention and economy', 36.4 *Economy and Society* (2007), 509–525, 514.

Bataille, George, *Visions of Excess: Selected Writings 1927–1939* (Minneapolis: University of Minnesota Press, 1985).

BBC News, 'Coronavirus: Easter egg crackdown over essential status 'wrong'', (30/03/2020) https://www.bbc.co.uk/news/business-52090441.

Beasley-Murray, Jon, *PostHegemony: Political Theory and Latin America* (Minneapolis: University of Minnesota Press, 2010).

Behkalam, Kaya, 'Augmented Archive', http://augmented-archive.net (viewed 30/03/2020).

Benite, Zvi Ben-Don, Stefanos Geroulanos, and Nicole Jerr (eds), *The Scaffolding of Sovereignty: Global and Aesthetic Perspectives on the History of a Concept* (New York: Columbia University Press, 2017).

Benjamin, Walter, 'Critique of Violence', in *Reflections: Essays, Aphorism, Autobiographical Writings* (New York: Schocken Books, 1986), 280.

Bentham, Jeremy, *A Fragment on Government* (NJ: The Lawbook Exchange, 2001).

Benvenuto, Sergio, 'Forget about Agamben', *European Journal of Psychoanalysis* (26/02/2020) http://www.journal-psychoanalysis.eu/coronavirus-and-philosophers / (viewed on the 27/03/2020).

Berlant, Lauren, *Cruel Optimism* (Durham: Duke University Press, 2011).

Berlant, Lauren, 'The commons: Infrastructures for troubling times', 34.3 *Environment and Planning D: Society and Space* (2016), 393.

Berlant, Lauren, *The Queen of America Goes to Washington* (Durham: Duke University Press, 1997).

Berlant, Lauren, and Jordan Greenwald, 'Affect in the end times: A conversation with Lauren Berlant', 20.2 *Qui Parle* (2012), 71.

Bishop, Kyle, *American Zombie Gothic* (Jefferson: MacFarland & Co, 2010).

Bitner, Mary Jo, 'Servicescapes: The impact of physical surroundings on customers and employees', 56.2 *Journal of Marketing* (2015), 57–71.

Blackman, Lisa, 'Reinventing psychological matters: The importance of the suggestive realm of Tarde's Ontology', 36.4 *Economy and Society* (2007), 574–596.

Booth, Mat, Dayu Zhang, Wallis Wang, 'Hong Kong 'Christmas shopping' protests', *South China Morning Post* (15/12/2019) https://www.scmp.com/video/hong-kong/3042200/hong-kong-christmas-shopping-protests (viewed on 30/03/2020).

Borch, Christian, *The Politics of Crowds: An Alternative History of Sociology* (Cambridge: Cambridge University Press, 2013).

Boyd, Robert, *The Office, Powers and Jurisdiction of His Majesty's Justices of the Peace and Commissioners of Supply* (Edinburgh: E Balfour, 1787).

Brennan, Teresa, *The Transmission of Affect* (Ithaca: Cornell University Press, 2004).

Brighenti, Andrea Mubi, 'Tarde, Canetti and Deleuze on crowds and packs', 10.4 *Journal of Classical Sociology* (2010), 291.

British Guiana, *Drill Manual* (1945), The National Archives of the UK, CO 111/796/6.

British Guiana, *Riot Manual* 13 (1944), The National Archives of the UK, CO 111/796/6.

Broeker, Galen, *Rural Disorder and Police Reform in Ireland*: 1812–36 (Abingdon: Routledge, 1970).

Buck Morss, Susan, 'Compatings and loosenings', in Jeffrey Schnapp and Matthew Tiews (eds), *Crowds* (Stanford University Press, 2006).

Burke, Edmund, *Letters on a Regicide Peace, Volume 3* (Carmel, IN: Liberty Fund, 1999), 65. For an insightful examination of the corporeal and vital forces see Catherine Packham, *Eighteenth Century Vitalism: Bodies, Culture, Politics* (London: Palgrave Macmillan, 2012).

Burke, Edmund, *Philosophical Inquiry into the Origin of our Ideas of the Sublime and the Beautiful* (London: Thomas McLean, 1823).

Burke, Edmund, 'Reflection on the revolution in France, and on the proceedings in certain societies in London relative to that event', [1790] in Edmund Burke (ed), *Revolutionary Writings* (Cambridge: Cambridge University Press, 2014).

Burke, Edmund, *The Writings and Speeches of Edmund Burke, Volume II: Party, Parliament and the American Crisis 1766–1774* (Oxford: Clarendon Press, 1981).

Burke, Jason, 'South African police fire rubber bullets at shoppers amid lockdown', *The Guardian* (28/03/2020) https://www.theguardian.com/world/2020/mar/28/south-africa-police-rubber-bullets-shoppers-covid-19-lockdown (viewed on 30/03/2020).

Bushman, Richard, *The Refinement of America: Persons, Houses, Cities* (New York: Vintage Books, 1993).

Butler, Judith, *Notes Toward a Performative Theory of Assembly* (Cambridge, MA: Harvard University Press, 2016).

Butler, Judith, *The Force of Non-Violence* (London: Verso, 2020).

Callewaert, Staf, 'Foucault's concept of dispositif', in 1–2 *Praktiske Grunde* (2017), 29.

Canetti, Elias, *Crowds and Power* (New York: Viking Books, 1963).

Carlyle, Thomas, *Sartor Restatus: The Life and Opinions of Herr Teufelsdrockh* (1831) (Oxford: Oxford University Press, 2008).

Carson, Craig, 'The king's virtual body: Image, text and sovereignty in Edmund Burke's 'reflection on the revolution in France', 2.2 *Republic of Letters: A Journal for the Study of Knowledge, Politics and the Arts* (2011), 120.

Césaire, Aimé, *Discourse on Colonialism* (New York: New York University Press, 2000).

Chambers, Samuel, *The Lessons of Rancière* (Oxford University Press, 2014), 42.

Cheung, Gary Ka-wai, *Hong Kong's Watershed: The 1967 Riots* (Hong Kong: Hong Kong University Press, 2009).

Christaens, Tim, 'Must society be defended from Agamben?', https://criticallegalthinking.com/2020/03/26/must-society-be-defended-from-agamben/ (viewed on the 27/03/2020).

Christodoulidis, Emilios, 'Against substitution: The constitutional thinking of dissensus', in Martin Loughlin and Neil Walker, (eds), *The Paradox of Constitutionalism: Constituent Power and Constitutional Form* (Oxford: Oxford University Press, 2008).

Ciccariello-Maher, George, 'Identity against totality: The counterdiscourse of separation beyond the decolonial turn', (PhD Thesis, UC Berkeley https://escholarship.org/uc/item/3c66g2x0, 54.

Ciccariello-Maher, George, 'To lose oneself in the absolute: Revolutionary subjectivity in Sorel and Fanon, 5.3 *Human Architecture* (2007), 102.

Clark, Terry, 'Introduction', in Gabriel Tarde (ed), *On Communication & Social Influence: Selected Papers* (Chicago: University of Chicago Press, 1969).

Clarke, Sarah, 'Hong Kong's Carrie Lam: Protestors now people's enemy', *Al Jazeera* (11/11/2019) https://www.aljazeera.com/news/2019/11/hong-kongs-carrie-lam-protesters-peoples-enemy-191111184126199.html (viewed on 19/03/2020).

Clover, Joshua, *Riot, Strike, Riot: The New Era of Uprisings* (London: Verso, 2016).

Collings, David, *Monstrous Society: Reciprocity, Discipline and the Political Uncanny at the End of Early Modern England* (Lewisburg: Bucknell University Press, 2009).

Colón-Ríos, Joel, *Constituent Power and the Law* (Oxford: Oxford University Press, 2020).

Connolly, William, *A World of Becoming* (Durham: Duke University Press, 2011).

Cornell, Drucilla, and Stephen Seely, *The Spirit of Revolution: Beyond the Dead Ends of Man* (London: Polity Press, 2016).

De Landa, Manuel, *Assemblage Theory* (Edinburgh: Edinburgh University Press, 2016).

Dean, Jodi, *Crowds and Party* (London: Verso, 2018).

Deane-Drummond, Anthony, *Riot Control* (London: Royal United Services Institute for Defence Studies, 1975).

Derrida, Jacques, 'Declarations of independence', 7.1 *New Political Science* (1986), 7.

Derrida, Jacques, *The Beast and the Sovereign, Volume 1* (Chicago: University of Chicago Press, 2009).

Diken, Bulent, 'From refugee camps to gated communities: Biopolitics and the end of the city', 8.1 *Citizenship Studies* (2004), 83.

Doussan, Jenny, *Time, Language, and Visuality in Agamben's Philosophy* (London: Palgrave MacMillan, 2013).

Douzinas, Costas, *Philosophy and Resistance* (Polity Press, 2013).

Downey, Anthony, 'Zones of indistinction: Giorgio Agamben's 'bare life' and the politics of aesthetics', 23.2 *Third Text* (2009), 109.

Duff, Cameron, 'On the role of affect and practice in the production of place', 28 *Environment and Planning. part D, Society and Space* (2010), 881.

Duffy, Tom, 'Kids joke 'we've got coronavirus' while coughing in NHS workers' faces', *Liverpool Echo* (28/03/2020) https://www.liverpoolecho.co.uk/news/kids-saying-coronavirus-cough-nhs-17999054 (viewed 30/03/2020).

Durant, Henry, 'Morale and its measurement', 43.7 *American Journal of Sociology* (1941), 408–412.

Duschinsky, Robbie, and Emma Wilson, 'Flat affect, joyful politics and enthralled attachments: Engaging with the work of Lauren Berlant', 28 *International Journal of Political Culture and Society*, (2015), 179.

Eagleton, Terry, 'Aesthetics and politics in Edmund Burke', 28.1 *History Workshop Journal* (1989), 57.

Eagleton, Terry, *Holy Terror* (Oxford: Oxford University Press, 2005).

Eagleton, Terry, *Ideology: An Introduction*, (London: Verso, 2007).
Eagleton, Terry, *The Ideology of the Aesthetic* (Hoboken: Blackwell, 1990).
EIRP and Interrights v Egypt (2011) ACHPR 85.
Eiseman-Renyard and Ors v United Kingdom (2019) ECHR 110.
El-Enany, Nadine, "Innocence charged with guilt': The criminalisation of protest from Peterloo to Millbank', in Francis Pakes, and David Pritchard (eds) *Riot: Unrest and Protest on the Global Stage* (London: Palgrave Macmillan, 2014).
Elden, Stuart 'Terror and territory' 39.5 *Antipode* (2007), 821.
Ellis, Darren, Ian Tucker, and David Harper, 'The affective atmosphere of surveillance', 23.6 *Theory and Psychology* (2013), 716.
Ellison, Graham, and Jim Smyth, *The Crowned Harp: Policing in Northern Ireland* (London: Pluto Press, 2000).
Esposito, Roberto, 'Cured to the bitter end', *European Journal of Psychoanalysis* (26/02/2020) http://www.journal-psychoanalysis.eu/coronavirus-and-philosophers / (viewed on the 27/03/2020).
Evans, Rob, and Paul Lewis 'Undercover police had children with activists', *The Guardian* (20/01/2012) https://www.theguardian.com/uk/2012/jan/20/undercover-police -children-activists (viewed on 19/03/2020).
Fanon, Frantz, *The Damned* (Paris: Presence Africaine, 1963).
Fanon, Frantz, *The Wretched of the Earth* (New York: Grove Press, 2004).
Farnell, Chris, 'The royal wedding zombie flash mob: Breach of the peace (of the dead)', http://chriswritesapocalypses.blogspot.co.uk/2011/05/17-royal-wedding-zombie -flash-mob.html (viewed on 28/02/2020).
Fassin, Didier, *Enforcing Order: An Ethnography of Urban Policing* (London: Polity Press, 2013).
Feltham, Oliver, *Alain Badiou: Live Theory* (New York: Continuum, 2008).
Ferguson, Adam, *Principles of Moral and Political Science* (London: Strahan, 1792).
Fisher v. Oldham Corporation (1930) 2 KB 364.
Ford, Lisa. 'The pig and the peace', in Dorsett, S, and Hunter, I, (eds), *Law and Politics in British Colonial Thought: Transpositions of Empire* (London: Palgrave MacMillan, 2010), 171.
Foss, Sonja, 'Theory of visual rhetoric' in Ken Smith, Sandra Moriarty, Gretchen Barbatsis, and Keith Kenney (eds), *Handbook of Visual Communication: Theory, Methods, and Media* (London: Routledge, 2011), 141.
Foucault, Michel 'On the genealogy of ethics: An over view of work in progress', in Hubert Dreyfus, and Paul Rabinow (eds), *Michel Foucault: Beyond Structuralism and Hermeneutics* (Chicago: University of Chicago Press, 1983), 229.
Foucault, Michel, *Power/Knowledge: Selected Interviews & Other Writings, 1972–1977* (New York: Pantheon, 1980).
Foucault, Michel, *Security, Territory, Population* (New York: Palgrave MacMillan, 2009).
Foucault, Michel, *Security, Territory, Population: Lectures at the College de France 1977–1978* (New York: Picador, 2007).
Foucault, Michel, *Society Must Be Defended: Lectures at the College de France 1975–76* (New York: Picador, 2003).
Foucault, Michel, *The Birth of Biopolitics: Lectures at the College de France 1978–1979* (London: Palgrave MacMillan, 2008).
Foucault, Michel, *The History of Sexuality, Volume 1: An Introduction* (London: Penguin, 1979).
Frank, Jason, *Constituent Moments: Enacting the People in Postrevolutionary America* (Durham: Duke University Press, 2010).

Furniss, Tom, 'Stripping the queen: Edmund Burke's magic lantern show', in Steven Blakemore (ed), *Burke and the French Revolution, Bicentennial Essays* (Athens: University of Georgia Press, 1992), 69.

Gallagher, Nancy, 'Sexual harassment in Tahrir Square', *E-International Relations* (27/06/2013) http://www.e-ir.info/2013/06/27/sexual-harassment-in-tahrir-square/.

Galloway, Alexander, *French Theory Today: An Introduction to Possible Futures* (New York: Public School, 2011).

Gibbons, Luke, *Edmund Burke and Ireland: Aesthetics, Politics and the Colonial Sublime* (Cambridge: Cambridge University Press, 2009).

Gibbs, Anna 'Panic! Affect contagion, mimesis and suggestion: In the social field', 14.2 *Cultural Studies Review* (2008), 130.

Gilles Deleuze, and Felix Guattari, *A Thousand Plateaus: Capitalism and Schizophrenia* (Minneapolis: University of Minnesota Press, 1987).

Gillham, Patrick, 'Securitizing America: Strategic incapacitation and the policing of protest since the 11 September 2001 terrorist attacks', *Sociology* (2011), 12.

Gillham, Patrick, Bob Edwards, and John Noakes, 'Strategic incapacitation and the policing of the occupy wall street protests in New York City, 2011', 23.1 *Policing and Society* (2013), 82.

van Ginneken, Jan, *Crowds, Psychology and Politics 1871–1899* (Cambridge: Cambridge University Press, 1992).

Ben Golder, *Foucault and the Politics of Rights* (Stanford: Stanford University Press, 2015).

Goldhammer, Jesse, *The Headless Republic* (Ithaca: Cornell University Press, 2005).

Goodrich, Peter, *Oedipus Lex Psychoanalysis, History, Law* (Berkeley: University of California Press, 1995).

Goodrich, Peter, 'Specula laws: Image, aesthetic and common law', 2 *Law and Critique* (1991), 239.

Gordillo, Gaston, 'Resonance and the Egyptian revolution', *Critical Legal Thinking* (22/02/2011) http://criticallegalthinking.com/2011/02/22/resonance-and-the-egyptian-revolution/ (viewed on 27/02/2020).

Gordillo, Gaston, 'The speed of revolutionary resonance', *Critical Legal Thinking* (14/03/2011) http://criticallegalthinking.com/2011/03/14/the-speed-of-revolutionary-resonance/.

Gordon-Zolov, Terri, and Eric Zolov 'The walls of Chile speak of a suppressed rage', *The Nation* (07/11/2019) https://www.thenation.com/article/chile-protest-art/ (viewed on 19/03/2020).

Gould, Deborah, *Moving Politics: Emotion and ACT UP's Fight against AIDS* (Chicago: University of Chicago Press, 2009).

Grove, Nicole, 'The cartographic ambiguities of harass map: Crowdmapping security and sexual violence in Egypt,' 46.4 *Security Dialogue* (2015), 358.

Hale, Erin, ''Be water': Hong Kong protestors adopt Bruce Lee tactic to evade police crackdown', *The Independent* (07/08/2019) https://www.independent.co.uk/news/world/asia/hong-kong-protest-latest-bruce-lee-riot-police-water-a9045311.html (viewed on 30/03/2020).

Hale, Erin, 'Hong Kong protesters use flashmob strategy to avoid arrest', *The Guardian* (13/10/2019) https://www.theguardian.com/world/2019/oct/13/hong-kong-protesters-flashmobs-blossom-everywhere (viewed on 30/03/2020).

Hamacher, Werner, 'Afformative, strike, Benjamin's 'critique of violence'', in Andrew Benjamin, and Peter Osborne, *Destruction & Experience*, (Manchester: Clinamen Press, 2000), 108.

Harrison, Graham, and Verna Yu 'Hong Kong voters deliver landslide victory for pro-democracy campaigners' *The Guardian* (25/11//2019) https://www.theguardian.com/world/2019/nov/24/hong-kong-residents-turn-up-for-local-elections-in-record-numbers (viewed 30/03/2020).

Henriques, Julian, 'The vibrations of affect and their propagation on a night out on Kingston's Dancehall Scene', 16.1 *Body & Society* (2010), 57.

Her majesty's inspectorate of policing, *Adapting to Protest* (London: HMIC, 2009) (https://www.justiceinspectorates.gov.uk/hmicfrs/media/adapting-to-protest-20090705.pdf (Viewed on 04/04/2020).

Hibou, Beatrice, *The Force of Obedience: The Political Economy of Repression in Tunisia* (Polity Press, 2011).

Hocking, Ernest, 'The nature of morale', 47.3 *American Journal of Sociology* (1941), 302.

Hoffman, Marcelo, *Foucault and Power: The Influence of Political Engagement on Theories of Power* (London: Bloomsbury, 2013).

Hong Kong Police, 'History: Police training institutions', https://www.police.gov.hk/info/doc/history/chapter06_en.pdf (Viewed on 22/07/2019).

Hong Kong Police 'History: The modern era 1945–1967', https://www.police.gov.hk/info/doc/history/chapter02_en.pdf (Viewed on 22/07/19).

Honig, Bonnie, *Antigone, Interrupted* (Cambridge: Cambridge University Press, 2013).

Honig, Bonnie, *Democracy and the Foreigner* (Princeton: Princeton University Press, 2003).

Howard, Dick, 'Foreword', in Zvi Ben-Don Benite, Stefanos Geroulanos, and Nicole Jerr (eds), *The Scaffolding of Sovereignty: Global and Aesthetic Perspectives on the History of a Concept* (New York: Columbia University Press, 2017).

Hudson, Chris, 'ION orchard: Atmosphere and consumption in Singapore', 14.3 *Visual Communication* (2015) 301.

Ibbett, Katherine, 'When I do, I call it affect', 40.2 *Paragraph* (2017), 244–245.

Jebnoun, Noureddine, 'Ben Ali's Tunisia: The authoritarian path of a dystopian state', in Noureddine Jebnoun, Mehrdad Kia, and Mimi Kirk (eds), *Modern Middle East Authoritarianism: Roots, Ramifications and Crisis* (London: Routledge, 2013), 109.

Jenkins, Fiona, 'Bare life: Asylum-seekers, Australian politics and Agamben's critique of violence', 10.1 *Australian Journal of Human Rights* (2004), 79.

Jones, Carol, and Jon Vagg, *Criminal Justice in Hong Kong* (London: Routledge, 2007).

Jones, Nate, 'A brief history of riot control', *Time Magazine* (06/08/2010) http://content.time.com/time/world/article/0,8599,2009006,00.html, (viewed on 07/08/19).

Jones, Rhys, *Peoples, States, Territories: The Political Geographies of British State Transformation* (Hoboken: Royal Geographical Society Book Series, Blackwell, 2007).

Jones, Sam, and Ben Quinn 'Osama Bin Laden dead: Aftermath', *The Guardian* (02/05/2011) https://www.theguardian.com/world/2011/may/02/osama-bin-laden-death-live (viewed on 28/02/2020).

Justices of the Peace Act (1361) 34 Edw 3.

Kalmár, Stefan, *The ICA Daily* (27/03/2020) https://www.ica.art/ica-daily/saturday-28-march-2020 (viewed on 30/03/2020).

Kalyvas, Andreas, 'Democracy and the poor: Prolegomena to a radical theory of democracy', 26 *Constellations* (2019), 538.

Kalyvas, Andreas, 'The sovereign weaver: Beyond the camp', in Andrew Norris (ed), *Politics, Metaphysics and Death: Essays on Giorgio Agamben's Homo Sacer* (Durham: Duke University Press, 2005).

Kane, Anne, *Constructing Irish National Identity* (London: Palgrave Macmillan, 2011), 129.

Kantorowitcz, Ernst, *The Kings Two Bodies: A Study in Medieval Political Theology* (Princeton: Princeton University Press, 1957).

Keech, Arthur, *Public Order* (London: Jordan and Sons Ltd, 1952).
Kelly, Margaret, 'King and crown: An examination of the legal foundation of the British king', (PhD Thesis, Macquarie University, 1998).
Kennedy, Liam, 'Seeing and believing: On photography and the war on terror', 24.2 *Public Culture* (2012), 266.
Kershaw, Baz, *The Radical in Performance: Between Brecht amd Baudrillard* (Abingdon: Routledge, 1999).
Khalil, Andrea, *Crowd and Politics in North Africa: Tunisia, Algerian and Libya* (London: Routledge, 2014), 2.
Krimmer, Elisabeth, *The Representation of War in German Literature* (Cambridge: Cambridge University Press, 2010).
Kuo, Lily, and Verna Yu 'Where were the police? Hong Kong outcry after masked thugs launch attack', *The Guardian* (22/07/2019) https://www.theguardian.com/world/2019/jul/22/where-were-the-police-hong-kong-outcry-after-masked-thugs-launch-attack (viewed on 30/03/2020).
Laclau, Ernesto, *On Populist Reason* (London: Verso, 2007).
Laing, Aislinn, and Natalia Ramos Miranda, 'Chile's Piñera extends state of emergency, says 'we are at war', *Reuters* (20/10/2019) https://uk.reuters.com/article/uk-chile-protests/chiles-pinera-extends-state-of-emergency-says-we-are-at-war-idUKKBN1WZ0F0 (viewed on 19/03/2020).
Le Bon, Gustave, *The Crowd: A Study of the Popular Mind* (London: T Fisher Unwin, 1903).
Lechte, John, and Saul Newman, *Agamben and the Politics of Human Rights: Statelessness, Images, Violence* (Edinburgh: Edinburgh University Press, 2013).
Legg, Stephen, 'Assemblage/apparatus: Using Deleuze and Foucault', in 43.2 *Area* (2011), 128.
Lemke, Thomas, 'Beyond Foucault: From biopolitics to the government of life', in Ulrich Brockling, Susanne Krasmann, and Thomas Lemke (eds), *Governmentality: Current Issues and Future Challenges* (Abingdon: Routledge, 2011), 165.
Leung, Gilbert, 'Breach of the peace, or violence and/of silence', in Elena Loizidou (ed), *Disobedience: Concept and Practice* (Abingdon: Routledge, 2013), 37.
Leys, Ruth, 'The turn to affect: A critique', 37.3 *Critical Inquiry* (2011), 437.
Lilleby, Sabrina, 'Extraordinary happenings, ordinary affects', 1.1 *Capacious* (2017), 20–21.
Lindahl, Hans, 'Constituent power and reflexive identity', in Martin Loughlin, and Neil Walker (eds), *The Paradox of Constitutionalism: Constituent Power and Constitutional Form* (Oxford: Oxford University Press, 2008), 19.
Lindeman, Eduard, 'Recreation and Morale', 47.3 *American Journal of Sociology* (1941), 397 & 398.
Lobban, Michael, 'From seditious libel to unlawful assembly: Peterloo and the changing face of political crime c1770-1820', in 10.3 *Oxford Journal of Legal Studies* (1990), 308.
Loughlin, Martin, 'The state, the crown and the law', in Maurice Sunkin, and Sebastian Payne (eds), *The Nature of the Crown: A Legal and Political Analysis* (Oxford: Oxford University Press, 1999), 41.
Loughlin, Martin, and Neil Walker, *The Paradox of Constitutionalism: Constituent Power and Constitutional Form* (Oxford: Oxford University Press, 2008).
Marcus, George, and Erkan Saka 'Assemblage', 23.2–3 *Theory, Culture & Society* (2006), 101.
Marinetti, Filippo, 'The founding and manifesto of futurism', in Umbro Apollonio (ed), *Futurist Manifestos* (London: Cengage, 1973), 22.

Martel, James, *Divine Violence: Walter Benjamin and the Eschatology of Sovereignty* (Abingdon: Routledge, 2011).
Marx-Longuet, Jenny, 'Articles on the Irish question' https://www.marxists.org/archive/marx/bio/family/jenny/1870-ire.htm (viewed on 27/02/2020).
Massumi, Brian, 'Histories of violence: Affect, power, violence: The political is not personal', *Law Review of Books* (13/11/2017) https://lareviewofbooks.org/article/histories-of-violence-affect-power-violence-the-political-is-not-personal (viewed on 02/04/2020).
Massumi, Brian, *Parables for the Virtual: Movement, Affect, Sensation* (Durham: Duke University Press, 2004).
Matthews, Daniel, 'Narrative space and atmosphere: A nomospheric inquiry into Hong Kong's pro-democracy 'umbrella movement'', 26.1 *Social and Legal Studies* (2017), 25.
Mawani, Renisa, 'Atmospheric pressures: On race and affect', York University Department of Sociology Annual Lecture (26/02/2019), draft with the author.
Mazzarella, William, 'The myth of the multitude, or, who's afraid of the crowd?', 36 *Critical Inquiry* (2010), 697.
Mbembe, Achille, *Necropolitics* (Durham: Duke University Press, 2019).
Mbembe, Achille, *On the Postcolony* (Berkeley: University of California Press, 2001).
Mbembe, Achille, 'The society of enmity', 200 *Radical Philosophy* (2016).
McBain, Graham, 'Modernising the law: Breaches of the peace & justices of the peace', 8.3 *Journal of Politics and Law* (2015), 172.
McConville, Brendan, *The King's Three Faces: The Rise and Fall of Royal America* (Chapel Hill: University of North Carolina Press, 2006).
McCurdy, Patrick, Anna Geigenbaum, and Fabian Frenzel, 'Protest camps and repertoires of contention', 15.1 *Social Movement Studies* (2016), 97.
McFarlane, Megan, 'Visualising the rhetorical presidency: Barak Obama in the situation room', 23.1 *Visual Communication Quarterly* (2016), 3.
Mead, David, *The New Law of Peaceful Protest: Rights and Regulation in the Human Rights Act Era* (Oxford: Hart Publishing, 2010).
Merkelson, Suzanne, 'Osama's dead, but how much does it matter?', *Foreign Policy* (02/05/2011) https://foreignpolicy.com/2011/05/02/osamas-dead-but-how-much-does-it-matter-2/ (viewed on 28/02/2020).
Mignolo, Walter, 'Coloniality is far from over and so must be decoloniality', 43 *Afterall* (2017), 40.
Minikkinen, Panu, *Sovereignty, Knowledge, Law* (Abingdon: Routledge, 2009).
Mitchell, William J T, *Iconology: Image, Text, Ideology* (Chicago: University of Chicago Press, 1987).
Momboisse, Raymond, *Riots, Revolts and Insurrections* (Springfield IL: Charles Thomas Publisher, 1967).
Morrill, John, *Revolt in the Provinces: The People of England and the Tragedies of War, 1630–1648* (London: Routledge, 1999).
Morton, Stephen, *States of Emergency, Colonialism, Literature and Law* (Liverpool: Liverpool University Press 2013).
Nail, Thomas, 'What is an assemblage?', 46.1 *SubStance* (2017), 21.
Nair, Sheila, 'Sovereignty, security and the exception: Towards situating postcolonial homo sacer', in Gerard Delanty, and Stephen Turner (eds), *Routledge International Handbook of Contemporary Social and Political Theory* (Abingdon: Routledge, 2011), 386.
Nally, David, ''The coming storm': The Irish poor law, colonial biopolitics and the great famine', 98.3 *Annals of the Association of American Geographers* (2008), 719.

Nancy, Jean-Luc, *The Inoperative Community* (Minneapolis: University of Minnesota Press, 1991).

Nancy, Jean-Luc, 'Viral exception', *European Journal of Psychoanalysis* (26/02/2020) http://www.journal-psychoanalysis.eu/coronavirus-and-philosophers/ (viewed on the 27/03/2020).

Nazra, El-Nadeem, and New Woman Foundation, 'Sexual assault and rape in Tahrir Square and its vicinity: A compendium of sources, 2011–2013', https://nazra.org/sites/nazra/files/attachments/compilation-_of_sexual-violence_-testimonies_between_20111_2013_en.pdf (viewed on 06/04/2020).

Neal, Andrew, Sven Opitz, and Chris Zebrowski, 'Capturing protest in urban environments: The 'police kettle' as a territorial Strategy', 37.6 *Environment and Planning D: Society and Space* (2019), 1047.

Nebehay, Stephanie, '1.5 million Muslims could be detained in China's Xinjiang: Academic', *Reuters* (13/03/2019) https://www.reuters.com/article/us-china-xinjiang-rights/15-million-muslims-could-be-detained-in-chinas-xinjiang-academic-idUSKCN1QU2MQ (viewed on 30/03/2020).

Negri, Antonio, *Insurgencies: Constituent Power and the Modern State* (Minneapolis: University of Minnesota Press, 1999).

Neocleous, Mark, *The Fabrication of Social Order: A Critical Theory of Police Power* (London: Pluto Press, 2000).

Neocleous, Mark, *War Power, Police Power* (Edinburgh: Edinburgh University Press, 2014).

Nieuwenhuis, Marijn, 'Breathing materially: Aerial violence at a time of atmospheric politics', 9.3 *Critical Studies on Terrorism* (2016), 513.

Northam, Gerry, *Shooting in the Dark: Riot Police in Britain* (Faber and Faber, 1989).

O'Connell, Daniel, 'On the motion for defraying the charge of the yeomanry and volunteer corps for Great Britain and Ireland', Hansard: HC (Deb 27 June 1831), vol. 4 cc388–402.

Oberweter v Hilliard and Salazar, Civil Action No. 09–0588, http://voices.washingtonpost.com/crime-scene/jeffersondecision.pdf (viewed on 04/04/2020).

Olarte, Carolina, 'From territorial peace to territorial pacification: Anti-riot police powers and socio-environmental dissent in the implementation of Colombia's peace agreement', 67 *Revista de Estudios Sociales* (2018), 26.

Organisation for Security and Cooperation in Europe, *Human Rights Handbook on Policing Assemblies* (Warsaw: Office for Democratic Institutions and Human Rights) https://www.osce.org/odihr/226981?download=true (viewed on 03/04/2020).

Orr, Jackie, *Panic Diaries: A Genealogy of Panic Disorder* (Durham: Duke University Press, 2006).

Owens, Patricia, 'Beyond 'bare life': Refugees and the 'right to have rights', in Alexander Betts and Gill Loescher (eds), *Refugees in International Relations* (Oxford: Oxford University Press, 2011), 133.

Owens, Patricia, *Economy of Force: Counter-Insurgency and the Historical Rise of the Social* (Cambridge: Cambridge University Press, 2015).

Owens, Patricia, 'Reclaiming 'bare life'?: Against Agamben on refugees', 23.4 *International Relations* (2009), 567.

Passavant, Paul, 'I can't breathe: Heeding the call of justice', 11.3 *Law, Culture and the Humanities* (2015), 330.

Passavant, Paul, 'Policing protest in the post-Fordist city', 2.1 *Amsterdam Law Forum* (2009), 93.

Pearce, Ruth, 'Queer zombies plan royal wedding 'celebration'', http://www.lesbilicious.co.uk/campaigns-politics/queer-zombies-plan-royal-wedding-celebration/ viewed on 28/02/2020).

Pedwell, Caroline, *Transforming Habit: Affect, Assemblage and Change in a Minor Key* (McGill-Queens University Press, forthcoming)

Pedwell, Caroline, 'Transforming habit: Revolution, routine and social change', 31.1 *Cultural Studies* (2016), 93.

Peel, Robert, *Sir Robert Peel from His Private Papers, Volume. 1* (London: John Murray, 1891).

Petti, Alessandro, Sandi Hilal, and Eyal Weizman, *Architecture after Revolution* (New York: Sternberg Press, 2013), 171.

Philippopoulos-Mihalopoulos, Andreas, *Spatial Justice: Body, Lawscape, Atmosphere* (Abingdon: Routledge, 2015).

Phillips, John, '*Agencement*/Assemblage', 23.2–3 *Theory, Culture & Society* (2006), 109.

Pilsch, Andrew, 'Lachrymator: Persuasion's tear gas', in 17th Biennial RSA Conference (2016), https://oaktrust.library.tamu.edu/handle/1969.1/159126 (viewed on 15/09/2020).

Poggi, Christine, '*Folla/Follia*: Futurism and the crowd,' 28.3 *Critical Inquiry* (2002), 727.

Poggi, Christine, 'Mass, pack and mob: Art in the age of the crowd', in Jeffrey Schnapp, and Matthew Tiews (eds), *Crowds* (Stanford: Stanford University Press, 2006), 193.

Policante, Amedeo, 'Of cameras and balaclavas: Violence, myth and the convulsive kettle', 8.4 *Globalizations* (2011), 457.

Pollock, Frederick, *Oxford Lectures, and Other Discourses* (London: MacMillan and Co, 1890).

Pollock, Frederick, and William Maitland, *The History of English Law before the time of Edward I, Volume I* (Cambridge: Little, Brown & Co, 1895).

Powell, Kashif Jerome, 'Making #blacklivesmatter: Michael Brown, Eric Garner, and the spectres of black life: Towards a hauntology of blackness', 16.3 *Cultural Studies ↔ Critical Methodologies* (2016), 253.

Power, Nina, and Alberto Toscano, 'Politics', in Adam John Bartlett, and Justin Clemens (eds), *Alain Badiou, Key Concepts* (London: Routledge, 2014).

Puar, Jasbir, *Terrorist Assemblages: Homonationalism in Queer Times* (Durham: Duke University Press, 2007).

Public Order Steering Group, 'Suggested draft introduction', The National Archives of the UK, HO 325/524.

Purbrick, Martin, 'A report of the 2019 Hong Kong protests', 50.4 *Asian Affairs* (2019), 1.

Putnam, Bertha Haven, *Early Treatises on the Practice of the Justices of the Peace in the Fifteenth and Sixteenth Centuries* (Oxford: Clarendon Press, 1924).

Putnam, Bertha Haven, 'The transformation of the keepers of the peace into the justices of the peace 1327–1380', 12 *Transactions of the Royal Historical Society* (1929), 12–48.

R (Hicks and Ors) v Commissioner of Police of the Metropolis (2012) EWHC 1947 (admin).

R (Hicks and Ors) v Commissioner of Police of the Metropolis (2014) EWCA Civ 3.

R (Hicks and Ors) v Commissioner of Police of the Metropolis (2017) UKSC 9.

R v Secretary of State for the Home Department (ex parte Northumbria Police Authority) (1989) 1 QB 26.

Rajaram, Prem Kumar, Carl Grundy-Warr 'The irregular migrant as homo sacer: Migration and detention in Australis, Malaysia and Thailand, 42.1 *International Migration* (2004), 33.

Ramadan, Adam, 'Spatialising the refugee camp', 38.1 *Transactions of the Institute of British Geographers* (2013), 65.

Rancière, Jacques, *Disagreement: Politics and Philosophy* (Minneapolis: University of Minnesota Press, 2004).

Robinson, Andrew, 'Walter Benjamin: Critique of violence', *Ceasefire Magazine* (21/12/2013) https://ceasefiremagazine.co.uk/walter-benjamin-critique-state/ (viewed on 30/03/2020).

Rose, Nicholas, Pat O'Malley, and Marianna Valverde, 'Governmentality', 2 *Annual Review of Law and Social Science* (2006), 83–104.

Rude, George, *The Crowd in Popular History: A Study of Popular Disturbances in France and England, 1730–1848* (Oxford: Oxford University Press, 1959).

Rumsfeld, Donald, 'US Department ofDefence Briefing' (12/02/2002) https://archive.defense.gov/Transcripts/Transcript.aspx?TranscriptID=2636 (viewed on 19/03/2020).

Rush, Benjamin, *Benjamin Rush's Lectures of the Mind* (Philadelphia: American Philosophical Society, 1981).

Rush, Benjamin, *Letters of Benjamin Rush, Volume I* (Lyman Henry Butterfield (ed), Princeton University Press, 1951).

Said, Rania, '-Z-: Flamingos, Francophonie, and the arts of urban dissent in Tunis' 17.2 *Journal of Romance Studies* (2017), 215.

Sayers, Frederick 'untitled paper', The National Archives of the UK, CO 968/146/4.

Schmitt, Carl, *Constitutional Theory* (Durham: Duke University Press, 2008).

Sedgwick, Eve, *Shame and Its Sisters: A Silvan Tomkins Reader* (Durham: Duke University Press, 1995).

Shapiro, Nick, 'Unknowing exposure: Toxic emergency housing, strategic inconclusivity and governance in the US Gulf South', in Emelie Cloatre, and M Pickersgill (eds), *Knowledge, Technology and Law* (London: Routledge, 2014), 189.

Shenhav, Yehouda, 'Imperialism, exceptionalism and the contemporary world', in Marcelo Svirsky, and Simone Bignall (eds), *Agamben and Colonialism* (Edinburgh: Edinburgh University Press, 2012), 19.

Shoemaker, Robert, 'The London 'mob' in the early eighteen century', in Peter Borsay (ed), *The Eighteenth-Century Town, A Reader in English Urban History* (London: Routledge, 1990), 1688–1820, 221.

Shokr, Ahmad, 'The 18 days of Tahrir', 258 *Middle East Report* (Spring, 2011) http://www.merip.org/mer/mer258/18-days-tahrir.

Sidis, Boris, *The Psychology of Suggestion: A Research into the Subconscious Nature of Man and Society* (New York: D Appleton and Co, 1898).

Simmons, Kier, 'Inside Chinese camps thought to be detaining a million Muslim Uighurs', *NBC News* (04/10/2019) https://www.nbcnews.com/news/world/inside-chinese-camps-thought-detain-million-muslim-uighurs-n1062321 (viewed on 30/03/2020).

Simpson, Brian, *Human Rights and the End of Empire* (Oxford: Oxford University Press, 2004).

Sinclair, Georgina, 'The 'Irish' policeman and empire: Influencing the policing of the British empire-commonwealth', 36.142 *Irish Historical Studies* (2008), 179.

Siverleib, Alan, 'Obama on Sunday: A photo for the ages?', *CNN* (04/05/2011) https://edition.cnn.com/2011/POLITICS/05/03/iconic.obama.photo/index.html (viewed on 28/02/2020).

Sloterdijk, Peter, *Bubbles: Sphere, Volume I: Microspherology* (Los Angeles: Semiotext(e), 2011).

Sokhi-Bulley, Bal, *Governing Through Rights: Human Rights in Perspective* (Oxford: Hart Publishing, 2016).

Sorel, Georges, *Reflections on Violence* (London: George Allen & Unwin, 1916).

Sotiris, Panagiotis, 'Against Agamben: Is a democratic biopolitics possible?' https://criticallegalthinking.com/2020/03/14/against-agamben-is-a-democratic-biopolitics-possible/ (viewed on 27/02/2020).

Spiegel, Jennifer, 'Masked protest in the age of austerity: State violence, anonymous bodies, and resistance 'in the red'', 41.4 *Critical Inquiry* (2015), 786.
Stewart, Kathleen, 'Atmospheric attunements', 29 *Environmental and Planning D: Society and Space* (2011), 445.
Sullivan, Shannon, *Revealing Whiteness: The Unconscious Habits of Racial Privilege* (Bloomington and Indianapolis: Indiana University Press, 2006).
Tabbi, Matt, *I can't breathe: A killing on bay street* (New York: Spiegel & Grau, 2017).
Tagg, John, 'A discourse (with shape of reason missing)', 15.3 *Art History* (1992), 351.
Taine, Hippolyte, *The Ancient Régime* (1876) (Gloucester, MA: Peter Smith, 1962).
Tarde, Gabriel, *Penal Philosophy* (Boston: Little, Brown and Company, 1912).
Tarde, Gabriel, *Social Laws: An Outline of Sociology* (1897) (MA: Macmillan, 1899).
Tarde, Gabriel, 'Sociology, social psychology, sociologism', in *On Communication & Social Influence: Selected Papers* (1894) (Chicago: University of Chicago Press, 1969).
Taussig, Michael, *The Nervous System* (Abingdon: Routledge, 2001).
Taylor, Kenneth, 'Fanon, violence and the struggle against colonialism', *Philosophy Talk* (29/01/18) https://www.philosophytalk.org/blog/fanon-violence-and-struggle-against-colonialism (viewed on 31/08/19).
Taylor, Serena, Amy Tan, Phoebe Sloane, Maggie Tiernan, and Faiqa Mahmood, ''When she stands among men': Sexual harassment of women at political protests in Cairo, January 2011–August 2013', *Al Nakhlah; Online Journal of Southwest Asia and Islamic Civilisation* (2014), 1–19.
The Telegraph, 'The Queen's coronavirus speech transcript: 'We will succeed and better days will come'', *The Telegraph* (05/04/2020) https://www.telegraph.co.uk/news/2020/04/05/queens-coronavirus-speech-full-will-succeed-better-days-will/ (viewed on 06/04/2020).
Warrington Guardian, 'Police stop group of youths for coughing at NHS workers', *Warrington Guardian* (28/03/2020) https://www.warringtonguardian.co.uk/news/18341961.police-stop-group-youths-coughing-nhs-workers/ (viewed on 30/03/2020).
Thomas, Martin, ''Paying the butchers bill': Policing British colonial protest after 1918', 15.2 *Crime, History and Societies* (2011), 57.
Thomas, Martin, *Violence and Colonial Order: Police, Workers and Protests in the European Colonial Empires, 1918–40* (Cambridge: Cambridge University Press, 2012).
Thompson, Edward P, *Customs in Common* (London: Penguin, 1993).
Thompson, Edward P, 'The moral economy of the English crowd in the eighteenth century', 50 *Past & Present* (1971), 76–136.
Thrift, Nigel, *Non-Representational Theory: Space, Politics, Affect* (London: Routledge, 2007).
Tilly, Charles, *From Mobilization to Revolution* (New York: McGraw-Hill, 1978).
Tilly, Charles, 'Repertoires of contention in America and Britain 1750–1830', in Mayer Zald and John McCarthy (eds), *The Dynamics of Social Movements* (Cambridge: Winthrope, 1979), 126.
Tombs, Alastair, and Janet McColl-Kennedy, 'Social-servicescape conceptual model', 3.4 *Marketing Theory*, 447.
Tomlins, Christopher, *Freedom Bound: Law Labour and Civic Identity in Colonizing English America, 1580–1865* (Cambridge: Cambridge University Press, 2010).
Toscano, Alberto, 'Divine management: Critical remarks on Giorgio Agamben's the kingdom and the glory', 12.3 *Angelaki: Journal of the Theoretical Humanities* (2011), 128.
Toscano, Alberto, 'Powers of pacification: State and empire in Gabriel Tarde', 36.4 *Economy and Society* (2007), 597–613.

Townshend, Charles, *Making the Peace* (Oxford: Oxford University Press, 1993).
Trey 'A history of Hong Kong's contentious politics: 'It was you who taught us…', *Comparativist* (28/08/2019) https://www.comparativist.org/2019/08/28/a-history-of-hong-kongs-contentious-politics-it-was-you-who-taught-us/ (viewed on 30/03/2020).
Tuastad, Dag, "'State of exception' or 'state in exile'? The fallacy of appropriating Agamben on Palestinian refugee camps', 38.9 *Third World Quarterly* (2017), 2159.
Turner, Victor, *Dramas, Fields and Metaphors: Symbolic Action in Human Society* (Ithaca: Cornell University Press, 1975).
UK College of Policing, *Public Order: Tactical Options* https://www.app.college.police.uk/app-content/public-order/planning-and-deployment/tactical-options/#containment (viewed on 03/04/2020).
Venn, Couze, 'A note on assemblage', 23.2–3 *Theory, Culture and Society* (2006), 107.
Venn, Couze, 'Individuation, relationality, affect: Rethinking the human in relation to the living', 16.1 *Body & Society* (2010), 129.
Waddington, Peter AJ, *Liberty and Order: Public Order Policing in a Capital City* (London: University College London Press, 1994).
Wall, Illan rua, 'Atmospheres of protest', in Shirin Rai and Silvija Jestrovic (eds), *Oxford Handbook of Politics and Performance* (Oxford: Oxford University Press, forthcoming a).
Wall, Illan rua, *Human Rights and Constituent Power: Without Model or Warranty* (London: Routledge, 2012).
Wall, Illan rua, 'Law's ordinary affects', *Law, Culture and the Humanities* (forthcoming).
Wall, Illan rua, 'Policing atmospheres: Crowds, protest and 'atmotechnics'', 36.4 *Theory, Culture & Society* (2019), 143.
Walters, William, *Governmentality: Critical Encounters* (London: Routledge, 2012).
Weber, Jack, 'The king's peace: A comparative study', 10.2 *Journal of Legal History* (1989), 135.
Weheliye, Alexander, *Habeas Viscus: Racialising Assemblages, Biopolitics and Black Feminist Theories of the Human* (Durham: Duke University Press, 2014), 31–36.
Weinberger, Barbara, *Keeping the Peace? Policing Strikes in Britain 1906–1926* (Oxford: Berg Publishers, 1990).
Wetherell, Margaret, *Affect and Emotion: A New Social Science Understanding* (London: SAGE, 2012).
Williams, Glanvlle, *Criminal Law: The General Part* (2nd Edition, London: Stevens and Sons, 1961).
Williams, Raymond, *Marxism and Literature* (Oxford: Oxford University Press, 1977).
Williams, Rosalind, *Dream Worlds: Mass Consumption in Late Nineteenth-Century France* (Berkeley: University of California Press, 1982).
Wong, Kam C, *Policing in Hong Kong: Research and Practice* (London: Palgrave MacMillan, 2015).
Wood, Andy, *Riot, Rebellion and Popular Politics in Early Modern England* (London: Palgrave MacMillan, 2002).
Wood, Lesley, *Crisis and Control: The Militarization of Protest Policing* (London: Pluto Press, 2014).
Young, Alison, 'Arrested mobilities: Affective encounters and crime scenes in the city', *Law, Culture and the Humanities* (forthcoming), 17.
Young, Alison, 'Japanese atmospheres of criminal justice', 59.4 *British Journal of Criminology* (2019), 765.

Yung, Wing Kwong, and Sandy Chai, 'Paradigm shift in Hong Kong public order policing', in John Eterno, Arvind Verma, Aiedeo Das, and Dilip Das, *Global Issues in Contemporary Policing* (Boca Raton: CRC Press, 2019), 166.

Zaharia, Marius, Felix Tam, and Claire Jim 'Frontline protesters make case for violence in Hong Kong protests', *Reuters* (22/08/2019) https://www.reuters.com/article/us-hongkong-protests-violence-analysis/frontline-view-making-the-case-for-violence-in-hong-kong-protests-idUSKCN1VB2LV (viewed on 30/03/2020).

Zumthor, Peter, *Atmospheres: Architectural Environments: Surrounding Objects* (Switzerland: Birkhauser GmbH, 2006).

INDEX

For Product Safety Concerns and Information please contact our EU representative GPSR@taylorandfrancis.com
Taylor & Francis Verlag GmbH, Kaufingerstraße 24, 80331 München, Germany

www.ingramcontent.com/pod-product-compliance
Ingram Content Group UK Ltd.
Pitfield, Milton Keynes, MK11 3LW, UK
UKHW021720240926
475702UK00029BA/1717
9780367333706